Glimpses of WORLD RELIGIONS

Glimpses of
WORLD RELIGIONS

JAICO PUBLISHING HOUSE
Ahmedabad Bangalore Bhopal Bhubaneswar Chennai
Delhi Hyderabad Kolkata Lucknow Mumbai

Published by Jaico Publishing House
A-2 Jash Chambers, 7-A Sir Phirozshah Mehta Road
Fort, Mumbai - 400 001
jaicopub@jaicobooks.com
www.jaicobooks.com

GLIMPSES OF WORLD RELIGIONS
ISBN 81-7224-156-9

First Jaico Impression: 1958
Seventeenth Jaico Impression: 2011

Printed by
Repro India Limited
Plot No. 50/2, T.T.C. MIDC Industrial Area
Mahape, Navi Mumbai - 400 710

CONTENTS

PREFACE

IN presenting this book in the present form to the readers, I lay myself open to some criticism. What impelled me to gather these glimpses of the religions of the world, when there are in existence innumerable renderings of each of them in a more scholarly and in a fuller form? To this criticism my reply is that scholastic and fuller renderings of the subject may be of the greatest possible value to the man of letters, to philosophers and metaphysicians, but to a general reader they are uninspiring and uninviting, for it is usual for them to stress controversial and other issues which destroy the intrinsic interest of the subject.

My endeavour has been modestly to steer clear of such controversial and other issues and to give the readers the essence of the religions. To me feeling and reverence for each of the subjects dealt with are of more meaning and of greater consequence than anything else. It will be admitted that the field of this work is much too wide to be covered with first hand knowledge by any one scholar. These glimpses may only be considered as an initiation in the subject; for more detailed knowledge of any particular religion, recourse may be had to works with a larger perspective written by scholars possessing special knowledge of the subject. In the presentation of the several religions an attempt has been made to give a sketch of religious conceptions as they appear from history, ethics—theology and religious philosophy. The limitation of space has restricted me from giving a large number of illustrative extracts and citations from the sources. I have endeavoured to bring out the individuality of each of the religions. The reader who surveys this field of religion can hardly fail to discern unity in apparent diversity, and a general trend of evolution.

In conclusion.I wish to acknowledge my deep gratitude to the various scholars, philosophers and teachers whose great works led me to the study of the religions, and who have been the source of my knowledge; for I humbly acknowledge myself to be a student and shall remain content with that appellation.

— **Author.**

Bombay

INTRODUCTION

THE dominant factor in the pursuit of knowledge in every department of science is to seek to exhibit the unity of law amid the multiplicity of diverse phenomena with which it has to deal; to gather up the manifold into one or to show how the one has given rise to many. This factor will prominently appear in the study of religion as in science. We must believe that the diverse religious beliefs and practices of mankind are not a mere medley, not a mere outburst of indiscretion and want of reason, but that they form a cosmos and may be known as a part of human life from which prudence and reason have never been absent and in which a growing purpose has fulfilled and still fulfils itself. In setting out on the inquiry into the unity of religion we shall have to start with certain assumptions.

The first principal assumption is that religion is a growth which is perennial and that its evolution has gone on obeying the primary laws of human progress. To inquire into anything means to know how it has come to be what it is and for this purpose one has to trace its history upto the root, and in order to trace its process of evolution it is necessary to define it. There are some scholars who maintain that religion is an intellectual activity. They say that there is only one way in which men can come to believe in higher things and that is by an intellectual process. This idea divorces from religion the practical side of religion which consists chiefly in worship. Belief and worship are inseparable sides of religion. Some others say that the basis of all religion is in the inscrutableness of the power which the universe manifests to us. This definition traces religion to the inadequacy in man's knowledge. It shows a negative rather than a positive element in man's experience. There is an absence of the practical ideas of worship and belief in this definition. Some other scholars have explained religion as the action of the curiosity or an impulse of the human mind, which prompts man to investigate the causes of things, particularly the first cause of all things. This does not tell us what religion is. This curiosity or the impulse to know is not religion. It belongs to the domain of philosophy. Religion is something more than curiosity. No definition of religion can be regarded as complete in which the motive of worship is left undetermined.

Religion is still in the process of growing and until the growth is complete an adequate definition of religion cannot be found. We shall, therefore, have to satisfy ourselves with an elementary definition of religion which is "Religion is a worship of higher powers from a sense of need." Though this appears to be a very modest definition yet if we would consider its implications we would find that it is not so. In the first place it implies an element of belief in the existence of higher powers with which there could be no worship. This is the intellectual factor of religion. If there is no belief in the existence of higher powers there can be no true worship. Primarily a belief must exist that the Being worshipped is capable of supplying the needs. In the second place there must be a conviction that these powers which are worshipped are higher. It is the sense of incapacity of an individual to supply his own needs which evokes in him a belief in the existence of higher powers and he, therefore, keeps up intercourse with these powers by offering worship to them. In the third place, these higher powers are worshipped with the object of cultivating a relation with them. In every act of worship there is an impulse that the Being addressed is supreme and mightier than the worshipper. Belief in higher powers, and the worship offered to them do not, alone, constitute religion; faith arising from the sense of need must also be there. These three together—feeling, belief and will—constitute religion both in the lowest and in the highest form of civilisation. Even a savage living in entire isolation and buffeted by chance from misery to happiness will not seek benefits from his god without some sense of attachment. It is the first gleam of religion, when this sense of attachment has arisen. At its lowest level religion was considered to be an individual affair between the savage and his god, who supplied his material needs and comforts; at a little higher stage it becomes an affair of the tribe or family and at this stage the material needs grow broader and less personal. At both these stages the conditions of his life do not allow his higher faculties to grow and his religion, as a whole, is a mass of puerile fancies and of fixed traditions. His gods are fancied as petty and capricious.

It is a momentous event in human progress when the tribes unite to form a nation. At this stage they learn to act as members of a greater community than the tribe. This is the beginning of civilisation. With such union of tribes a new type of religion makes its appearance. While each of the tribes may long retain its own gods, some one god assumes a higher position than the rest and his worship becomes the central religion of the community. Religion becomes a common worship for public ends and a national religion comes into being. With the growing conception of worship for public ends, lives of men also grow richer and deeper and a new consciousness of personal human dignity springs up, and men come to feel the infinite value and an infinite responsibility of personal life. At this stage the old national religion for public ends is felt to be cold and unsatisfying and the individual sets out to seek a consistent intellectual view. He aims at a higher moral law. He becomes conscious of a new call for personal strivings and a new force for establishing identity. He wilfully breaks through old ties and obligations. Thus the individualist stage of religion succeeds the national.

The individualist stage becomes also in part the universal stage inasmuch as it seeks to establish identity. Thus religion, having developed from tribal to national, and from national to individual and to universal forms an integral and inner part of civilisation. It expresses the essential spirit of human life in various ages and nations. The religion of a race is the truest expression of its character; and a study of the religions of the world is the study of the desires and aspirations of humanity. Just as civilisation is the result of progressive development from the- savage state to a higher level of culture, in the same way religion which is one of the integral parts of civilisation gradually develops from the lower to the higher stage. There can be really no religion which could be created de novo or rather ab novo; for, religion is everywhere an historical growth and a new system has always to begin by adjusting and adopting what it can, from the older system. The great religions of the world exhibit features which they have inherited from their uncivilised predecessors. There has been no entirely new religion since the beginning of the world. The elements and roots of religion were there as far back as we can trace the history of mankind; and the history of religion has always shown the same radical elements, which are a measure of human weakness and dependence, an intuition of god, a belief in the divine government of the world, a distinction between good and evil and a hope of a better life; these form some of the radical elements of all religions. At all stages of existence mankind has felt that the world of which he is aware outside him, and the world of feelings and desires within him are in conflict, but the conviction lives within him that in some way they can be brought into harmony; and that a power exists which rules in both these discordant realms and in which, if he can identify himself with it, he also can escape from this discord. Such a belief has been entertained by mankind from early ages. Where the sense of human weakness and dependence has inspired him to hold communion with a higher power, there religion has made its appearance.

We shall now see the principal features of the religion of the savages. In the lower levels of civilisation, the worship of objects by mankind may be arranged in four categories : (1) Parts of nature, great or small (2) Spirits of ancestors and other spirits (3) objects supposed to be haunted by spirit i.e. fetish worship and (4) Supreme Being.

The early man turned to the great elements of nature as those who could help him. He conceived the elements as living like himself and having feelings and motives similar to his own. At first it was simply the natural being conceived as living that was worshipped and not as the spirit of a being indwelling in it. Rivers and springs, trees and groves, crops and fruits, rocks and stones, formed the minor nature-worship. The worship of nature was not of the objects alone but of their living process. Immediately after, or contemporaneous with nature-worship, came the worship of the dead and of ancestors. This worship is to be found throughout antiquity and was practised by the savages. They imagined that at death the spirit leaves the body and after traversing the distant regions, comes back to the body. Much was done to gain the sympathy of the departed to increase their own joy and comfort. It was the universal belief that the person continued to exist after the dissolution of the body. The third kind of worship known as fetish worship in which objects were revered not for their intrinsic worth but because of the spirits supposed to be connected with them. Lastly the savage worshipped a deity who was supposed to be a principal one who subordinated the minor deities.

In course of time the worship of natural objects was followed by giving them names and weaving their histories; but the final step in the development took place when gods were imagined in the likeness of human beings and possessing human characteristics. The gods were thus separated from the objects. As one god grows after another, or as the gods of other countries are added, they become manifold and none of them is held to be the supreme one. It was by a gradual process- of thought that it was conceived that one of them was prominent and supreme. These diverse developments of thought about gods did take place in primitive times. In each of the higher religions, these beliefs are prehistoric and what remained for the great religions was to infuse them with new forms and new sanctions.

Religion is not merely knowledge but it is faith and communion and these can be deep and true. It was conceived by mankind from the beginning of its development that there was within man an ideal being which was all perfect and powerful and which would not be grasped by the senses and with which he could have communion.

Religion thus is a link between man and God and the essence of religion has always been understood to be the establishment by man of a relation between himself and the Infinite Being.

Having thus conceived God as an ideal being, all perfect and powerful, the human instinct cannot rest satisfied and it strives and struggles to transcend the limitations which circumscribe it. The inner consciousness in man is ever striving to conquer the lower—the tiny-self. This struggle is the beginning of his awakening in the arena of spiritual life. The spiritual struggles of men are represented by the various existing religious creeds which form the roots of the prevalent ideas of God, inspiring men to have communion with Him. In the midst of all his strivings he realises that, however sense perceptions may appear to be real, they are powerless to satisfy his longing soul which strives to establish oneness with Him. He, therefore, directs his search inwards and experiences facts which are reduced to abstractions either in the shape of abstract personality called God or as an Abstract Essence or Ideal or Moral Law. These nomenclatures establish that they are outside the domain of the senses.

In all the existing religions one fact stands out prominently and that is, that there is an Ideal or Infinite power towards which mankind struggles, which cannot be realised except through self-abnegation or self-renunciation. This forms the background of ethics in all religions. An ethical code cannot be framed on considerations of social utility, for, all the social conventions are derived from society as it exists; and it must not be forgotten that society is in constant evolution and any code of ethics, developed from one form of society, is transitory and cannot cover the vast field of human existence. But an Ethical Code which is based on religion has a wider and unlimited scope, for, it takes up an individual in relation to the Infinite. Man acting on the mere utilitarian concept of ethics can be good, but a man who intends to bring mass magnetism, whose life would emit spiritual sparks and ignite other lives, must have a spiritual or religious background for his ethics. Such man directs his search inwards from where he gets the knowledge of laws which govern his inner being. This movement towards the inner man and this knowledge of the subtle workings which are within the human mind, belong to the field of religion; and its study is the highest impelling power which moves mankind to realise the (Infinite Power which is within each individual, bringing with it peace and bliss to him and to all others. Such study must be on a broader basis, and one must abandon all narrow, sophisticated and limited ideas of religion and believe that religion is realisation, and not arguments and discourses, not theories and doctrines, not discussions and disputations. One must learn that though religions may be founded and fashioned into strange shapes by the hand of man, true religion is one and eternal. The keynotes of all religions are the feeling of the Infinite, the bowing down before the incomprehensible, the yearning after the unseen, love of God and oneness with Him. One must remember that however imperfect, however puerile, a doctrine, philosophy or creed may be, it always places the human soul in the presence of God and however imperfect the conception of God may be, it always represents the highest ideal of perfection which the human mind for the time being can reach. It is true that each religion possesses its own doctrines, creeds and rituals, and though it is difficult to find universal features in all the religions, there is one feature which is common to all and acknowledged by all religions in the form of God. It is He who forms the golden string in all the religions and it is He who establishes oneness in the diversified universe. On the plane of individuality one feels oneself separate from all the living creatures but taken as a living being, one finds that all are comprised in the universal existence which is God the ultimate reality in the universe. One must realise that, that one reality is expressed in innumerable ways and each expression is as true as the other. Different religions arc nothing but milk in vessels of different shapes and forms, and one reality is comprised in each of them. All creeds have a common source as their origin. The real coincidences between all the religions of the world teach us that all religions spring from the same soil—the human heart, that they all look to the same ideals. Differentiation may appear in the external forms of the various creeds, theories and doctrines but there is no real difference between them for each is not contradictory but supplementary to other. There is no creed which is entirely without some Truth, and there is none which contains the whole Truth. From the study of the different religions it would be found that each expresses an essential part of the Truth and elucidates it with full force. They are all but varying patterns of the original Truth which is the life spring of all religions and wherever it exists, it must manifest itself.

"In every religion there are precious grains and we must draw in every religion a broad distinction between what is essential and what is not, between the eternal and the ephemeral, between divine and human; and though the non-essentials can fill volumes, the essentials can be comprehended in a few words." Every religion has some mission to fulfil and nothing can thwart its aim or annihilate its purpose. In order that religion may be a perennial living force, one should esteem and revere all the different creeds, doctrines and theories and realise that they are like so many radii proceeding to the same centre. God is the centre of all religions and each one of us is proceeding towards Him along any of the paths. All religions admit that apart from the body which perishes, there is a certain part, which is changeless—eternal and perfect. This is the idea of Soul. The end of all religions is realising of God in Soul. This is the universal religion; and for realising this, ideas and methods may differ, but all converge to the same centre. There is that beyond all books, beyond all creeds, beyond all the varieties of the world, that is realisation of God within oneself.

HINDUISM

THE ancient civilisation of mankind was determined by natural causes and was confined to four areas of the world. The valley of the Nile was the seat of a powerful empire. The Euphrates and the Tigris witnessed the civilisation of Semitic nations; the Assyrians and Babylonians flourished within its limits. In the valley of the Hoang Ho and the Yangste Kiang flowered Turanian civilisation. The valley of the Indus was the birth place of the earliest civilisation which was developed by a section of Aryans. Rome and Greece lighted the torch in the East and carried it to the West.

The earliest expression of Hinduism was not recorded In writing but was handed down from generation to generation through the faithful memory of the people. India presents a continuity of civilisation and progress. From the year 2900 B.C., the age ascribed to Mohenjo-Daro, to the present age of Mahatma Gandhi, we find that faith reverberated within and acted upon the minds of the People of the vast country. From barbarous idolatry, sorcery and witchcraft the people made headway towards subtle and spiritual pantheism. Philosophers wove monotheism from the Upanishads; scientists studied astronomy, astrology, medicine and all other useful subjects in their minutest details; statesmen and politicians carved out democratic institutions of unknown antiquity in the villages; poets and dramatists portrayed life in vivid colours; and artists raised from stones beautiful figures of Gods and Goddesses. These turn our thoughts to the earliest progenitors of this civilisation and one asks who these Aryans were and whence did they come? It is assumed that these Aryans came from the Caspian sea region. About the period of time when Aryan Kassits overran Babylonia, the Vedic Aryans began to pour themselves into the Indus valley. These Aryans were emigrants, strong in physique, courageous, skilful, and loved life in all its fullness. They entered the valley in search of agricultural prospects. These emigrants, by slow degrees, gained mastery over Northern India and formed themselves into miniature states. Families grew into clans and clans into tribes. Each tribe was ruled by a chieftain. The village community was ruled by assemblies of family heads. The history of Hinduism begins with the Aryan settlements in the Punjab between 2000-1400 B.C. during which period they vanquished the northern provinces from the dark-skinned aboriginals.

From the Punjab they began to spread along the course of the Ganges and within a few centuries the whole of the Gangetic basic, from the North to Benares and Bihar, came under the banner of Aryan civilisation. Prominent amongst the races, who settled alongside the Ganges, were the Kurus who settled along the upper course of the Ganges to the East of Delhi. Their great rival, the Panchalas, settled down along the lower banks and the Vedelha to the North; between the Kurus and the Vedelha lived Kosals. These and smaller races were bound by common language, literature, religion and social and religious scriptures. The Vedic Age (2000 B.C. to 1000 B.C.) is the history of the conquest of the Punjab by Aryans from the aboriginals. During this age, they cleansed the forest and beat back the dark skinned children of the soil to the South. From generation to generation they widened the sway of their civilisation, religion and culture. In the Vedic age, the banks of the Ganges were the homes of the most renowned and civilised Hindu dynasties. Until 14 B.C. they had formed flourishing kingdoms on the upper banks of the Ganges. The Kurus and Panchalas lived in peace and friendly rivalry for a long time and developed a civilisation surpassing the one of their ancestors. Jealousies amongst different races often broke out and ended in hostilities. There was a great war in 13 B.C. in which all the known Hindu tribes of Northern India participated. This forms the subject matter of the great epic of Mahabharata. It is said that the war was waged between the Kurus and the Panchalas. Neither the Kurus nor the Panchalas, however, are the heroes of the epic as it has come down to us. In the epic the five Pandavas are the heroes. It is certain that this central story is a myth. The most probable supposition is that the Pandavas were a distinct race who assisted the Panchalas in the war. It is supposed that, subsequently, when the Pandavas wielded the supreme power, the epic was compiled from the recollections relating to the great war, and the supposed forefathers of the ruling race were represented as heroes of the strife; although they belonged to the different race they were represented as cousins of the Kuru princes so that later generations might not look upon them as usurpers. It is apparent that we Shall search in vain in the epic for the real incidents of the war. Yet the epic is useful as it throws much light on the age,

Having dealt in this brief manner with the history of the Aryans, who were the progenitors of the religious and social structures which they established in India we shall now deal with Hinduism.

Of all the living religions, Hinduism is the most ancient. It was not founded by any individual prophet and is not composed of the teachings of any particular group of them. The Vedas are the fountain-heads of Hinduism. The ancient Rishis and sages of India have expressed their intuitive spiritual experiences in the Upanishads; these experiences are direct and are regarded as authoritative.

Hinduism allows the maximum freedom in matters of faith and worship and does not assert that final perfection can be attained through the means prescribed by it. Hinduism does not lie in the acceptance of any particular form of worship. It inspires everyone to reflect, investigate, search and cogitate. Hence it is found that Hinduism has absorbed all sorts of religious faiths, various forms of worship, and diverse kinds of rituals and customs. According to Hindu tenets there is an essential unity in the conception of religion and outlook on life. Rig Veda says: "Truth is one; sages call it by different names." Again we find in the Upanishad "That all the Paths lead to the same goal just as cows of variegated clours yield the same white milk."

The philosophy of Hinduism is not meant for intellectual curiosity and vain speculation. It is a guide to the path of life; it spiritualises human existence.

Hindu scriptures can be classified under six heads:—(1) Srutis, (2) Smritis (3) Itihasas (4) Puranas (5) Agamas and (6) Darshanas. 'Srutis' literally mean that which is heard. The great Rishis (Sages) heard and experienced the eternal truths and recorded their experiences for the benefit of posterity. These constitute the four Vedas. The truths of the Vedas are revelations. They are the most authoritative sources of religion.

The 'Smritis' literally mean that which is remembered. They are traditions. They stand next in importance to Srutis. Smritis are founded on the teachings of the Vedas. They explain and elucidate religious obligations. They form the parts of the code of laws which guide the individuals, families and communities in their daily conduct, their manners and customs. The injunctions and prohibitions of the Smritis are related to particular social surroundings and as society changes sages of different ages made alterations, adaptations and readjustments to suit the changing social and cultural environment. Manu, Yagnavalkya and Parasara are the most celebrated sages who have readjusted the teachings.

The Itihasas (histories) are the two well known epics, the Ramayana and Mahabharata. They contain stories of absorbing interest through which the fundamental teachings of Hinduism are impressed upon the minds of common people. The religion of the Vedas and the laws of the Smritis are depicted through the noble and elevating deeds of great men. The common men could not grasp the philosophy of the Upanishads. Hence these Itihasas were written for the benefit of the common people. The essence of philosophy is presented through analogies and parables.

The Puranas are of the same class as Itihasas. They were written to popularise the religion of the Vedas. The aim of Puranas is to give in a concrete form to the teachings of the Vedas, by means of myths, stories, legends, the lives of saints and kings and through allegories. They present religion in a concrete form. There are eighteen Puranas such as Skanda, Markandeya, Siva, etc. of which the Bhagavath, and the Vishnu Purana are the most popular. Another class of popular scripture is Agamas. Though they do not derive their authority from the Vedas they are not antagonistic to the teachings of the Vedas. They are predominently Vedic in spirit and character. They are theological treatises and manuals of worship. The three chief sects, Saivism, Saktism and Vaishnavism base their doctrines and dogmas on the Agamas.

There are six Darshanas. Darshanas literally mean light or vision. The six schools of philosophy are the six instruments of true teachings. Each Darshana prescribes a way of looking at Truth. Each has developed, systematised and corrected the various parts of the Vedas in its own way. Each system is a step or rung in the spiritual ladder. Their object is to demonstrate Truth, They are highly philosophical.

We shall now have a look into the religion as propounded in the Vedas.

The four Vedas (1) Rig Veda, (2) Yajur Veda, (3) Sama Veda and (4) Atharva Veda are the Srutis which are direct intuitional revelations. They form the foundation of all other Hindu scriptures. Prof. Max Muller says: "The Rig Veda is the most ancient book in the world. The sacred hymns of the Brahmanas stand unparalleled in the whole world and their preservation might be called miraculous." It is the precious treasure which the Aryans brought with them from their ancient home. The first three Vedas are identical in form, language and character. The chief among them is Rig Veda.

Yajur and Sama Vedas are purely liturgical and were useful for conducting religious ceremonies. In the Vedic age, sacrifice was considered to be an act of high devotion; the performance of which was not entrusted to priests alone but could be performed by any one who offered it, along with chanting of hymns from Rig Veda or Sama Veda. In course of time, the simple formulae became strict in most of the details and was called Yajur, which has its root in "Yag" and means sacrifice. Atharva Veda occupied a position next in importance to Rig Veda, but for a long time was not held in high esteem. The early Aryans had to mix with the aboriginals. It can be seen from the hymns of Atharva Veda that a spirit of compromise was adopted by the early Aryans in their recognition of the Gods worshipped by the aboriginals.

Each Veda consists of three parts known as (1) Mantras, (2) Brahmanas and (3) Upanishads.

The collection of Mantras is called the Samhita. The Brahmanas lay down religious duties to be observed; and the Upanishads discuss philosophic problems which form the concluding portions of the Brahmanas. The hymns are the creation of inspired poets; Brahmanas are the works of priests and Upanishads, the meditation and reflections of sages. From the study of Rig Veda we get knowledge of the social organisations of the time as also of the subsequent trends of thought prevalent in India.

It would be mere conjecture to fix the date of the composition and collection of these hymns. A safe conjecture would be 4500 B.C.

The Rig Veda consists of 1017 hymns and it is divided into eight chapters. Some of them are addressed to Agnh some to Indra and further some to others. One also finds speculative hymns as to the origin of creation. There are hymns expressing superstitions, charms and exorcisings. These hymns were not written by one individual or by a particular sect, nor are they the product of one age. The composers of these hymns were poetic souls who were moved by the beauties of nature and the wonders of the world. Their intense feelings suffused the objects of nature with personalities having souls. To them nature was a living entity to which they attuned themselves.

There are conflicting opinions on the spirit of these Vedic hymns. Rammohan Roy considers that these are allegorical representations of the attributes of Supreme Deity. These Vedic hymns are the products of several ages and contain various shades of thought.

The Brahmanas and the Upanish'ads develop the earlier views. We find in the Upanishads that the sages were not satisfied with the outward worship of nature and they proceeded to develop the suggestions contained in the Vedas.

In Rig Veda we find the inspired aspirations of the primitive souls who were in search of some retreat from the doubts and despair of the Senses and outward being. We read in them an intense desire to understand the world for its own sake. The earliest religion was the worship of nature in its manifold aspects. Physical phenomena first attracted attention and were subsequently assigned personalities. The deification of natural phenomena came at a later stage. People deified natural phenomena and worshipped them as Gods and Goddesses. They attributed to them a human sense of justice, and believed they were capable of being influenced by human attributes of love, hatred and passion. In the beginning the Gods were imagined to be great and powerful rather than good and gentle. So in course of time this deification proved wearisome and dissatisfying. From this dissatisfaction grew a tendency to place all Gods together. The Supreme, in some of the advanced hymns, is addressed as 'He' or 'It'. The Gods of the Vedic period are the reflections of the needs of the time. In this Universe therefore there exists a good number of unexplicable mysteries and whenever men failed to reason out a happening they attributed it to be the work of an unknown power which was conveniently called a God.

Sacrifice represents the second stage of the Vedic religion. It does not appear that Vedic religion was an idolatrous one. There were no temples. People had direct communion with Gods without the mediation of priests. Gods were supposed to be the friends of the Worshippers, and heaven and earth were addressed in a Moving manner 'father heaven' and 'mother earth'.

The conception of 'Rta' that is order contained in the Veda is the harbinger of the law of Karma which the predominant note of Hindu philosophy. Rta swings the world of men and of God an3 it influences everyone. It is conceived as a standard of morality and the good are those who trod its path. It is the truth and kernel of things. The opposite of Rta was disorder and falsehood.

Hospitality is considered a great virtue. "He who is possessed of food, hardens his heart against a feeble man finds no consolation." Sorcery, withcraft, charms, seduction and adultery are condemned as vicious. Gambling is taboo. Asceticism does not occupy a high place. Tama', the God of death, is not conceived as a terrible lord of vengeance. A man at his death throws off his mortal coil and the soul takes a bright spiritual, form and enters the realms of 'Yama' where he dwells with his forefathers and God Yama. Heaven is believed to be the abode of the pious and Hell of the wicked.

From its inception the religion of the Aryans was tolerant, and expansive, and so, it adapted itself to the new surroundings, found new growth and new vitality. They thought it undignified to stamp out of existence the religion of the aboriginals. They disliked fanaticism in religion. They were in search of Truth and believed that any god which satisfied the human mind in any particular way is a form of Truth.

In Artharva Veda these influences are evident. This Veda compromised with the religion of the aboriginals with the result that it elevated the religion of the aboriginals and partly degraded its own. So we find in Artharva Veda strange utterances of incantations and spells, charms, witchcraft, hymns to devils and demons. Some such stray references are also found in Rig Veda.

Madame Rogozine writes: "We have here, as though in opposition to the bright cheerful pantheon of beneficent deities so trustingly and gracefully addressed by the Rishis of Rig Veda, a weird repulsive world of crawling demons inspiring abject fear, such as never sprang from Aryan fancy."

The religion of Artharva Veda is an admixture of Aryan and non-Aryan religions. This was the religion practised by the common people. It was not practised by the priestly class and was not held in high esteem.

When we pass from Rig Veda to Yajur Veda, Sama Veda and the Brahmanas, there is a distinct change of atmosphere. The buoyancy and simplicity of the former gives place to artificiality, coldness and unnaturalness.

Presentation assumes greater importance than the matter and spirit of religion.

The second part of the Vedas are the Brahmanas. They are purely formal. There is no poetic fervour and inspiration is lacking. The words were selected to produce artificial sounds and prayer was considered to be muttering of certain Mantras in a set form. Brahmanas can be classed as text books for priests for the performance of sacrificial rites and ceremonies. They laid high importance on sacrifice. During this period, important changes were introduced in religious thought which permanently affected the future history of the Hindu religion. They laid great stress on the observance of caste and Ashram Dharmas. They gave a high and predominant authority to Vedas. The priests assumed a dignity equal to that of God. Asceticism was held in high repute and four Ashram Dharmas (1) Brahmacharya (studentship), (2) Garhastya (Householder), (3) Vanaprastha (hermit), (4) Sanyasa (Ascetic) were introduced. As regards the religion propounded in the Brahmanas it has been remarked, "A rigid soul-deadening commercialist creed based on a contractual motive took the place of the simple devout religion of Vedas." Priesthood became a profession and a hereditary one; priests became the mediators between men and Gods. By giving importance to Vedas and as men who preached them they created a sanctity around them. The Vedas which were merely transmissions of Truth came to be regarded as divine revelations which were communicated to the seers. At times we find in the Brahmanas exalted sentiments. People were enjoined to observe certain duties and obligations to all creations of God. Though the religion is formal, the high sentiments, and lofty ideas of truth, godliness, respect for parents, kindness, charity, mercy and abstinence from evil doing, enabled it to endure and influence subsequent thought in Hinduism. In the Brahmanas we find suggestions of rebirth.

The Upanishads form the concluding portions of the Vedas and are therefore called Vendanta or the end of Vedas, on which rest the later philosophies of-India. It has been remarked : "There is no important form of

Hindu thought which is not rooted in the Upanishads.' The springs of Upanishads are ever sought, for revival of idealistic thought. Their poetry and idealism are of such a high strain that they have swayed the hearts and heads of men. The oft quoted eulogy of Arthur Schopen-hauer regarding the philosophy as expressed in the Upanishads may be repeated. "It is the most rewarding and most elevating reading which there can be in the world. It has been the solace of my life and will be of my death." They are the earliest records of ideal speculations in India. Their aim is to bring peace and tranquillity to the searching soul. Metaphysical questions are put in the form of dialogues and discus - sions. "They express the restlessness of a striving human mind to grasp the true nature of reality." They are not written by a single individual. They reveal fundamental conceptions. "So numerous are the suggestions of truth and so various are the guesses of God that almost everybody may seek in them what he wants and find what he seeks."

They are 108 in number, of which ten constitute chief ones. They are the oldest and most authoritative. It is difficult to assign any date to them. The earliest of them are pre-Buddhistic, a few of them are post-Buddhistic. The probable date is sixth century B.C. The chief among them are (1) Chandogya, (2) Brihad-Aranyaka, (3) Taittriya (4) Aitareya, (5) Kaushitaki, (6) Katha, (7) Isa, (8) Mandaka, (9) Prasana, and (10) Maitri. Very little is known about the lives of these great thinkers whose reflections are embodied in the Upanishads. The reflections of the sages are original and are expressed in such form that they can be regarded as pieces of literature which can be distinguished from the hymns of the Vedas and the Brahmanas. The Upanishads placed new values on the religion propounded in the Vedas. They successfully stressed the monistic suggestions of the Vedic hymns. They probe from the external to the internal. Unlike the Brahmanas they are indifferent to the sacredness of Vedas. They denounce the external Vedic practices. They recognise only one god who is defined as eternal self-existent, incomprehensible and omniscient. He alone creates, preserves and destroys. He is the light lord and life of the world without any second and He is the sole object of adoration and worship. "How many Gods are there really, Yagnavalkaya?" "One" he said. Now answer another question, "Some do meditate on Agni Brahma, Rudra, Shiva, Vishnu. Say which of these is best for us." He said unto them "There are but chief manifestations of the highest, the immortal, the incorporeal Brahman. Brahman indeed is all these, and men may meditate, worship or discard also those which are its manifestations." The nature of this monistic Brahma is given as "Verily this whole world is Brahma He who consists of mind, whose body is life, whose form is light, whose conception is truth, whose soul is space, containing all works, containing all desires, containing all odours, containing all tastes, encompassing the whole world, the unspeaking and the unconcerned, smaller than the grain of rice or a barley corn or a mustard seed or a grain of millet or the kernel of a grain of millet and yet greater than the earth, greater than the atmosphere, greater than the sky, greater than these worlds."

It must be capable of all contraries. "It moves, it moves not. It is far, it is near. It is within all these. It is outside all these." The polytheistic conceptions had captured the imaginations of the people and it was found difficult to overthrow them. This process was accomplished by co-ordinating the many gods into one.

The object of the Upanishads is not to impart metaphysical knowledge but to guide the people into the new way of thinking. The soul of a man is the pivot on which revolves the philosophy of the Upanishads. They exhort the people to worship and adore the Atman within and not innumerable gods. "Whoever worships another deity (than this self) thinking He is one and I am another he does not know."

The philosophy of the Upanishads has been impugned as pessimistic; but the type of pessimism which is found in them is the common note of all philosophy. Man constantly desires to escape from doubt and despair. In the Upanishads we do not find that kind of pessimism which calls upon a being to suppress all efforts. In the philosophy of the Upanishads we find a constant faith in life, a zest for living, an effort at self-conquest and a search for truth. The meaning attached to life is a constant endeavour to attain perfection. They declare that neither sacrifice, nor rites and ceremonies, nor worshipping many gods nor much knowledge shall lead to perfection. Adoration of God is not by outward observances, but by internal purity and goodness.

Yagna (sacrifice) which was supposed to be an act of merriment, joy and feasting has undergone a tremendous change. It is declared that all around us the divine nature sacrifices itself and a man lives in, by, and with sacrifice. Sacrifice is made the synonym of self-effacement, self-surrender, self-renunciation. We are exhorted to put at the altar of God every thought, feeling and action. The worship of the spirit is urged and not the ceremonies. The philosophy of the Upanishads restrained and arrested the strict rituals of the Brahmanas which did not satisfy the super-consciousness of man's mind. The Upanishads do not give sanctity to the Vedas. It has been said by Narada "I know the Rig Veda, the Yajur Veda, the Sama Veda, with all these I know the Mantra and the sacred books; but I do not know the Self."

The Upanishads seek to solve the main problem of life. "Whence are we born, where do we live and whither do we go. Should time and nature or necessity or chance or the elements be considered the causes or He who is called the Purusha or the man that is the supreme spirit." These are the doubts and questions which they attempt to solve. The objects and the senses, the mind and-knowledge are all finite. The joys of the earth are short lived, Only the infinite is ever enduring and ever lasting. The central thought on which the Upanishads discourse is "There is infinite existence (i.e. Sat), Absolute Truth (i.e. Chit), and pure delight (i.e. Ananda)."

In the dialogue between the teacher Prajapati and the pupil Indra narrated in the Chandogya Upanishad there appears the definition of self in a progressive manner as-(1) Bodily Self, (2) The Empirical Self, (3) The Transcendental Self, and (4) The Absolute Self. What is the nature of the Self of Man? Prajapati answers thus 'The Self which is free from sin, free from old age, from death and grief, from hunger and thirst, which desires nothing but what it ought to desire and imagines nothing but what it ought to imagine. That it is which we must try to understand. It is the subject which persists throughout the changes, the common factor in states of walking, dreaming, sleeping, death, rebirth and final deliverance. Prajapati says distinctly that the Self of a man is subjective and not objective. The Self of man is not a heap of qualities comprised in the "Me" but is that which remains detached from "Me" and inspecting all the qualities. In the above dialogue Prajapati exhorts his pupil to realise this Self which continually exists even when all experiences are suspended.

In the Mandakya Upanishad we find analysis of consciousness. The soul has four conditions; the last condition includes all the previous ones. They are waking, dreaming, sleeping and Turiya. The first condition makes a being conscious of all the external objects of the world and enjoys them. The second is that of dreaming, where the Self enjoys the subtle things of the experience gathered during waking hours, upon which it forms a fresh world of new forms. In this state the spirit is at large, .liberated from the chains of the body. The third is the condition of sound sleep in which there is no desire and no dream. In this state the soul experiences oneness with Brahma. We are transported, having been liberated from vexations and desires. This state gives a foretaste of Bliss, but the highest state is not merely a dreamless sleep or desirelessness but it is pure intuitional consciousness. There is vacuity of knowledge of the inner and outer objects. This state is unseen, transcendental, incomprehensible, uninferrable, unthinkable, indescribable and which is the sole essence of the consciousness of Self, which has been symbolised by Omkara. The pure Brahman cannot be found in matter, Prana, Manas or Vignana, but can be realised in Turiya state, the highest conceivable state of Bliss of the human mind. It is called the Nirpudhika state or Nirguna Brahmana. Brahman is the Atman and Atman is the Brahman, the infinite is not beyond the finite but it is in the finite. It is "Tat Twam Asi" that thou art. The pairs of opposites, the subjective and objective,. lose all distinction and are formed into one. The conception of Ishwara is the Summum Bonnum (highest happiness) of the religious consciousness.

According to the Upanishads every individual is equipped with a force of energy which would enable him to attain spiritual perfection. An individual has divine instinct in him by which the "unheard becomes the heard, the unknown becomes the known". Yoga is the practical method suggested by the sages for the realisation of the highest. It has been said "Let a Brahmin renounce learning, and become a child. The Atman is attained, not by learning nor by genius and much knowledge of books. It is attained in moments of illumination." The soul, when it once seizes the reality, loses itself in its contemplation and enjoyment. He becomes one with God. It is an indescribable and ineffable vision. A realised soul would say: "God put it into my head and I cannot put it into yours," Kena Upanishads say: 'It is unknown to those who know and known to those who do not know." The sages of the Upanishads lived in a world of nature with intense feelings and emotions. To them the world did not appear as a baseless fabric and a mere phenomenal show. To them the world was throbbing and pulsating with life, love and harmony. It is God's revelation of Himself, it is His joy that assumes all forms. The everyday experiences of life present two aspects of consciousness. Our problem arises when we try to reconcile the two aspects. It is this seemingly irreconcilable quality which causes all the misery and unhappiness. Vedanta conceives of it as Maya. The truth of oneness of things is brought out in a dialogue between the father and son in the Chandogya Upanishad. The father points out to his son some characteristic objects of nature and exhorts him to realise the unity of life,—the continuity of life—with that of the universe. It is difficult to conceive this one reality which is being over-shadowed and overpowered by several objects. This difficulty is aggravated by the imperfection of the human mind which is circumscribed by space, time and cause.

When it is said that there is one reality and there is no other reality outside the Atman, it is meant that Atman is the universal, supreme and the all-pervading spirit which embraces everything. "The Atman, of which we are in search, is not the object of knowledge but the basis of knowledge." The Upanishads inform us that of all the finite objects the individual soul possesses the highest potentiality, which is capable of realising the Supreme. To the sages of Upanishads, the world seemed to be striving to become infinite. (It is said in one of the Upanishads, "Two birds of beautiful plumage, inseparable companions, sat upon the same tree, one on the top and another below. The beautiful bird below was eating the fruits of the tree which were sweet and bitter, at one moment a sweet one and at another a bitter one. The moment he ate the bitter fruit, he was sorry but after a while he ate another and when it was too bitter, he looked up and saw the other bird who ate neither the sweet nor the bitter but was calm and majestic, immersed in his own glory. And when the poor bird below forgot and went on eating the sweet and bitter fruits again, until at last he ate one that was extremely bitter, he stopped again and once more looked up at the glorious bird above. Then he came nearer and nearer to the other bird and when he had come near enough the rays of light shone, upon him and enveloped him and he saw that he was transformed into the higher bird. He became calm, majestic, free, and found there had been but one bird all the time on the tree."

The bird was but a reflection of the one above. Even so in the tree of the world man is in reality one with God but frets, fumes and grieves over his own helplessness, and when he reflects that he and his God are one all his helplessness passes off. It is in human consciousness that the tension between the finite and the infinite reaches its highest pitch. No doubt the human soul, when struggling with the gross self, is the highest in the world, but that is not the highest realisable. Freedom of spirit is reached when the God in him realises itself. The ideal which the Upanishads set forth is that man must become one with God, and this is the goal of life. Duty is a means to that end, and morality is valuable only as it leads to it. The passion and pride of the animal self and the ambitions and craving of egoism anchor the vital energies to the shores of lower self and atrophy the vitality of the soul. In the Taitriya Upanishad it has been said: "Know the Atman as the Lord who sits in the chariot of the body, Buddhi is the charioteer, mind is the reins, senses are the horses and objects are the roads." Cravings are to be kept under restraint for when craving seizes a man the soul is shattered. It has been said in Katha Upanishad "Man is not in the least elevated above animalism by the possession of reason, if his reason is only employed in the same fashion as that in which an animal uses its instinct." If instead of being guided by reason we are guided by senses our life would be shipwrecked.

Reason informs us that a man possesses no interest which he can call his own apart from the whole of which he is part. A man of reason must have an unselfish devotion to the world. Each man falsely differentiates himself from whatever that exists outside his physical body and mental history. The only door of escape from sin is to annihilate all selfish desires, longings and possessions, and to subordinate individual to social ends. This would be a life of reason and then we should be able to see that all things are in God and of God. A man who has realised this truth will deny all selfish desires, will long to lose his life and will follow the path of universal life. It appears in Isa Upanishad "That moral life is a God-centered life, a life of passionate love and enthusiasm for humanity, a life seeking the infinite through the finite,"

The Upanishads direct us to have inward morality, and to attach a primary importance to motive in conduct. Yagnavalkya says: "Self-love lies at the root of all other kinds of love; love for wealth and prosperity, clan and country are special forms of selfish love." All that the Upanishads insist upon is to renounce selfish desires. and endeavours. "Detach from thyself and attach thyself to God" is what is demanded of an individual. Even an ideal sage has desires, but his desires are pure and unselfish. We are asked to eschew animal desires, lust, and impulsive cravings of the brute in man. The desire for knowledge and for attaining perfection is to be pursued. The tender feelings of love, compassion, charity, sympathy, kindness, mercy, etc. are to be intensely developed and their opposites to be rooted out The Upanishads say: "It is not by 'Kama' (Desire) nor by offspring, nor by wealth, nor by sacrifice that immortality is gained. It is gained through renunciation and sacrifice. As has been said in lsa Upanishad "By renunciation thou mayest enjoy." In effect there is a direction to cast off all possessions, call nothing your own and then enjoy life. But the attitude towards renunciation should not degenerate into a senseless asceticism, for such an attitude has been described as self love. The seeker after perfection, does not relinquish the world but would live in it, love the objects of the world, for the infinite they contain and fulfil the duties that are cast upon him. "Every common duty fulfilled, every individual sacrifice made, helps to realise the self." Things of the world are not baits but alloys of supreme bliss.

Solitude, continence, fasting and purity are enjoined for purification of the body. For attaining spiritual heights physical discipline is absolutely essential. The Upanishads do not encourage the idea that life is a dream and the world a shadow. In Isa Upanishad it is said "Even while doing deeds here one may desire to live a hundred years."

The Upanishads also enumerate a code of duties to be performed. It is said that an act of an individual coordinates him in the divine scheme of things. An individual must practise virtue, self-restraint, be merciful, kind and liberal "Give with faith, give in plenty, with modesty, with fear, with sympathy" so declares a verse in the Taitriya Upanishad. The Chandogya Upanishad exhorts us to practice meditation, charity, right dealings, non-injury to life and truthfulness. This is declared to be the right form of conduct. It is considered to be a great virtue to love the brute creation.

A true Sanyasin is he who, with spiritual vision, restrains and immolates himself for mankind. Right living and right knowledge as distinguished from mere intellectual ability, accompanied by virtue, a sense of duty and a desire for attaining perfection are the pathways of self-realisation. Without realisation of self, life has no aim, no purpose, no support, and so is futile. Until the Grosser self is entirely spiritualised the ideal will not be achieved. The Upanishads declare: "Religion is the inspiration of Morality; without religion, morality is but an eternal struggle; in religion it is turned into realisation." If an individual casts off the selfish ego, morality will become the condition of his being and the eternal law will be fulfilled in love. Every man has the innate potentiality to rise and reach the divine stature, or what is called the tabernacle of God, if he strives for it.

There are three stages in the attainment of religious consciousness viz. (1) Shravana which means listening, (2) Manana (Reflection), and (3) Nididhyasan (contemplative meditation). The first stage points to the place of tradition in religious life. Some kind of traditional revelations are necessary to initiate oneself in the faith of a living God. The second stage points to the need for rational thought. The understanding of truth is not to be confused with the attainment of reality, which is distinguished from mere reason. The third stage helps us to transmute the rational idea into spiritual perception. The pursuit of truth is the constant endeavour for building up the life of truth in the soul. "The worshippers must intuit Brahma to become Brahma."

The central feature of religion as evidenced from the teachings of the Upanishads is that there is one Supreme Being who is to be worshipped with love, reverence and faith. "The Upanishad holds that the absolute and the God are identical, we name it supreme Brahma to emphasise its transcendence of the finite, its inexplicability and its all comprehensiveness. We call it Ishwara to emphasise the personal aspect so necessary for religious devotion."

The highest state of realisation is 'Mokhsa' or Release. It has been said in Mundaka Upanishad: "As the flowing rivers disappear in sea losing their names and forms, thus a wise man freed from name and form, goes to the divine person who is beyond all." The highest is a state of rapture and ecstasy which is called 'Ananda', where the being is absorbed and becomes one with Brahma the Creator, and experiences oneness with Him. Yagnavalkya explains this state to Maitreyi in the following words: "As a lump of salt which is thrown into water dissolves, and cannot be gathered up again, but wherever water is drawn it is salty, so is it with this Great Being, the Endless, the Unlimited. It is this Being which imparts the knowledge and absorbs it, at one and the same time. There is no consciousness after death."

Maitreyi says: "This aspect of thy argument that there is no consciousness after death perplexes me."

Yagnavalkya replies. 'I tell thee nothing perplexing, it is quite comprehensible."

Where there is duality of existences one can see the other, can smell the other, but where everything has turned into his Atman by whom shall he see, smell, speak, hear, think or apprehend? By whom shall he apprehend him through whom he apprehends this universe? In the absolute, all duality is said to be lost. "Traversing these worlds, having the food he likes, taking the form he likes he exists singing songs."

Mundaka holds it to be the companionship with God. The self is not annihilated any more than the rays of the sun are lost in the sun, waves of the sea in the ocean and notes of music in harmony.

According to the Upanishads evil is neither an illusion nor is it permanent. It is unreal in so far as it is bound to transform into good and its reality consists in its transforming nature with a struggle. The path to perfection is through suffering, strife and sacrifice.

"The good is one thing, the pleasant another, these two have different objects and chain a man. It is well with him to choose the good; he who chooses the pleasant misses the end."

Struggle is the law of freedom. Strife carries sacrifice in its womb and sufferings and sacrifice are the axles of evolution. In Chandogya Upanishad it is said "Marc verily is the sacrifice."

The law of Karma is the conservation of moral energy. According to this law there is nothing indefinite or accidental; we reap what we sow, and every action, every thought produces an effect on character. Unconscious tendencies are the result of past conscious deeds and thoughts. It is impossible to evade the Law of Karma. "Man is a creature of will, according to what he believes in this world so will he be when he is departed." It is held that we can liberate ourselves from the preceding conditions by performing selfless actions. Man is not a mere products of nature. He has the capacity to transcend his Karma. The essence of spirit is freedom. The spiritual in him is the basis of his initiative and endeavour. There is a Soul in him of which he is the master. Nothing external can compel it. The more we live in the Living Presence of God, the more we assert the rights of the spirit, the more free we are. The more selfish we are, the more is our bondage to Karma. Karma has two aspects. The cosmic and the psychological. Every deed must produce its natural effects in the world. At the same time it leaves an impression or forms a tendency on the mind of man; it is this tendency or 'Samaskara' that inclines us to repeat the deed we have once done. By self-discipline we can strengthen our good impulses. Karma is not a blind unconscious principle governing the whole universe. The moral law of Karma is the expression of the nature of the Absolute. Freedom and Karma are two aspects of the same reality. "Karma implies hope for the future and resignation to the past."

The concept of rebirth occupies a dominant position in the Upanishads. Their view is that the soul is not annihilated at death. They have a strong conviction as to the continuity of life. It is a corollary to the law of Karma. In the Upanishads the belief is transformed into the doctrine of rebirth in the world, in contrast to the belief in the Brahmanas of birth in the next world. The highest kind of immortality is becoming one with Brahman. So life eternal is, union with Brahman. The undelivered soul is subject to the law of births and deaths and has to work out its destiny by lives on earth. The kind of birth depends upon the nature of work. Between one life and another there is a persisting identity though our consciousness may not testify to it; the reality of life is the character, and not the body and the mind. It survives the disruption of death. The Upanishads hold that "Karma changes, but the universal self endures."

Having dealt in a summarised way with philosophy and religion as propounded in the Upanishads we now propose to have a glimpse of the teachings of the Gita.

Like a jewel the Gita is set in the epic of Mahabharata. Its authorship is unknown but is attributed to Vyas, and its date, Dr. Radhakrishnan fixes in the fifth century B.C. The book is called Bhagwat Gita because Lord Krishna is known as Shree Bhagwan. The doctrine which he preaches is the Bhagwat Creed.

The Gita derives its main inspiration from the Upanishads and is counted as one of them. The Gita restates the central teachings of the Upanishads. The fundamental ultimates such as the Self, the Absolute, God, the Universe have been borrowed bodily from the Upanishads. It appears that at the time of the composition of the Gita, varied ideologies, theories and speculations were in vogue. The author of the Gita has transformed them and created an inward religion, profound and subtle but simple. The dogmatic formulas and external forms are superseded by presenting an integrated eirenicon for all men and for all time. It has been said "That the author has refined and reconciled the different currents of thoughts, the Vedic cult of sacrifice, the Upanishads' teachings of the transcendent Brahma, the Bhagwat theism of tender pity, the Sankhya dualism, and the Yoga meditation, the diverse has been concentrated into one whole by discrimination rather than by denial, by refinement rather than by doubt, by converging the several waters rather than diverting them."

The teachings of the Gita have been put forth as a tradition. 'If expresses the Truth in positive language, It represents not any particular sect of Hinduism but in its entirety. It envelops within its fold ethics and metaphysics. There is no divorce of the life of spirit from the actual day-to-day life. The author has offered a practical and simple religion to the lowly and the lost to realise his goal in life. "We are not called Jo solve the meaning of life but to find out the deed demanded of us and to work; and so by action to master the riddle of life." Aldous Huxley has spoken about the philosophy of the Gita in the following words: "The Gita is one of the cleverest and more comprehensive summaries of the perennial philosophy ever to have been made. Hence its enduring value not only for the Indians but for mankind ... The Bhagwat Gita is perhaps the most systematic spiritual creature of the perennial philosophy."

Some students of the Gita attach an allegorical meaning. They picture the Pandavas and the Kauravas to be respectively the forces of good and evil in the human frame; some others draw out suggestive meanings from the names of the Various characters of the epic denoting Dhristarashtra as the individual ego holding fast to the flesh and listening to the dialogue between Krishna the silent within, and Arjuna, the humble, self-surrendering and pure obeying his advice and fighting the forces of evil and gaining victory; yet some others would typify Arjuna as a struggling soul eaten up by inward agony and hold that these doubts, despair and search of Arjuna are the facsimile of the fate of man. The soul is symbolised by the battlefield of Kurukshetra. The Kauravas are the enemies who impede the progress of Arjuna who strives to regain freedom for man. Krishna stands for the voice of God. The Gita manifests to its devotee a vision of the Supreme, guides him how to know Him in His true glory and power, how to seek Him, how to enter in Him and how to be one with Him.

In the opening the Gita brings Arjuna into the battlefield fully convinced of the justness of the cause but in a short while he becomes despondent and desires to shrink from his duty by putting forward various arguments. He argues that it is nobler to desist from killing those whom he loved and be killed by them unresisting and unarmed. This gives occasion to Lord Krishna to explain to Arjuna—the representative man who is feeling a sense of the emptiness of earthly possessions, pleasures.

and powers—philosophic problems in a simple and logical way.

The divinity which is ascribed to Krishna is the ultimate reward of all spiritual seekers. He is now as he was then, and shall be hereafter, to everyone of us and is ready to speak to us, at every moment of time. He is the Indwelling spirit, our rest and our spiritual consciousness.

For attaining perfection apparently three different paths are shown. These are: (1) The Karma Yoga i.e. the path of work. (2) The Jnana Yoga, i.e. the path of knowledge. (3) The Bhakti Yoga i.e. the path of devotion. These can be broadly classified under three heads, the practical, the theoretical and the emotional methods. Men possess varied aptitudes, inclinations and tastes. They are of active, reflective and emotional temperaments, but do not possess any of these traits exclusively. In the perfect state there is a fusion of knowledge, action and love. "To those seeking knowledge He is eternal light, to those struggling for virtue He is eternal righteousness, and to those emotionally inclined He is eternal Love."

In the beginning the Gita explains in a variety of ways the nature of the immortal self. The self is distinguished from the non-self. It is said "The (Imperishable self which inhabits impermanent bodies, pervades the whole universe; Him no weapons can cut, no fire can burn, no water can wet, no wind can dry. Thou art that permanent Imperishable Self and not the ever-changing ever-perishing vestment of the self, called the body." The delusion of 'mine' and 'thine' is caused because one identifies the Self with the perishing self. It is one's attachment to the physical self that makes one lament the death and destruction of things which are foredoomed to perish. One should therefore detach oneself from the false sense of the 'I', destroy ignorance and with unswerving faith and devotion attach himself to that Imperishable Self and thus attain freedom from bondage.

The Gita says in unequivocal terms that action surpasses renunciation of action. The Gita does not teach that the world is a shadow and a illusion. It exhorts men to live in fullness of active life with the spirit chained to the Supreme. It says that Nature is ever at work in her fullness and it is impossible for an individual to abstain from action even for a moment. Freedom from bondage cannot be achieved through inaction. Man is asked not to renounce action but to perform with the detachment of spirit and without desire for the fruit thereof. The action may be altruistic but whether it binds the soul, or otherwise depends upon the motive or the desire which impelled one to do it. If one performs all actions including daily duties dispassionately, without anger, without attachment, in the spirit of selflessness, in dedication to God, without desire for the fruit, such action will free the individual soul and will lead him to perfection. We must cut the knot of ignorance which impedes progress.

Shankara has said: "Liberation is accomplished by wisdom, but wisdom does not spring without the purification of the heart. Therefore, for the purification of the heart one should perform all acts of speech, mind and body in a prescribed manner dedicating them to the supreme Lord." Action performed in such a manner becomes Yagna or sacrifice. Disinterested action is sacrifice. Mahatma Gandhi gives the meaning of sacrifice thus: "Sacrifice, according to the Gita, means an act (which includes thought, speech or deed) directed to the welfare of all life without receiving or desiring a return for it of a temporal or spiritual nature. The world cannot subsist even for a single moment without sacrifice in this sense and therefore the Gita after having dealt with the true wisdom in the 2nd chapter takes up in the third the means of attaining it and declares in so many words that 'Yagna' or 'sacrifice' came with creation itself. This body therefore has been given us only in order that we may serve all creation with it and therefore, says the Gita, he who eats without offering Yagna, eats stolen food. Every single act of one who would lead a life of purity should be in the nature of Yagna. Yagna having come with our birth, we are debtors all our lives and thus for ever bound to serve the universe. And even as a bond slave receives food, clothing and so on, from the master whom he serves, so should we gratefully accept such gifts as may be assigned to us by the Lord of the Universe" (from Yervada Mandir).

The whole creation has sprung from sacrifice. The righteous ever works and thinks for the common good. The spring of his delight is his soul, and with untiring energy he performs all work without attachment, with a desire for the welfare of all creation. He is not deluded by the sense of 'I'. He feels himself not the doer.

For those who do not possess the knowledge to isolate the self, the Gita presents another way, and that is, of surrendering all actions to God as an offering, with the mind transfixed on the soul, and being indifferent to the fruit of action or the sense of mineness, resting in faith, and without coming under the sway of senses, and skilfully doing and discharging his own duty however low it may be in a spirit of selflessness.

Lust and wrath, which are seated in the senses, the mind and reason, obscure knowledge, stupify man and impel him to sinful acts and conduct. Therefore it is necessary that a man must first restrain his senses, then control his mind, then reason, and then overcome his self by the Self, so that he will not be overcome by lust and wrath which destroy knowledge and discrimination.

The freed soul performs the duties of the world assigned to him, spontaneously and unruffled by the events of the world. "They live in the world but as strangers. They endure all hardships of the fiesh and yet they live not after the flesh. Their existence is on earth but their citizenship is in Heaven." The Gita says: "As an ignorant man acts from attachment to action so should the wise act without attachment, wishing the welfare of the world. A man, who frees himself from passion, fear, lust and wrath, who relies on Him, and is ever full with Him and is refined by the ordeal of knowledge, finds union with him. The enlightened soul takes up every undertaking that comes to him. He is free from desire and selfish purpose and has reduced to ashes all his actions in the fire of knowledge. He has renounced attachment to the fruit of action, he is ever content and free from all dependence, he performs actionless actions, he expects nothing, he holds his mind and body under restraint, puts away every possession, is content with whatever he gets and is rid of the pairs of opposite. He is free from ill-will, even-minded in success and failure, his mind is grounded in knowledge, he acts only for sacrifice. He sees all beings in himself and thus sees the Lord in all beings."

Sanyasa, according to the Gita, is the renunciation of desire and not the renunciation of action. 'Tyaga' is the renunciation of the fruits of all works. "Not by Karma (action) nor by progeny, nor by wealth but by Tyaga is release obtained." Action without selfish desire or expectation of gain, performed in the spirit of "I am not the Doer" is the ideal set before us. The Gita does not teach the complete renunciation of action but the conversion of all work into desireless action. Salvation is not a matter of outward action or inaction. It is the possession of the impersonal outlook and inner renunciation of the ego.

Act of sacrifice, gifts, austerity and the like should be performed without attachment and desire for their fruits. To one who is fillcd with the spirit of surrender all actions are welcome; he is not affected by pleasure or pain; nor does he feel elated by performing pleasant action nor does he find unhappiness when performing unpleasant action. By doing the action in the right spirit he acquires purity of heart and mind and through that purity he realises the immortal, actionless self.

The Gita says that the Self has no connection with activity. The Prakriti does the actions, but through delusion the individual takes the credit for the performance. All actions are spoken of as done by the body, speech or mind; the fruit is also enjoyed through them. To those who consider the body as consciousness, it appears that the Self is the agent. They cast a net over themselves and are shut up in the prison of their bodies.

When selfishness and egoism are destroyed and, when desire and personal gain are renounced, action cannot bind the individual soul. He who has a trained intellect, a pure understanding and who is equipped with knowledge, is absolutely free from the egoistic notion. Obstacles that hinder the realisation must be removed and when obstacles are removed knowledge will illumine; just as where light is, darkness cannot prevail, so, where knowledge is, ignorance cannot stand.

The Gita shows another path for attaining the goal and that is the knowledge of reality or the path of knowledge. It is action which keeps the world in motion, action in turn is the outcome of desire and attachment and these spring from ignorance. Ignorance consists in identifying the self with the Self and believing that the individual self is permanent. Thus so long as one is shrouded in ignorance one lives in bondage. In order to obtain freedom, one must dispel the darkness of ignorance by knowledge. Knowledge does not mean the acquisition of theoretical learning or intellectual acumen. If one desires to reach the higher self through the path of knowledge one must have a detached passion for acquisition of knowledge. Ignorance or spiritual blindness cannot be removed with theoretical learning and intellectual acumen; but one has to cleanse the soul, gain mastery over his mind and all his senses, and become one with all creation. The rabble of desires and fumes of passion must be conquered. The inconstant mind and the unwieldy senses must be reined in.

The Jnanayogi is undeluded, knows and rests in Brahman, detaches himself from contacts, finds bliss in the Atman (soul), becomes one with nature, attains oneness with Brahman, has acquired mastery over himself and is forever engrossed in the welfare of all beings. The Gita gives us some of the means for disciplining the mind and its activities.

A man who seeks to attain perfection must renounce selfish purpose, conquer himself, rest in perfect calm, be self-composed in cold or heat, pleasure or pain, honour or dishonour; must master his senses, regard a clod of earth, stone or gold as one and the same; hold with equal reverence a boon companion, a friend, an enemy, a stranger, an alien, an ally, a saint, or a sinner; he must be firm, like a rock, and must be discriminative, of knowledge. These are some of the spiritual qualifications to be cultivated. The physical conditions which facilitate the path of one who is determined to enter the sanctuary of self, are a clean spot, a firm seat, concentrated mind; control of the functions of thought and sense and steadfastness in the vow of Brahmacharya. He must be disciplined in food, recreation and sleep and in effort he must be free from longing for objects. He sees Atman in all beings and all beings in Atman. Although the mind acts like a rabble yet it is possible to curb it by constant practice and by dispassion, and so produce mental calm which would give rise to inward silence; so the soul will establish contact with the eternal spirit. Both Karma Yoga and Jnana Yoga lead to the same goal but Karma Yoga is Simpler. Jnana Yoga is difficult without Karma Yoga.

We shall now see Bhakti Marga—that is the way of devotion. Devotion is the bond of trust and love to a personal God. This is the kingly science, the kingly secret, the supreme purifier, and easier to practise. It can be realised only through direct experience or spiritual intuition. It is the loving attachment to God, a longing for God for its own sake. "The human soul draws near to the divine by contemplation of God's power, wisdom and goodness, by constant remembrance of Him, with a devout heart." The devotee directs his whole being to God. And God declares to him: "This is my word of promise, that he who loveth me shall not perish."

Such devotion is not merely the flight of the lone to the Alone:—The soul detaching itself from the earth and attaching itself to the Supreme,—but is active love and faith towards the Divine. The faith that is required is the firm conviction that knowledge of the Self alone can give one supreme peace.

We are given the knowledge of God as He is, in various ways. He is described as the Imperishable Unmanifest. He is the sustainer of all beings though He is not in them. He contains all, and all beings move in Him without affecting Him. He is the creator, the sacrifice, the herb, the fire, the offering, the Mantras, father, mother, friend, goal, abode, source, dissolution, death and deathlessness, the giver, the withholder and acceptor of all sacrifice, the birthless, the ageless, the being, the finite and the infinite. He presides over all only as a witness.

A devotee may worship Him as creator and the source of all that is good, or he may worship Him as a sustainer and preserver of all, or he may worship Him as a destroyer; in whatever manner he worships Him he must realise that his worship may not limit his God who transcends all. A Devotee must ever bear in mind that the God of his worship is merely a symbol of the Supreme.

When a devotee beholds nothing separate from Him and has taken sole refuge in God, God expects very little of him and He Himself looks after his bodily wants and preserves him from all evils. "As for those who worship Me thinking on ME alone and nothing else, ever attached to Me, I bear the burden of what they need."

A true devotee has three distinctive qualities: Even-mindedness, undivided devotion and skill in action. These are completely harmonised in a true devotee. He does everything as a sacrifice to Him and His glory. When a devotee acquires such a self-effacing devotion he wins the Lord. "He who does my work, who makes ME his goal, who is my devotee, who has cast off all attachment and shed all ill-will, comes to ME."

Lord Krishna says in the Gita that a devotee who is dear to him is he "Who bears no ill-will to any being, who is from attachment and egoism, even-minded in pleasure and pain, who is ever content, self-controlled, patient, firm in determination, who has surrendered his mind and his intellect to Him, who causes fear to none and does not fear anyone, who is free from anger, fear and agitation, who expects nothing, is pure, skilful in action, unconcerned and untroubled, who has given up all initiative, who neither rejoices nor hates, neither grieves nor desires, who is indifferent to good or evil repute, who is alike in cold and heat, pleasure and pain, free from attachment, who is restrained in speech, content with everything and who has no fixed abode and is firm in mind."

A true devotee, says the Gita, possesses the knowledge of the identity of all lives. In a liberated soul there is annihilation of the mind and in him there is no ignorance. The Gita gives a series of attributes of an individual whose mind is turned upwards and on whom the knowledge of the Self has dawned. Such a man is humble, unpretentious, forgiving, upright, serving the teacher, pure, steadfast, self-controlled, indifferent to objects of senses, unegoistic, unattached; realises the painfulness and evil of birth, death, age and disease, is not wrapped up in wife and children, home and family and is even-minded whether good or evil befall him. He has an unwavering devotion to Him, resorts to solitary places, and has a distaste for the haunts of men. He does not injure. He has the settled conviction that there is nothing higher than Him and that He is the sole refuge. His mind has merged with Him and has a constant awareness of the Atman and for him knowledge of Atman is the only true knowledge and the reverse of it is ignorance.

The Gita has worked out most elaborately the doctrine of Gunas (modes or attributes) as the constituents of Prakriti. All mental and material phenomena spring from the evolution of Prakriti. The Prakriti has three Gunas or. attributes which are: (1) Sattva, (2) Rajas, and (3) Tamas. On the material level Sattva denotes lightness, Rajas denotes movement, Tamas denotes heaviness, and on the mental level these three Gunas act as goodness, passion and dullness respectively. They appear and act in varied proportions and thus produce diversity in actual existence. The soul ascends or descends in accordance with the dominance of one or the other of the Gunas. On the human level the three Gunas indicate triple mentality; which are Sattva, that is the best; Rajas comes next, and Tamas is the lowest and the worst. The individual gets himself ensnared by identifying himself with the body consciousness. To attain perfection one has to transcend the Gunas. Any effort to transcend the Gunas is not in vain but the aspirant moves forward towards perfection.

Sattva has the characteristic of effulgence, harmony, goodness, produces knowledge, happiness, purity, sublime thoughts and it moves inward. Rajas is passion, activity and ambition. It produces desires and craving, greed.

restlessness, attachment and authorship of action. Tamas produces inertia, torpor and ignorance. Under its influence the actions of an individual are on the plane of instinct.

All the three Gunas cannot operate at one and the same time; when one Guna asserts itself, it overpowers the other two and produces its own effects.

The Gita therefore exhorts an individual to analyse all phenomena in terms of these Gunas, know their characteristics and to stand firm as a witness to the processes of the Gunas. To attain supreme bliss one must become 'Gunatita' i.e., he should transcend the Gunas. The supreme self is in no way affected by the Gunas, the liberated man feels that he is the witness of the processes of the Gunas, that he is neither the enjoyer nor the doer. The "Gunatita" or he who has transcended the Gunas, is he who sits like one unconcerned, unperturbed by the Gunas, who stands apart without wavering and knowing that it is only the interplay of the Gunas.

The Gita says that this Samsara or the universal manifestation can be viewed in two ways. The tree of Samsara can be pictured with its roots above in Brahma which is the support of everything and the resting place of all. The branches of this tree grow downwards. They evolve into grosser and grosser states. Egoism which is one of its branches goes downwards in three directions. From roots of actions done with expectation of gain a new branch of rebirth comes up forming a series without beginning or end. It can be cut by the sword of knowledge.

The other way to look at this tree of Samsara is that the branches of this tree are above and below. It is nourished by the three qualities, the sense objects are its buds. and the roots which grow downwards are the bonds of Karma. The branches of this tree are the objects of senses and the original root is ignorance. The branch which goes upward is the branch of Dharma; another is dispassion which leads to self-realisation. The highest root is Brahma; the secondary roots are the latent impressions which spread in this world and impel men to perform virtuous and vicious actions. This tree can be cut with the axe of non-attachment.

We are given three aspects of divine existence. The first is perishable, which comprises the whole world of changing forms; the second is Imperishable which manifests itself in diverse forms of illusions.. .Purshottam or the highest is distinct from these two. He is not affected by the limiting adjuncts of the perishable and the imperishable. He pervades the three worlds and sustains them.

The Gita exhorts us to develop Sattva qualities by controlling the senses, doing selfless service and practising introspection and meditation and inquiring "Who am I?"

The "Daivi Sampat" (Divine wealth) helps the aspirant to attain self-knowledge. The divine attributes are twenty-six in number: they are fearlessness, purity of heart, steadfastness, knowledge of Yoga, alms-giving, control of senses, sacrifice, study of Sastras, austerity, straightforwardness, harmlessness, truthfulness, absence of crookedness, compassion to beings, uncovetousness, gentleness, modesty, absence of fickleness, vigour, forgiveness, fortitude, purity, absence of hatred and absence of pride. An individual must cultivate fearlessness in word, deed and thought. If one leads a life of honesty and truthfulness, observes right conduct and surrenders himself to God, he becomes fearless. Fearlessness is the first virtue to be developed. It will induce discrimination and dispassion. In order to acquire self-knowledge he must check the outgoing tendencies of the mind and the senses.

A man of demoniac nature knows not what to do and what to refrain from. Neither purity, nor right conduct nor truth is found in him. He is harsh, arrogant, self-conceited and hyprocritical. He is beset with cares, worries and anxieties and his mind is engrossed in acquiring and preserving countless sensual objects. "Bound by hundred ties of hope, given over to lust and anger, they strive to obtain by unlawful means, hoards of wealth for sensual enjoyment." The Gita says "Triple is the gate of this hell leading to the ruin of the soul and they are lust, anger and greed, and therefore one should abandon these."

"The Gita describes to us the three kinds of people who are endowed with three kinds of faith. Faith assumes a three-fold character under the influence of the three

Gunas. When Sattva is strongly developed, it is easy for an aspirant to attain self-realisation; if Rajas is predominant then faith becomes the handmaid of activity and if Tamas dominates faith is annihilated.

The tendency of an individual determines his desire, the desire determines his action, his action determines his birth into another being after death.

The Gita says that there are three kinds of food that a man can eat. They are either sattvic, Rajasic or Tamasic according to its character and effect on the body and the mind. The Sattvic food produces cheerfulness, mental clarity and serenity; the Rajasic food stimulates passion, restlessness, evil thought, craving, disease, pain and anxiety and the Tamasic food produces lethargy, indolence and stupefaction.

Virtues like charity, austerity and sacrifice can become vices if they are not performed unselfishly, without attachment, without desire for fruit, and unless as an offering to God.

Self-discipline must begin with the mind first. The practice of 'Sama' control of the mind comes first and then comes 'Dama' control of the senses. A man must observe austerity of body, mind and speech.

In conclusion the Gita says, 'Fix thy mind on ME, be devoted to ME, and make sacrifice to ME.' Bow down to ME, thou shalt come ever to ME and truly do I promise unto thee for thou art dear to ME."

BUDDHISM

"BUDDHISM, that wonderful teaching which declares life to be sorrow and yet is free from pessimism; which apparently inculcates the profoundest egoism and yet is extolled for its loftiest morality; which denies the 'I', the soul, and yet teaches absolute responsibility for our deeds through rebirth; which is without God, or prayer and yet offers the most certain salvation—this wonderful teaching was founded by Gautama, of the aristocratic Sakya clan."

Buddha was born about the year 560 B.C. in a grove called- Lumbini near the city of Kapilavastu (modern Bhinla) in Nepal. His personal name was Siddhartha. His family name was Gautama. His father's name was Suddhodana, his mother's Mahamaya; she died seven days after giving birth to Siddhartha. Hearing of his birth a great sage, Asita, came to see the child and saw in him several marks of greatness one associates with a deliverer of the world. The birth of the Prince was celebrated in great eclat. After the death of his mother, Siddhartha was nursed and educated by his mother's sister Pajapati, who was also his step-mother and later became the first woman member of his order.

From his early age, Siddhartha was of a quiet, retiring and contemplative disposition and was full of compassion and pity. His father noticed his spiritual inclinations and tried his best to protect the young prince from worldly sufferings. Siddhartha meditated upon the sufferings of mankind. He felt within himself an entrancing love for all living creatures and felt pity for their pains and sorrows.

Siddhartha was married to Yashodhara. His father built for him three stately palaces each adapted to the seasons of the year; and adorned these palaces with gardens. He provided the Prince with all the pleasures. The king had commanded that no one should mention death, old age, sorrow, pain or sickness in his presence.

The years which followed his marriage were spent in regal splendour. There was a surfeit of dancing, music, and courting. All sorrowful sights, all misery and all knowledge of misery were kept away from him and he did not know that there was distress in the world. In the midst of all these rejoicings, Siddhartha, however, felt dissatisfied and he pined for a change. As a chained elephant longs for the wilds of the jungles, he desired to be released from the prison house and wanted to see life beyond the walls, and asked his father, the king, for permission to do so. In his early twenties, he became acquainted with human suffering. On one occasion, the prince saw a shrivelled old man worn out with swollen veins, broken back, bending on a staff and trembling. On another occasion he saw a sick man writhing in pain, overcome by fever, exhausted and helpless. On the third occasion he saw a dead man being carried on a bier surrounded by people wailing and lamenting. Seeing these sights he exclaimed "O worldly men! how fatal is your delusion! Inevitably your body will crumble to dust. Yet carelessly, and heedlessly you live on."

On the fourth occasion the Prince saw an ascetic standing on the road quiet and tranquil, full of grace, having a fixed glance as if he had attained the path that brings peace of mind. His tender heart vibrated with grief at the miseries of existence. He loathed the first three sights and for the first time felt the miseries to which humanity is subjected, to decay and ultimate destruction. He saw the universal problem of misery in individual instances. These experiences moved him to reflect. He was lured by the sight of the ascetic. Coming to know of his son's thoughts his father tried to divert his mind. Siddhartha felt that he was living in death in the midst of life. He felt that from his sole to the crown, the body originated in impurity, is compounded in impurity and exhaled impurity without end.

In the silence of night he heard the fateful message and determined to forsake the world. He sought deliverance for himself and desired salvation for all. The sight of the carefree sage fired his imagination. This episode would have led to immediate renunciation had it not been for the fact that he received news of the birth of a son and he exclaimed "A new fetter (rahula) has been forged for me." The king thought it to be a good omen and ordered that the baby be named Rahula. The baby however did not prove to be a fetter, for Siddhartha thought that before the attachment grew stronger, it was better to end his worldly career. Intensely feeling the emptiness of the things of the senses and of the world, the young prince renounced for ever, regal power, glory and wealth to meditate upon the Eternal Spirit and to prepare the way for people to escape from the shackles of worldly life. He saw his wife Yashodhara fast asleep with the baby by her side. He tore himself away from worldly attachments and left his palaces, became homeless, begged for his food and necessities and wandered in search of the light of knowledge. The going forth of the Buddha into voluntary exile is called the great Renunciation. This was at his twenty-ninth year.

He first attempted to seek the Truth by philosophic thought. Thereafter, he, in accordance with the belief that the mind became elevated by emaciating the body, practised relentlessly for seven years self-mortification and self-torture. By these ascetic denials of the demands of the flesh he reduced himself so much that he swooned. Legend has it that a shepherdess who happened to pass by, gave him milk, and he regained consciousness. "My body has become weaker and weaker and my fasts have not advanced me in my search for salvation. This is not the right path. I should rather try to strengthen my body by drink and food and thus enable my mind to seek composure." He found that he could not attain the great Truth through such practices and realised their futility. He realised that it was impossible to attain spiritual enlightenment and peace by following austere asceticism or by following the path of knowledge as shown by the ancient schools of thought.

Gautama sat under a "Bodhi tree" steadfast and firm, with a mind determined to find the Eternal Wisdom. "Never from this seat will I stir until I have attained the supreme and absolute wisdom. Legend tells us that

Mara, the goddess of evil, hurled all her missiles to tempt him. But Mara failed in all her attempts and all her missiles were turned into flowers. This battle is a metaphorical conflict between the higher and the lower aspirations in Gautama's mind. Thus transfixed, he spent seven weeks under the tree which has been subsequently called the Bodhinada or the seat of intelligence where he got enlightened. According to historical tradition this great event occurred on the Full Moon of May 544 B.C. Having put to flight Mara he meditated," and all the miseries and sufferings of the world passed before his mental eye. Surely he concluded that if living creatures saw the result of all their evil deeds they would turn away from them in disgust. But consciousness of the self blinds them and they cling to their base desires. They crave for pleasure and they cause pain; when death destroys their individuality, they find no peace, their thirst for existence abides and the "self" reappears in new births. Thus they continue to move in the coil and can find- no escape. The world is full of sin and sorrow. Gautama discovered the law of causation. After being Enlightened he reflected "What shall I do, now that I have acquired this sacred knowledge, this clearness of comprehension? This race of mankind that only lives for pleasure, will not understand me; and if I make known this by teaching, born of sorrow, my only reward will be vexation and disillusionment."

The thought that some might understand, overcame his reluctance and so he went forth with the words "Opened be to all the gate of deathlessness; let him who has ears to hear come and listen!" He went out to Benares to announce his message to suffering humanity. At Sarnath (a few miles from Benares), he preached to his five ascetic friends his first sermon on "Dharmachakra Pravartana"—that is setting in motion the wheel of law. He preached the four noble Truths and the Eightfold Path. They accepted his teachings. Thus Gautama began his career as a teacher of the world.

As time passed, the appeal of his message soon spread far and wide and his disciples and followers increased and both high and low entered his fold. The Buddha sent forth singly his sixty disciples in all directions to proclaim the doctrine. He advised them in these words: "Go ye, O Bhikkus and wander forth for the gain of the many, for the welfare of the many, out of compassion for the world, for the good, for the gain, for the welfare of gods and men. Proclaim, O Bhikkus, the doctrine glorious; preach yet life of holiness, perfect and pure." He preached his doctrines to all without making any distinction between classes and castes. This was a great departure from the ideas which prevailed at that time. There is a very touching story of a poor outcaste whose duty was to sweep the floor of the temples. He was despised and shunned by everybody. One day he heard the Buddha preaching his doctrine and the latter intuitively felt that this outcaste was fit to enter his order. To his great surprise and joy the Buddha addressed him saying: Tome, O Bhikku." He was thus admitted to the Brotherhood and was made an equal of all others. The Buddha continued to spread his message until the day of his death. He converted Kings, nobles, Brahmins, merchants, labourers and outcastes. He adapted his speeches and dialogues to the capacity of his hearers. He often expressed himself in parables and sayings.

Shortly before his death, he called his disciples together and informed them of his coming end; but thereafter he resumed his wanderings. At Pava he was entertained in a mango grove by a smith called Cunda and was soon after attacked by a painful illness. He bore it patiently, but on the way from Pava to Kusinara he broke down. He refreshed himself with water, travelled further on, and finally arrived at a Sala grove of Kusinara, the last stage of his pilgrimage. Then Buddha spoke to Ananda "See! These Sala trees are full of blossoms out of their season, they let a rain of blossoms descend upon the body of the Tathagata as a token of respect for the successor of the Buddhas of old. But it is not thus, Ananda, that the Tathagata is rightly honoured, reverenced and venerated, but he who truly follows the Law, he it is who rightly honours, reverences and venerates the successors of the Buddhas of old."

He once more called his disciples together and asked them whether in any one of them there lurked any kind of doubt about his teachings "that ye may not later regret not having asked me whilst I yet tarried among you." All were silent and he began his final exhortation to them. The last words that left his lips were: "Behold now, Brethren, I exhort you, decay is inherent in all component things! Work out your own salvation with diligence." He breathed his last somewhere about 480 B.C. when he was eighty.

We know very little of the life of the Buddha. The Suttas, the sermons which the Buddha himself delivered do not sufficiently supply much information. Of his personality we learn little else but that at such and such time he stayed at such and such a place; sometimes in Savatthi at Anathpindika garden or in the bamboo grove at Rajagriha and so forth. Everywhere and always his style is the same. But it has been said in a legend that "The dignity of his appearance proclaims him as the embroidered flag, the temple." His sermons flow with sublime uniformity studiously moderate in tone. In the Buddha there was a fusion of two qualities. He was a man of rich and responsive human sympathy; he had unfailing patience, strength, gentleness and goodwill. To all seekers of Truth who approached him, he was sincere and unreserved. He inspired in his followers an affectionate devotion. At the same time he was a thinker of unexcelled philosophic power. He had an analytic understanding which enabled him to shift the right kernel of thought from the deceptions of the times. He adopted, abandoned, revised and revitalised wherever necessary the prevalent theories of the time. It is because of this characteristics of the Buddha, that Buddhism is consciously based on a systematic and rational analysis of the Problem of life and of the way to its solution. The earnestness and the enthusiasm of his love for all creatures, the wisdom and simplicity of his message won the hearts of the people.

Before we proceed with the doctrines of Buddhism we may peep into condition of the times in which the Buddha lived. For revolutionary thought reflects the spirit of the age and it is therefore essential to survey the habits of thought, the general atmosphere of the age and the ruling ideas of the time In those days India was divided into several small states ruled by chieftains and princes. India then was in a high state of civilisation. Industry and commerce flourished. The leading classes were the Brahmins and the nobles. The common people were happy and contented. People showed great interest in religious and philosophic questions. There were speculations about all things. Liberty of conscience and tolerance prevailed and there was no fear of criticising the existing religious creeds. Rival theories, speculations and ideas filled the atmosphere. "Discussions were rife about the finiteness or infiniteness or neither or both of the world, the end of the self and the distinction of truth and appearance, the reality of the world beyond, the continuance of the soul after death and freedom of will. Some held to the supremacy of God, others to that of man. Some argued that they knew nothing about it; others flattered their audiences with mighty hopes and confident assurances. Some were busy building elaborate metaphysical theories; others were busy demolishing them. Many theories independent of the Vedic tradition arose. There were some who sought peace in renunciation, those Who practised self-mortification, those who tried spiritual abstractions, the controversialists, the materialists and the sceptics. It was an age of speculative chaos full of inconsistent theologies and vague wranglings." There were no accepted principles which were recognised by all. Truth was lost in the dark clouds of metaphysics. From those discordant notes and conflicting ideals, theories and opinions and from the rise and fall of the divergent beliefs, the Buddha concluded that metaphysical thinking was a vain attempt to seek the Truth. It appeared to him that this chaos of speculation will not promote the self-searching and integral unity of understanding. In those days men freely created Gods to suit their purposes. The Vedic religion with its creeds and rituals, rites and ceremonies was held in high favour. Miracles were the order of the day. The philosophy of the Upanishads was not accepted as a living belief. Every sin was supposed to be a violation of God's law and people imagined that the only way to please God was by rolling in dust, self-mortification, sacrifices, and the torturing of the flesh. Though men believed in the law of Karma, they did not care to see the natural consequences of sin. They lived in constant fear of an offending God who presided over the activities of the human beings and minutely supervised them. The result was that religion was separated from life, and God and the world were placed at different centres. The Buddha was shocked at the conduct of worship which was accompanied with cruel rites. The Buddha felt it was necessary that natural law should triumph over the super-natural and he preached that it was possible for every man to seek salvation without fear of God. He exhorted every man to raise the tone of morality. "It is a foolish idea," he said "that another can cause us happiness or misery." To the people at large the philosophy of the Upanishads had not reached. People believed in puerile superstitions; in the rites and ceremonies prescribed by the priests. The Buddha described these priests as "Tricksters, droners of holy words for pay, diviners, ever hungering to add gain to gain." Religion was dominated by the priests. "Son, make a sacrifice to God and a payment to me and thy sins will be forgiven thee." This hope of salvation by silver could not satisfy the higher cravings of the human soul. He repudiated the prevailing belief that there is a supreme personal creator and the belief of the materialists that development of the world is due to innate independent power of things. He taught that the world is diverse because there is diversity of deeds. He started with the promise that a perfect creator cannot be the originator of an imperfect world. The Buddha saw the falsity of beliefs of the people. The faith of the people was based on false beliefs. The Buddha revolted against this faith and denied the authority of the Vedas. In his revolt he reacted to the spirit of the times. The Buddha intended to provide a firm foundation for religion. He realised that the chief task was to destroy the belief in gods. In this he had to oppose the prevailing views and declare that virtue and happiness, vice and suffering are co-related. He showed -that a man is born with his actions. "My action is my possession, my inheritance, the matrix which bears me, the race to which I belong, my refuge." The Buddha in the early days put on a higher level the services of man before the service of God. He did not care to establish a new scheme of universe but desired to teach a new sense of duty. He aspired to found a religion without dogma and desired to do away with priestcraft, sacrifice and sacrament. He asked men to look within for change of heart. He forcefully exhorted the people to fight against false dogmas and false creeds. True religion consisted in devotion to the good and true happiness was to be attained only by good thoughts.

He felt that people had lost all faith. He asked men to reason and to use their heads and hearts. He aspired to establish a "religion within the bounds of pure reason" and thus exterminate the belief of the people in superstitions and false dogmas. "Though a person be ornamented with jewels, the heart may have conquered the senses. The outward form does not constitute religion or affect the mind. A man who dwells in lonely woods and yet covets worldly things, is a worldling, while the man in worldly garments may let his heart soar high to heavenly thoughts. There is no distinction between the layman and the hermit if but both have banished the thought of self."

He argued and discussed with the sceptics and showed the path to right thinking. He boldly enumerated his own experiences in the various fields and asked his followers to verify for themselves the conclusions arrived at by him. Buddihism has no dogmas. Every man is free to investigate for himself the facts from which the Buddhist doctrines have been derived. The Buddha had no revelation other than the experience which every human being is confronted with. He only had a deeper insight into the nature of things and could, better than any other man, trace the cause of evil and propose a remedy. The Buddha does not liberate men but teaches them how to liberate themselves. "Men adhere to his preachings of truth not because it comes from him but because aroused by his word, a personal knowledge of what he preaches arises in the light of their minds." According to him 'If a man sees things as they really are he will cease to pursue shadows and cleave to the great reality of goodness. Understanding is to be limited to the field of experience the law of which it can explore.",

The Buddha could not dissociate himself entirely from the spiritual ideas prevalent in his age. He felt that he had the sympathy and the support of the Upanishads and their followers. As Rhys David has said: "Buddhism flourished within the fold of the orthodox beliefs." The Vedic religion was polytheistic and people began to read in the Upanishads the polytheism of the Vedic religion. The Buddha intended to present the teachings of the Upanishads in their pure form, unadulterated by the Vedic polytheism. Rhys David says: "Gautama was born and brought up and lived and died as Hindu; there was not much in the metaphysics and the principles of Gautama which cannot be found in one or other of the orthodox system and a great deal of his morality could be matched from earlier and later Hindu Books. Such originality as Gautama possessed lay in the way in which he adopted, enlarged, ennobled and systematised that which had already been well said by others in the way in which he carried out their logical conclusion, principles of equity and justice already acknowledged by some of the most prominent Hindu thinkers. The difference between him and the other thinkers lay chiefly in his deep earnestness and in his broad public spirit of philanthropy."

For an account of Buddhism we have to depend on the 'Pitakas' or the basket of leaves. The 'Pitakas' express doctrines taught by the Buddha in its nearest approximation. They represent what early Indian Buddhists believed to be the sayings and doings of their master, The 'Pitakas' were compiled twenty-four years before Christ. They contain the most authoritative account of the teachings of the Buddha. His teachings for a long time were transmitted through memory of teachers and disciples. They were reduced to writing in 80 B.C. They are written in Pali language. The Pali canon has three divisions: (1) Sulta (tales), (2) Vinaya (Discipline), and (3) Adhidharma (Doctrine). About Sulta Pitakas Rhys David says: "In the depth of philosophic insight in the method of secretive questionings, often adopted in the earnest and elevated tone of the whole, in the evidence they afford of the most cultured thought of the day, these discourses constantly remind the reader of the discourses of Plato."

The Vinayak Pitakas deal with the ecclesiastical discipline and prescribe rules and regulations to govern the life of the monks. The Adhidharma Pitakas deal with psychological ethics, philosophy and metaphysics.

In the Pali canon at times there is found the questions of King Milinda—a dialogue between the Buddhist teacher and the dialectician Nagsena and King Menander. We find that this work is greatly used in Ceylon. It appears to have been written in the beginning of the Christian era. Rhys David classed it as a masterpiece of Indian prose and the best book of its class.

Buddhagosha's Visuddhimagga is a later work. It was written by a Brahmin convert to Buddhism in the year 400 A.D. He is the first Buddhist commentator. Besides there are other Pali works of historical importance. It may be observed that the Buddha's speeches are always prefaced by the words: "Thus have I heard." The reason of this is that after the death of the Buddha his disciples held a council in which each repeated the speeches he had heard and remembered. It is, therefore, possible, that we have in many places not only the Buddha's ideas but even his own words.

Buddhists designate their religion by the word Dhamma which has been variously interpreted as doctrine, low, norm, religion, truth or world order. (In reality it includes all these ideas.

To understand the doctrine of the Buddha we may commence with the first sermon which he gave to his five ascetic friends known by the name of "Dharmachakra Pravertana" that is setting in motion the wheel of law. It is generally called the speech of the foundation of the Kingdom of Righteousness and is in reality the foundation of the whole doctrine. The doctrine is based upon two axioms; first, all life is sorrow, and, second, always keep the path of the mean. Both these are summed up by the Buddha himself in the four noble Truths. The first three of these Truths contain the philosophy of the teaching; the last, the morality of the teaching as seen through this philosophy. The two are interwoven in such a way that the one cannot be understood without the knowledge of the other. Before explaining the four noble Truths he exhorted his five ascetic friends to keep to the path of the mean in the following words: "These two extremes, monks, are not to be practised by one who has gone forth from the world. What are the two? That conjoined with the passions and luxuries, low, vulgar, common, ignoble and useless; and that conjoined with self-torture, painful, ignoble and useless. Avoiding these two extremes the Tathagata (The Perfect one) has gained the enlightenment of the Middle Path which produces insight and knowledge and tends to calm, to higher knowledge, enlightenment, Nirvana.

"And what monks, is the Middle Path, of which the Tathagata has gained enlightenment, which produces insight and knowledge, and tends to calm to higher knowledge, enlightenment, Nirvana? This is the noble Eight-fold Path—namely, right view, right aspiration, right speech, right action, right livelihood, right effort, right mindfulness, right concentration. This, monks, is the Middle Path of which Tathagata has gained enlightenment which produces insight and knowledge and tends to calm, to higher knowledge, enlightenment, Nirvana." The Buddha then informed his ascetic friends of the Four Noble Truths which run as follows: "This is the noble Truth of pain: birth is suffering, old age is suffer ing, disease is suffering; death is suffering, sorrows, mentation, dejection and despair are suffering. Contact With unpleasant thing is suffering; not getting what one craves is suffering. In brief the five groups of clinging are suffering. "Now this is the Noble Truth of the cause suffering: Verily it is this thirst, the craving for existence and enjoyment which leads to renewed rebirths, seeking satisfaction; now in this way now in another. It is the craving for gratification of the passions, the craving for existence in the present life or hereafter, or the craving for annihilation.

"Now this is the Noble Truth of the cessation of suffering; verily, it is the complete destruction, conquering annihilation of this craving.

"Now this is the Noble Truth which leads to the cessation of suffering; verily it is this noble Eight-fold Path, namely right views, right aspirations, right speech, right deeds, right livelihood, right effort, right mindfulness, right concentration."

These few sentences are the foundation of the Buddhist religion and philosophy. The Buddha declares that life in every form and in every expression is suffering because it is transient and unenduring; it is unenduring because it has arisen from some causes and it must come to an end as soon as these causes cease to act. And this is the reason why wherever there is transiency there is suffering. The Buddha has said "There are three things which you cannot find in the world: (1) That which whether conscious or unconscious is not subject to decay and death; (2) That quality of anything which is not permanent that you will not find; (3) And in the highest sense there is no such thing as being possessed of being." The Buddha asked "And that which is transient O! Monk, is it painful or pleasant" and the reply was "It is painful." The Buddha established that everything is transient and there is nothing which is permanent. He established that if self or Atma is permanent then nothing on earth is self. All things are not self. "All are impermanent; body, sensation, perception, Sanskaras and consciousness. All these are sorrows; since they are not self."

To elucidate this further I must here relate the parable of the mustard seed. A young woman named Kisa Gotami had an only child who died. In her grief she could not believe that her child was dead. At last she was told that the only one who could give her consolation was the Buddha. She hastened to him and he saw that mere words of consolation would not assuage her grief. He therefore told her to bring him a handful of mustard seed from a house in which nobody had died. She went, for it seemed easy to get such a simple remedy, but wherever she asked for it and mentioned the condition of her request, the householders replied "What are you thinking of? The living are few but the dead are many". She understood that her grief was not an exception but the common lot, and that suffering was universal. In this story two of Buddha's most important doctrines are disclosed. Firstly, that the phenomenal existence is in constant flux and is transitory. Every living creature, like all other things is a compound of elements which must sooner or later dissolve and decay and therefore death must be accepted in a realistic manner; and the second is the connection between the realistic acceptance of death and a projection of the outward compassion towards all living creatures, who like ourselves are subject to decay and death. One's absorption in one's own grief prevents him from gaining victory over his pain as also identifying his feelings with the feelings of others in the like circumstances. One is freed from his own grief if one feels compassionate oneness with all living creatures. Love according to the Buddha did not mean an attachment to a person or an object through which one hopes to satisfy his selfish cravings, but an endless self-immolating compassion freely flowing towards all creatures and possessing an inherent condition of enlargement. It is defined as "State Divine". In brief the five aggregates i.e. body, sensation, perception, psychic disposition (subconsciousness) and consciousness which spring from attachment are painful. And he proves that each of them singly and therefore also altogether are transitory and that the craving for such transitory things, leads sooner or later to suffering.

Men asked, "What does this weary round of existence mean?" The Buddha showed an escape and declared the final goal to Nirvana. In Dhammapada it is said Not in the sky nor in the depths of ocean nor having entered the caverns of the mountains, nay such a place is not to be found in the world where a man may dwell without being overpowered by death." There is transitoriness in all things, we are deceived by chance, oppressed by the great weight of obligation, there is fear of death, and a feeling of passing into another life where there would be a repetition of this feeling of human tragedy. All this a man cannot help himself sighing "Let me escape". The Buddha declared that escape from the agonies of earth was to get out of it. The Buddha laid great stress upon the sufferings of life but he also said this with a great feeling for humanity like a mother warning her child against danger. He has truly remarked "The pilgrimage of being has its beginning in eternity. No opening can be discovered from which proceeding, creatures mazed in ignorance, fettered by thirst for being stray and wander. What think ye disciples where is more? The water which is in four oceans or tears which have flown from you and have been shed by you strayed and wandered on this long pilgrimage and sorrowed and wept because that was your portion which ye abhorred and that which ye loved was not your portion."

It has been said that the Buddhist creed is pessimistic for the Buddha rather emphasized the dark side of life. But a little consideration will show that that is not so. Buddhism boldly faces the sufferings of life, but it does so in order to show to mankind the way of escape from the sufferings of life. The doctrine of the Buddha is not a doctrine of suffering. He has said at one place "Of whatever doctrine ye are convinced that it leads to peace and not to passion, to humility and not to pride, to frugality and not to greed, to contentness and not to quarrelsomeness; of that ye may be certain that it is the truth, the law, the doctrine of the Master." Buddhism does not preach annihilation, but salvation. It does not teach death but life. He has himself said "Verily I say unto you The Blessed One has not come to teach death, but to teach life, and thou dost not discern the nature of living and dying. This body will be dissolved and no amount of sacrifice will save it. Therefore seek thou life that is of mind. Where self is, truth cannot be; yet when truth comes, self will disappear. Therefore let thy mind rest in the Truth, propagate the truth, put thy whole soul in it and let it spread. In truth thou shalt live for ever. Self is death and truth is life. The clinging to self is a perpetual dying while moving in truth is partaking of Nirvana which is life everlasting." Hit enjoins the right way of living. Its aim is Nirvana, the abandonment of selfhood and leading a life of truth which is attainable here upon earth in this life of ours."

He has declared "Nirvana is where precepts of justice and morality are followed: when fires of greed, of hatred and of delusion and the flames of all other passions are extinguished then Nirvana is reached." The Buddha does not preach the mere futility of life and therefore to resign oneself to the inevitable doom. The Buddha teaches to lead a life of purity and detachment to objects. He said to Anathapindika: "I say unto thee, remain in thy station of life and apply thyself with deligence to thy enterprises. It is not life, wealth and power that enslave men, but the clinging to life, weatth and power. The Bhikku who retires from the world in order to lead a life of leisure will have no gain. For a life of indolence is an abomination and lack of energy and is to be despised." His doctrine is not of despair and dejection nor of inaction and indolence. He exhorts us to arm ourselves against the evil, exterminate it and attain life of higher quality an Arhata state. And what is evil, and what is the root of evil? To this the Buddha has said "Killing is evil, stealing is evil, yielding to sexual passion is evil, lying is evil, slandering is evil, abuse is evil, gossip is evil, envy is evil, hatred is evil, to cling to false doctrine is evil; all these things, my friend, are evil" and he goes on further to say that desire is the root of evil, hatred is the root of evil, illusion is the root of evil. The Buddha perceived nothing but suffering; strove for nothing but freedom from this suffering and that was his sacred goal. "Not only by discipline and vows, not only by such learning do I earn the happiness of release which no worldling can know, O! Bhikkus, be not confident as long as thou hast not attained the extinction of thirst."

The illusion of self originates and manifests itself in a clinging to things. The desire to live for the enjoyment of self entangles us in the net of sorrow. Just as the entire world depends upon the six senses so also does this "I" depend upon the six senses. All suffering depend upon our senses. Everthing, yet Monks, is a burning fire. And in what wise, ye monks, is everything a burning fire? The eye is aburning; objects are aburning; the mental impressions that depend upon the eye is aburning; the sensation that arises out of the attachment of the eye is aburning; whether it be pleasant or unpleasant or neither the one nor the other. And what sort of fire is it that burns here? Verily it is the fire of Lust, of Hate and of Error that burns here; it is the fire of being born, of old age, and of death, the fire of grief, distress, sorrow, misery and despair. The fire of individuality is kindled through Lust, Hate and Illusion that is to say through the three kinds of willing. As one fire kindles fresh fire and this in turn fresh fire again, so from the life that once has arisen ever new life flames come forth afresh and from this, new life, again in endless succession. In our will to live, our attachment to life has the force that maintains the eternal play of action and reaction. Therefore "without beginning or without end is this Samsara." Deliverance is only possible when the senses cease to bring fresh fuel to the flame of life. The Buddha has said more than once that no peace or quietitude can come by forcibly repressing the senses. So long as the senses are in existence, so long must they be in activity. It is not to matter but to form, to the 'I' consciousness that will arise, and to the willing adheres suffering—that is life. Hence if life, sorrow, is to cease willing also must cease; and when willing ceases the attachment of senses to objects also ceases. There is, then no contact, no friction, no willing, no deed and if there is no deed, there is also no consequence of deed, no arising and where there is no arising, there is no passing away. Where there is neither arising nor passing away, there is also no being born and dying, no personality, no suffering. As regards the annihilation of personality Buddha has said "Even the complete remainderless annihilation, rejection driving forth, abolition, and the disowning of this lust for life, this the Exalted One has said, is the annihilation of personality." In Buddha's view it is only cognition that is to be corrected, and if that is corrected, all the rest will follow. Whosoever has perceived life, world, 'I' in all their painful transiency, as Becoming, nowhere any longer finds anything to which it is possible to become attached. For to what shall he cling when he knows that in truth there is no "self" present that can cling, and no "other" to which can it cling. The'Buddha's teaching is an admixture of philosophy and the doctrine of conduct. In the fourth Noble Truth He teaches that the cessation of suffering can be attained by following the noble Eight-fold Path. Morality, however is nothing else than, willing, brought into certain forms. Without morality there can be no knowledge; without knowledge there is no morality. With the increase of knowledge, there is an increase of morality and with the increase of morality, there is an increase of knowledge. As a man washes hand with hand so right behaviour is perfected through wisdom and wisdom through right behaviour. An individual who, following the Eight-fold Path has attained the final goal of knowledge, no longer exists as a personality. Self is an illusion and the Buddha shows how to annihilate it.

Wrong acts issue from wrong beliefs and to do away with wrong views right views are essential. Right views are the correct knowledge of the four noble Truths. It is on this account that Right Belief has been assigned the first place. Then follows the Right Aspiration from which follow right vision. It is the firm determination to live according to the doctrine and to persevere till the goal is attained. "It is the longing for renunciation, the hope to live in love with all, renouncing the idea of separateness one must aspire for all." He must say "I must bear the burden of all the creatures." Aspirations are directed to activities and they must find expression in right speech, right deeds and right living." To abstain from falsehood, to abstain from back-biting, to abstain from harsh languages and to abstain from frivolous talks is called right speech. The Buddha said to his disciples "When you meet, two things are fit for you, instructive conversation or holy silence." Right deed is that action wh ich is free from selfishness or self interest. The Buddha does not believe in ceremonial prayer and ritual, spell and sacrifice. "Better homage to a man grounded in Dharma than to agni (fire) for a hundred years." A Brahmin once told him that bathing in Bahuka river washes a sinner of his sins. The Buddha retorted 'The Bahuka, the Adhika cannot purify the fool of his sins bathing himself ever so often—No river can cleanse the doer of evil, the man of malice, the perpetrator of crime. To the pure it is always the holy month of Phaggan. to the pure it is always a perpetual fast. To the man of good deeds it is a vow everlasting. Have thy bath here. even here O Brahmin, be kind to all beings. If thou takest not what is given thee, secure in self-denial. What wouldst though gain by going to Gaya? Any water is Gaya to thee."

Asoka has said "Not superstitious rites but kindness to servants and underlings, respect to those deserving of respect, self-control coupled with kindness in dealing with living creatures these and virtuous deeds of like nature are verily the rites that are everywhere to be performed." In the words of the Buddha "In what consists true religion? In causing as little suffering as possible, in doing as much good as possible and in showing love, compassion, truthfulness and purity as often as possible." The Buddha did not lay his axe on the ceremonials of the times but explained their significance and thus undermined them. "Neither abstinence, nor going naked, nor shaving the head, nor rough garments, neither offerings to priests, nor sacrifices to Gods will cleanse a man who is not free from delusions. "Buddhism stresses purity of motives, humility and service of all creatures. To attain Nirvana practice of certain conduct is absolutely essential. 'Sila' that is Morality, holds an important and supreme place. Sila is the putting into practice the codes of conduct such as non-violence, charity benevolence towards subordinates, esteem for those who deserve esteem, self-restraint joined to goodness and pity, these and similar acts are the customs ye ought to follow and not superstitious rites and ceremonies." It is the active self-sacrifice that is demanded of an individual. We are exhorted to practise the virtues actively. He exhorts us to keep in mind the saying. "As I am so are the others, as others are so I am." Right action plods the way to right living. An individual should not lie or be deceitful or practise chicanery and fraud. Right effort, right thought and right tranquillity are the subjective purifications needed to attain perfection. By right effort an individual is exhorted to control passions of all sorts. Passions generate bad qualities and therefore the root of bad qualities the passions are to be controlled with an iron will. "If a person conquers thousands in battle, know ye that he is the greatest conqueror who conquers himself," It is through right effort that an individual can subjugate and destroy anger, envy, pride, jealousy and attachment to objects. The Buddha teaches us to cast away hatred. "Blessed are those who live free from hatred amid the hating world." Right effort and right thinking go hand in hand. The roaming mind is to be settled and fixed and the mental waverings are to be controlled. It is said: "When evil thoughts and desires arise, we should try to let other wholesome ones arise from them, or should examine their sorrowful nature or should not pay any attention to them or should analyse and decompose them into their elements or should suppress them with the application of all our strength and energy. And when we shall see that these bad pernicious thoughts and desires dissolve themselves and disappear and the mind becomes firm, quiet and confident." All the right efforts are destroyed by emotions and false impulses. "Whosoever is pure and knows that he is pure and finds pleasure in knowing that he is pure becomes impure and dies with an impure thought; whosoever is impure and knows that he is impure and makes effort to become pure dies with the pure thought." Spiritual pride places an individual on the lowest rung of the ladder. "On the mind depends 'Dhamma' on practice of 'Dhamma' depends enlightenment." Right mindedness is the deep reflection on the body, sensations, thoughts and impulse, which emanate from certain causes and are therefore transitory.

Spiritual perfection is not attained by mere suppression of senses and sensations but by cultivation of the mind. It is then alone that an individual sees the truth and makes an effort to attain it. There must be a cultivation of senses. By training an individual he can discriminate between the right and the wrong and can arrive at the truth of things.

Prajna (insight) is the highest activity of a human mind. When an individual is merged with the whole, empirical knowledge is displaced by Prajna. Next after Prajna (insight) comes Dhyana (meditation) which calms and steadies the mental processes and takes the place of prayer in Buddhist thought. Dhyana (meditation) has four stages. The first is joy and happiness which is accompanied by contemplation, inquiry, stilling of senses and sensations and reflection. The second stage is of deep peace of mind, internal tranquillity and elation. In the third state all passions and prejudices are drowned. There is an absence of lust for life. In the fourth stage there is an entire self-possession supreme tranquillity, absence of joy. Right concentration according to Buddhist view will bring the mind and mental processes into harmony with all that is, eliminating egoism.

Life is a series of becomings and extinctions from which the Buddha drew the philosophy of transformation. He said "Whatever is subject to origination is subject to destruction." (In other words he said, Everything is, that is one extreme O! Kaccna. Everything is not another extreme. The truth is in the middle. Life flows continuously. Identity of things is a synonym for continuous becoming. :Law of causation is made the foundation of continuity. "Know, that whatever exists arises from causes and conditions and is in every respect transient." Again he declares "Anything whatever born brought into being or organised contains within itself the inherent germ of destruction." From this it is obvious that the Buddha represented the whole universe as a continuous flow. In a dialogue with Anathapindika, the Buddha said "Who is this that shapes our lives? Is Ishwara a personal creator? If Ishwara be the maker, all living things should have silently to submit to their maker's power. They would be like vessels formed by the potters' hand, and if it were so, how would it be possible to practice virtue? If the world had been made by Ishwara then there should be no such thing as sorrow, or calamity or sin; for both pure and impure deeds must come from him. If not, there would be another cause beside him, and he would not be the self-existent one. Thus you see, the thought of Ishwara is overthrown.

"Again it is said that the Absolute has created us. But that which is absolute cannot be a cause. All things around us come from a cause as a plant comes from the seed; but how can the Absolute be the cause of all things alike? If it pervades them then certainly it does not make them.

"Again it is said that self is the maker. But if self is the maker, why did he not make things pleasing? The causes of sorrow are real and objective. How can they have been made by self?

"Again if you adopt the argument, there is no maker; our fate is such as it is and there is no causation; what use would there be in shaping our lives and adjusting means to an end? Therefore we argue that all things that exist are not without cause. However neither Ishwara, nor the Absolute, nor the Self, nor the Causeless Chance is the maker but our deeds produce results both good and evil. The whole world is under the law of causation and the causes that act are not unmental, for the gold of which the cup is made is gold throughout."

Individuality of a being is unstable and possesses an inherent capacity to grow. The empirical self of an individual has therefore growth, change and destruction. In the words of Rhys Davids: "There can be no individuality without putting together, there can be no putting togeher, no confection, without a becoming and there can be no becoming indifferent without dissolution a passing away which sooner or later will be inevitably complete." It is said in Mahavagga: "Our form, feeling, perception, disposition and intelligence are all transitory and therefore evil, and not permanent and good. That which is transitory, evil and liable to change is not the eternal soul, so it must be said of all physical forms whatsoever. Past, present or to be, subjective or objective, far or near, high or low. This is not mine, this I am not, this is not my eternal soul." The very principle of all life is transitoriness. It would be futile to search for a permanent soul in the senses or in any of the constituents of a being. The Buddha remained silent about the soul and disputed the reality of superficial self. The objects with which we identify ourselves are not the true self. He maintained that "absolute 'attainment of our end is only to be found in the abandonment of everything." The Buddha has at several places said what the soul is not, but he has not said in definite words what it is. It would be dangerous to assume that according to the Buddha there is no permanent self. He neither affirms nor denies the "existence of soul. According to him what we ordinarily know is the phenomenal self and he asserts that there is something else than the phenomenal self. He does not speculate on what that something else is. The following conversation with a wandering monk will make it clear: Then the wandering Monk Vachhgotta spoke to the Exalted One saying 'How does the matter stand venerable, Gautama, Is there the ego'? When he said this the Exalted One was silent. 'How then, the Exalted One, is there not the ego;' and still the Exalted One maintained silence. Then the monk rose from his seat and went away but Ananda said to the Exalted One 'Wherefore has the Exalted One not given an answer to the question put by the monk.' 'Is there the ego' had answered 'the ego is" then that would have confirmed the doctrine of the Samanas and Brahmanas who believe in immortality of the soul. If I Ananda, when wandering Monk asked me 'Is there not the ego' had answered 'the ego is not' then that would have confirmed the doctrine of those who teach the absolute annihilation in death."

Nagarjuna in his commentary says: "He taught the existence of Atman (Soul) when he wanted to impart his hearers the conventional doctrine; he taught the doctrine of An-atman (non-soul) when he wanted to impart to them the transcendental doctrine. Buddhism deals with the individual life and it is indifferent to the immortality of the soul. It does not attach importance to the permanent self of which we know little and is abstruse. Whosoever is originated will be dissolved again. All worry about the permanent self is vain, the ego is like a mirage and all tribulations that touch it will pass away: They will vanish like nightmare when the sleeper awakes."

We shall now see how the Buddhist analyses the self. When one says 'I' what he does is that he refers to all the 'skandhas' (i.e. the five factors constituting an individual person) combined or any one of them and deludes himself that that was 'I'. "He who knows the nature of his self and understands how his senses act finds no room for the 'I', and thus he will attain peace unending. The world holds the thought of 'I' and from this arises false apprehensions." "Ye that are slaves of the 'I', that toil in the service of self from morn to night, that live in constant fear of birth, old age, sickness and death receive the good tidings that your cruel master exists not." Self is an error, an illusion, a dream. Open your eyes and awake. See things as they are and you will be comforted. He who has found there is no 'I', will let go all lusts and desires of egotism. The clinging to things, coveteousness and sensuality inherited from former existences are causes of misery and of vanity in the world. "As a mother even at the risk of her own life protects her son, so let him that has recognised the truth, cultivate goodwill without measure among all beings above, below, around, unstinted, unmixed with any feeling of making distinctions or of showing preferences." Once when the Buddha saw that some boys were tormenting fish, he asked them whether they dreaded pain and when they said they did, he admonished them saying: "If you dread pain, never inflict any on other, nor even on the meanest creature." This explains that goodwill and kindness that is demanded of us is all compassing.

The components of an individual are grouped into two broad heads, which are 'Nama' and 'Rupa' these constitute the phenomenal self. Even according to the Upanishads 'Nama' signifies the mental and 'Rupa' the form. Whatever is subtle is 'Nama'. There is an inherent connection between the two, and emerge into being simultaneously. The individuality of a man consists of both 'Nama' and 'Rupa'. Body and mind emanates from mental state 'Nama' (mental) includes Chitta, emotion, consciousness, and mind. Nama-Rupa are sub-divided into Skandhas (factors constituting an individual) which are: (1) material attributes (Rupa), (2) feeling (Vendha), (3) Perception (Samjana), (4) Mental dispositions and will (Samskaras), (5) Reason (Vijnana). These form the complex grouping of self.

The coming into being of life which is suffering as well its end is accounted by the doctrine of Pratityasumutpada or the doctrine of dependent origination. "Then the Blessed One during the first watch of night fixed his mind upon the chain of causation in direct and reverse order. By the destruction of ignorance which consists in the complete absence of lust the "Samskaras' are destroyed, by the destruction of 'Samskaras' consciousness is destroyed, by the destruction of consciousness, name and form are destroyed, by the destruction of name and form, the six provinces are destroyed, by the destruction of the six provinces, contact is destroyed, by the destruction of contact, sensation is destroyed, by the destruction of sensation, thirst is destroyed, by the destruction of thirst, attachment is destroyed, by the destruction of attachment, existence is destroyed, by the destruction of existence, birth is destroyed, by the destruction of birth, age and death, grief, lamentation, suffering, dejection and despair are destroyed. Such is the causation of the whole mass of suffering." The above is in short the whole of the Buddhist creed.

The chief agent in this series is ignorance; from which emanates the false sense of 'I'. It is the pivot of individual existence which conceals the true nature of life which hangs on sorrow. It is ignorance which assumes as real that which is false. It breeds egoism. It creates lust for life which is ignoble and stupid. It separates the individual from the rest of existence. It makes the individual to stick to his mean self and struggle to continue it against all odds; it is owing to the vital strengh of ignorance that an individual life is full of sufferings.

It is 'Tanha' or thirst which leads an individual from one birth to another. It is the chief cause both of life and sufferings. We are, because we thirst for life and we suffer because we crave for evanescent pleasures. "Whomsoever thirst holds in subjection, that thirst, that contemptible thing which pours its venom through the world, his suffering grows as the grass grows. Whomsoever holds it in subjection, sufferings fall from him as the water drops from the lotus flowers." The Buddha ascribes the origin of sufferings to desire (Tanha). The thirst or craving for life in the wide sense engenders a desire for life and pleasure which results in procreation, the craving for existence in the dying man which is translated into a new birth. The craving for wealth, power and gratification of personal ambition lead to misery and disappointment. It is what Carlyle called 'Divine discontent' which according to the Buddha is the root of all misery in this life.

We are ignorant of the true nature of 'I' and of the four noble Truths. The Buddha attacked ignorance and declared it to be the main prop of false desires and therefore acquisition of knowledge is necessary to end suffering. Human existence is beset with inward contradictions out of which the Buddha points a way out. He teaches us how to avoid suffering. The good of an individual consists in unmaking himself to escape from the evil existences. Nirvana is the **summum bonum** of life and all deeds, thoughts and craving which lead to it are good and their opposites bad. To arrest re-birth an individual must break up the composite self. The ideal of Buddhism is an escape from the chain of re-birth and enter the eternal that is Nirvana.

All acts are placed in two categories: (1) Those which are pure. (2) Those which are impure. The pure acts are those in which there is absence of desire, passion and ignorance. They prepare the path of an individual to Nirvana. Meditation on the four Noble Truths is a pure act which is set above good and evil consequences; all other acts which are contrary to these are impure. Acts which lead one to conquer passions, desire, illusion of the ego and in which there is absence of lust, hatred, delusion and the like are denominated good ones; and the bad acts are those which lead to unpleasant retributions. Good acts are those which are performed with an intention of gaining happiness in the world hereafter. Bad acts are those which have for their motive to acquire worldly happiness and are inspired by self-interest. He has said "Meditation on transitoriness leads to victory over greed; meditation on suffering leads to the annihilation of hatred; meditation on the non-existence of an immortal soul leads to cessation of selfishness."

He understood that knowledge cannot be acquired by mere exercise of will and that it required the exercise of mind too. He decided to follow the middle course of life, a path between self-indulgence and self-mortification. Sacrifices and penance did not bring divine wisdom. The ideal of life was life and he abandoned the form and ceremonial of conventional creed. The enlightenment which he got gave him the cause of human sufferings and the middle path was its remedy. He questioned "Who is a true Brahmin." The answer was "One free from evil and pride, self-restraint learned and pure."

According to Buddhism by proper endeavour and training an individual gets strength and virtue which can make him—independent of all objects. If an individual by strenuous training conquers himself he becomes a victor and all other things fall under him. "Not even God can change into defeat the victory of a man who has vanquished himself." The Buddhist morality is individual in the main. Convention, traditions and authority are discounted. When the Buddha was asked by Ananda about instructions touching the order, he said: "Be ye lamps unto yourself, be ye a refuge to yourself. Betake yourself to no external refuge, hold fast to truth as a lamp, hold fast to refuge: the truth; look not for refuge to any one beside yourself."

An individual must shun ten transgressions of which three are bodily sins, murder, theft, and adultery; four are of speech. They are, lying, slander, abuse and idle conversation, and the three sins of mind are coveteousness, hatred and errors. Sinful conduct is also classed under four heads (1) Sensuality, (2) Ignorance, (3) Desire for re-birth, and (4) Metaphysical speculations. There are five different instructions given for self-control. These are control of anger, desire for material acquisitions, the lust of the flesh, cowardice and malevolence and a desire for false excitements.

There are ten ideal virtues which are charity, purity of thought, patience, strenuousness, meditation, intelligence, employment of right means, resoluteness, strength and knowledge. According to Buddhist doctrine the path of knowledge is narrow. It is possible for every man to achieve Eternal Salvation. Freedom is merging into universal consciousness and enlarging the field of feelings and sympathy for every being. "The disciple lets his mind pervade one quarter of the world with thought of love and so the second—and these pervade the wide world."

The doctrine exhorts us not to be self-centred and envelop ourselves into the cloud of selfishness but to realise that the whole existence however small is linked together. The Buddha has repeatedly said that metaphysical and intellectual knowledge is of little avail; what is demanded of an individual is the knowledge of morality. This knowledge can be acquired by an individual by purging the soul from the dark clouds of passion and impulse. For the practice of Truth three conditions have been imposed : (1) Faith, (2) Sight, and (3) Devotion. The faith that is required of an individual is not that blind faith which accepts the authority of the others. The Buddha told his disciples, "Now, O ye monks, are you going to say we respect the master, and out of respect for him, we believe this and that? You must not say so. Is not what you will say to be true, that exactly which you have by yourself seen, known and apprehended?"

The Buddha believed that fulfilment of worldly duties is not directly helpful for attainment of eternal salvation. He has said "full of hindrances is the household life, a Path defiled by passion; free as air is the life of him who has renounced all worldly things. How difficult is it for a man who dwells at home to live the higher life in all its fullness, in all its purity, in all its bright perfection!" "Let me then cut off my hair and beard. Let me clothe myself in the orange coloured robes and let me go forth from the household life into the homeless state."

It has been contended by some that the ethics of Buddhism are ascetic, It would be classed as asceticism if it only exhorts us to suppress desires. The 'Tanha' can be destroyed after the destruction of desires which can only be achieved by strenuous and continuous effort. Buddhist doctrine does not favour passivity. We are not told to fly away from the world but we are exhorted to fight against evil. In a dialogue with Simha the Buddha said: "I teach Simha the not-doing of such actions as are unrighteous either by deed or by word or by thought, I teach the not-bringing about of all these conditions of heart which are evil and not good. However I teach Simha the doing of such actions as are righteous by deed, by word and by thought; I teach the bringing about of all those conditions of heart which are good and not evil. I teach Simha, that all conditions of heart which are evil and not good unrighteous actions by deed, by word, and by thought, must be burnt away. He who has freed himself, Simha, from all those conditions of heart which are evil and not good, he who has destroyed them as a palm tree which is rooted out so that they cannot grow up again such a man has accomplished the eradications of self."

It would be proper to say that Buddhist doctrine is a midway between asceticism and luxury. It calls upon us to avoid extremes and excesses. It urges us to tear asunder the ties which bind us to the lower plane of life and cultivate ourselves to rise above by strenuous efforts. "I preach asceticism in as much as I preach the burning away of all conditions of heart that are evil. One who so does is the true ascetic." The Buddha urged that one should root out egoism. "I proclaim, Simha the annihilation of egotism, of lust, of ill-will, of delusion. However, I do not proclaim, the annihilation of forbearance, of love, of charity and of truth." The Buddha teaches the complete surrender of self, but he does not teach a surrender of anything to those powers that are evil, be they men, or Gods, or the elements of nature- "Struggle must be" he says "for all life is a struggle of some kind. But he that struggles should look to it lest he struggle in the interest of self against truth and righteousness." According to him an ascetic is he who purifies the spirit and does not chastise the body. When nun Gautami asked the Buddha to teach her the quintessence of the Dhamma he said, "Of whatsoever teaching thou art sure that it leads to passion and not to peace; to pride and not to humility; to the desiring of much and not desiring of little; to the love of society and not the love of solitude; to idleness and to earnest striving to a mind hard to pacify and not to mind easy to pacify that Oh! Gautami that is not Dhamma." "A follower of the Buddha has to follow five precepts. These arc voluntary vows and are not in the form of commandments. They are: (1) The vow not to kill, (2) The vow not to take what is not given voluntarily, (3) The vow not to do any wrongful sexual acts, (4) The vow not to lie, (5) The vow not to take intoxicants or stupefying drugs."

The law of Karma is translating of justice in human existence. "It is through a difference in their Karma that men are not all alike; but some are longlived, some are shortlived, some healthy and some sickly, etc." The theory of Karma is an ancient doctrine. The records of an individual are carried from birth to birth. This does not mean that men must acquiese in whatever that happens. The Buddha preached freedom of action and taught how to conquer the law of Karma. The self of an individual has the capacity to rise and expand. According to him though the present is determined by the past, the future is open and under the control of an individual. He has said "O priests, if any one says that a man must reap according to his deeds, in that case there is no religious life; nor is any opportunity offered for the entire extincion of misery. But if any one says O priests, that a reward a man reaps accords with his deeds in that case; O priests, there is religious life and opportunity is afforded for the entire extinction of misery."

Karma ceases to have effect when the highest state is realised, then the struggle ceases and nothing remains to cause any effect on the existence to come.

In accordance with the Brahmanical doctrine, Buddhism has conceived a hell for the evil doers, and re-birth for the imperfect. Buddhism does not recognise migration of the soul or the passage of an individual from life to life. On the death of an individual both his physical and psychical lives are dissolved. It is another being who takes birth and not the dead man. The following conversation between Kutadanta and the Buddha makes this clear. The Tathagata said: "It is by a process of evolution that Samskaras came to be. There is no Samskara which has sprung into being without a gradual becoming. Thy Samskaras are the product of thy deeds in former existences. The combination of thy Samskaras is thy soul. Wheresoever they are impressed thither thy soul migrates. In thy Samskaras thou wilt continue to live and thou wilt reap in future existences the harvest sown now and in the past."

"Verily, O Lord," rejoined Kutadanta "this is no fair retribution. I cannot recognise the justice that others after me will reap what I am sowing now."

The Blessed One replied: "Is all teaching in vain! Dost thou not understand that those others are thou thyself? Thou thyself will reap what thou sowest, no others." "Verily I say unto you; Not in the heavens, not in the midst of the sea, not if thou hidest thyself away in the cliffs of the mountains wilt thou find a place where thou can escape the fruit of thy action. At the same time thou art sure to receive the blessings of thy good actions." It is the character that floats, which builds up a new individuality and gravitates itself to the new state of life for which it is worthy. In Buddha-gosha—Visuddhimagga it is thus stated "For in any existence one arrives at the gate of death., .all the members great or small are loosened and wrenched apart in every joint and ligament and the body, like a green palm leaf exposed to the sun dries up by degrees; and the eye sight and the other senses fail and the power of feeling and the power of thinking and vitality are making a last stand in the heart then consciousness residing in that last refuge, the heart continues to exist by virtue of Karma otherwise called pre-dispositions. This Karma, however, still retains something of what it depends on, and consists of such former deeds as were weighty, much practised and are close at hand, or else this Karma creates a reflection of itself or of the new mode of life now being entered upon, and it is with this as its object that consciousness continues to exist.

"Now, while consciousness still subsists, in as much as desire and ignorance have not been abandoned and the evil of the object is hidden by that ignorance, desire inclines the consciousness to the object; and Karma that sprang up along with the consciousness impels it towards the object. This consciousness being in its series thus inclined towards the objects by desire and impelled towards it by Karma like a man who swings himself over a ditch by means of a rope hanging from a tree on the higher bank quits its first resting place and continues to subsist in dependence on objects of sense and other things and either does or does not light on another resting place created by Karma. Here the former consciousness from its passing out of existence is called passing away, and the latter from its being re-born into a new existence is called re-birth but it is not to be understood that this latter consciousness did not come to the present existence from the previous one and also that it is only to causes contained in the old existence namely to Karma, or predisposition to inclination... that its present appearance is due."

The word 'Nirvana' literally means "blowing out" or "cooling". With the idea of blowing out come up the thought of extinction and with the idea of cooling the nought that the extinction is still incomplete presents itself. "The mind released is like an extinction of a flame." These two conceptions of Nirvana represent both the negative and the positive aspects of the one ultimate state which is indescribable. The Buddha himself has defined it. "Now this is the noble truth as to the passing of pain. Verily it is the passing away so that no passion remains, the giving up, the getting rid of the emancipated form, the harbouring no longer of this craving thirst." 'Nirvana' is not fellowship with God. It is the quenching of thirst. It is the extinction of the flames of lust, ignorance, hatred and the likes. "Final deliverance is declared by sage Buddha to be nothing other than flow of faultless state of consciousness." It is the destruction .of the limited self which partakes with the unlimited universe and merges therein. It establishes oneness with all that is. It is an existence which flows eternally with peace, tranquillity, freshness, purity and Bliss.

JAINISM

VARDHAMANA, also known as Vaisaliya, that is the man from Vaisali, who afterwards came to be known as Mahavir, the Great Hero or the Conqueror, was born the second son of a Kshatriya chieftain, named Siddhartha of the Naya clan by his wife named Trisala in Magadha (Modern Bihar) in the year 599 B.C. Legend has it that his mother Trisala had fourteen wonderful dreams revealing to her that not only would she bear a son but also that her son would win everlasting rest and renown. These dreams of Trisala are today often engraved round the silver treasuries in Jaina temples, Trisala related the dreams to Siddhartha and, interpreters, who were summoned, foretold them of the birth of a spiritual conqueror (Jina) Lord of the three worlds, and the universal emperor of the law. Legends inform us of his boyish prowess and how he used to excel his companions in strength, valour and physical endurance as also of the beauty of his mind and body. It is said that he lived with his parents till they died. At their death, Mahavir who was by then approaching his thirtieth year felt free to become an ascetic and after obtaining his elder brother's permission, he renounced the world. According to the Svetambara tradition, Mahavir married Yasoda and a daughter, Priyadarsana, was born to them. The Digambara traditions represent their Hero as choos- the sterner and more austere path and hold that he not marry. It has been said that Mahavir from his earliest days felt an urge to forsake the world and to betake himself to a homeless and an ascetic life but he nevertheless felt that he could not do this, during his parents life-time lest he should cause them pain. "It parents life-time lest he should cause them pain.It will no behove me" says a legend "during the life of my paresnts to tear out my hair and leave the house to enter the state of homelessness."

All the sects are in agreement that his initiation into spiritual life took place when he was about thirty, some time between the years 570 and 569 B.C. The Naya clan to which he belonged seemed to have supported a body of monks who followed the rule of Parasvanath, an ascetic who lived some two hundred and fifty years before Mahavir. It was to this order that the thoughts of Mahavir turned. These monks had their cells in a park called Sundarvana, outside Vaisali, and in the centre of this park grew one Asoka tree whose leaves were supposed never to know either grief or pain. Mahavir fasted f6r two and a half days and gave away all his property. He led a life of austerities for twelve years wandering from place to place, never staying longer than a single night in a village or more than five nights in a town. The rule was however relaxed during the rainy season when Mahavir made a practice of remaining for four months at some place. During these twelve years he meditated and walked, sinless and circumspect in thought, word and deed.

"As water does not adhere to a copper vessel or collyrium to mother of pearls, so sins found no place in him; his course was unobstructed; like the firmament he wanted no support, like the winds he knew no obstacles, his heart was pure like water; nothing could soil him, like a leaf of a lotus; his senses were well protected like those of a tortoise; he was single and alone like the horn of a rhinoceros, he was free like a bird, he was always like the fabulous bird Bharunda, valorous like an elephant, strong like a bull, difficult to attack like a lion, steady and firm like mount Mandara, deep like the ocean, mild like the moon, effulgent like the sun, pure like refined gold; like the earth, he patiently bore everything, like a well-kindled fire, he shone in his splendour." Many legends are told of Mahavir's absolute absorption in meditation and of his unconsciousness of outward circumstances during these years.

It is believed that Mahavir was born with three degrees of knowledge which are "Mati Jnana", "Sruta Jnana", and "Avadhi Jnana" and he acquired the fourth kind of knowledge "Manah Paryaya Jnana" by which he knew the thoughts of all sentient beings. After twelve years of wanderings and penance, he acquired the fifth degree of knowledge which is "Keval Jnana" or omniscience. He now possessed "complete and full, the unobstructed, unimpeded infinite and supreme knowledge and intuition called Kevalship." His meditations and austerities had been so deep and profound that he was able to destroy the past Karmas (i.e. the accumulated result of actions) which are enemies to enlightenment, knowledge and freedom. He received the title of Jina (or conqueror of eight Karmas) from which Jainism derives its name.

Equipped with supreme knowledge Mahavir began to preach and his first sermon was on the five great vows which we shall deal with later. Mahavir's great message to mankind was that birth and caste are of no consequence and that Karma is all in all, which must be destroyed to attain the perfect state. Mahavir's first disciple was Gautama Indrabhuti. After imparting his teachings to Gautama, he set off to teach a wider circle. It was received well by his warrior kinsfolk. He spent the last thirty years of his life in preaching and organising the order of ascetics which was patronised by the princes and chieftains who were related to him. About a year after gaining Kevalship Mahavir became a Tirthankara, one of those who guide along the right path. The path which he pointed out lay in becoming a member of one of the four Tirthsa,—monk or a nun, if possible, otherwise a devout layman or a laywoman. He died in his seventy-second year (some fifty years before the Buddha) at Papa, the modern Pavapuri, a small village in Patna District. Just before his death he delivered fifty-five lectures that explain the results of Karma and answered thirty-six unasked questions and having finished his great discourse on Marudeva he died in 527 B.C. By his self-denial and austerities he freed himself from the bondage of Karma.

The Jainas trace their history through the stories of Tirthankars, which are twenty-three in number before Vardhaman, he being the twenty-fourth. Thus Jainas believe that theirs is the oldest religion; and support their belief with passages from Vedas. Jaina tradition ascribes the origin of the system to Rashabadeva, the first Tirthankar who was born when the world had passed out of its happiest period. He taught men seventy-two arts and women sixty-four. He taught the Jaina faith. There is a mention in the Yajur Veda of the three Tirthankaras, Rsabha, Ajitnatha, and Aristameninatha. After Rsabha followed a succession of Tirthankaras ending with Mahavir. It is said that in the year 776 B.C. a creed known as Parasvanatha was founded by Parasvanath who preceded Mahavir. The Jainas say that Parasvanath was born in the city of Benares in or about 817 B.C. As a worldly man, Parasvanath bore himself with great credit. He was a brave warrior. At the age of thirty he renounced the world and became an ascetic. He practised austerities for eighty-three days. On the eighty-fourth day he obtained Kevalship. He became the head of an enormous community; his mother and wife were his first disciples. He preached his doctrines for seventy years until at last his Karma was exhausted and he attained his liberation on Mount Sameta Sikhara in Bengal which was thenceforth kno wn as the mount of Parsvanath. He made four vows binding upon his followers. They were: (1) not to take life, (2) not to lie, (3) not to steal, and (4) not to own property; the vows of chastity and celibacy being included in the last two. To these, Mahavir specifically added two, one that of chastity and another of confession. During Mahavir's life-time he attracted a great number of disciples of both the sexes and from these developed the four orders of his community which was organised by him. These as stated above are the monks, the nuns, the laymen and the laywomen. Among his followers were fourteen thousand monks; at the head of these were eleven chief disciples. He divided his fourteen thousand monks into nine regular schools and placed, each school under the guidance of one of his chief disciples. There was a large number of women who followed Mahavir and renounced the world to become nuns. At their head was Candana the first cousin of Mahavir.

Mahavir's third order consisted of laymen who were householders, who could not renounce the world. At the head of these laymen or Sravaka, that is hearers.

were Sankhaji and Salakji. The last order consisted in laywomen or Sravika whose household duties prevented them from becoming nuns. At their head were two women Sulasa and Revati. Sulasa is considered to be the highest type of woman devoted to her household and Revati is typical of a generous woman.

Mahavir was the head of all the four orders. After his death Gautama Indrabhuti succeeded him in spiritual leadership for twelve years; he was followed by Sudharma (the present Jaina monks are considered to be his spiritual descendants), who was in turn followed by Jambu Swami. He was the last Jaina to obtain Kevalship. He was succeeded by Prabhava who died in 397 B.C. It was during this time that the two sects, Osvala Jaina and Srimala Jaina arose. It is also said that it was at this time that the image of Mahavir was enshrined at Upakesa Pattana. The six spiritual leaders who followed Jambu Swami are called Sruta Kevali because a complete Kevalship was denied to them but they possessed a complete knowledge of the scriptures. They were followed by the Dasapurvi or the leaders who knew ten Purva of the Twelth Anga.

We are informed that in or about 296 B.C. half the community under the leadership of Bhadrabahu moved towards the South in Mysore. This is an important period in the history of the Jainas, for, it was at this time that the earliest canons of Jainism were fixed. In the third century B.C., Sthulabhadra summoned a Council of the Monks at Pataliputra (the modern Patna) to fix the canon of the sacred literature consisting of eleven Angas and fourteen Purvas. During this period not only was Jainism established in the South and the canon of the scriptures fixed but also the question of nudity was raised. The third and the second centuries must have been a period of great activity amongst the Jainas. It is said that under Asoka, the religion Penetrated as far as Kashmir. Another chief event in Jaina history is the great schism and the final division into Svetambara (white clothed) and Digambara (Nude) Sects which took place in A.D. 79 or 82. The philosophical views of these two sects are identical but there is difference in their ethical creeds. The Digambaras are strict in observing the austerities. They hold that a perfect saint can live without food, without any possession, even clothes and that it is not possible for women to attain sainthood. They pictured the Tirthankars as. nude and unadorned and with eyes fixed on the earth. They disown the canonical books of Svetambaras. Owing to the patronage of the Western Kings, the centre of Jainism gradually shifted from Bihar to Gujarat. In Gujarat at Vallabhipur (near Bhavnagar) a great council met in 454 A.D. In this year the whole canon was reduced to writing and a large number of copies were made. Recognition was given to eighty-four books as constituting canonical literature. Among them there are 41 Sutras, a number of Prakinahs or unclassified work; twelve Niryutes or commentaries and one Maha Bhasya or great commentary. The forty-one Sutras include eleven Angas; twelve Upangas; five Chedas; five Mulas and eight miscellaneous works. They were written in Ardha Magadhi language but after the Christian era Sanskrit became the language of Jainism. The zenith of Jainism lasted from the date of the Council at Vallabhipur down to the thirteenth century.

Jainism, like Buddhism, is indifferent if not opposed to the Vedas. The similarity between Buddhism and Jainism is apparent. It would not be just to say that the rise of Jainism was due to the sufferings of the common people. One must not loose sight of the fact that in the beginning of the epic period there was a general ferment of thought. It is common that when different views of life professed by different people came in sharp contact with each other, they gave rise to intense feelings and beliefs. Jainism is an outcome of this mental unrest which prevailed at the beginning of the era. The doctrine of re-birth enunciated by the Upanishads led to the belief that all things in the world possessed souls. Like Brahminism and Buddhism, Jainism might be defined as "a way of escape" not from death but from life; but unlike either of them, it hopes to escape not into nothingness, nor into absorption but into a state of being without qualities, emotions or relations and removed from the possibility of re-birth. Another difference is that while Buddhism repudiates the taking of life, Jainism permits it under certain circumstances. If one cannot resist passions and endure austerities suicide is permitted. As to the caste system both Buddhism and Jainism related it to character. It is by one's action, they say, that one is a Brahmin, Kshatriya, Vaishya or Sudra. In relation to the six schools of Indian philosophy, Jainas quote the old story of six blind men who each laid their hands on a different part of the elephant and tried to describe the whole animal. Jainas hold, in fact, that the six schools of philosophy are part and parcel of one organic whole and that if one be taken by itself it becomes a false doctrine. The Jaina claim not to be "Ekantavadin"—those who look at things from one angle but "Anekantavadin" that is, those who look at things from diverse points of view. The basic principles of Jainism are Ahimsa (Non-injury), Satyam (Truthfulness), Astiya (Non-stealing), Brahmacharya (celibacy), and Aparigraha (non-covetousness). Jainism teaches universal brotherhood and equality of all beings. The doctrines of Jainism are summed up in the maxim "Ahimsa Parmo Dharmah". All rules of conduct are based on mercy which has four forms: (1) To perform a kind act without expectation of a reward; (2) To rejoice at the well-being of others; (3) To sympathise with the distressed people and to relieve their sufferings; and (4) To pity the criminals.

The doctrine of Jaina philosophy is based on the foremost necessity of conquering the grosser self for the realisation of Truth. The Jainas believe that only the Tirthankaras can give a code of conduct for life. They are pure souls who have attained perfection. Jainism is not a theistic system. It does not believe in the existence of a God who is the creator and ruler of the world. The highest is a person and not a Being.

The Jains believe that the world is formed of everlasting atoms and therefore it will exist eternally. The World has developed and will continue to develop by the inter-play of substances. It has three divisions—the lower, middle and the higher. "There can be no destruction of things that do not exist nor can there be creation of things out of nothing. Things come into existence and cease to exist because of modes and attributes." The Jainas repudiate the theory of the creation of the world out of nothing or by accident. There are six substances which constitute the world. These are time, space, matter, soul, fulcrum of action and fulcrum of inaction. The diversities of the world are traced to cooperating conditions of time (Kala), nature (Swabhava), necessity (Niyati), Activity (Karma), and desire to be and to act (Udyama). A seed may have a potentiality to grow into a tree but it must have the help of time, natural environments, the act of being placed in soil.

The universe, according to Jainism, is divided into two main divisions, the sentient beings and the non-sentient beings. They have been interplaying since time immemorial. The soul which is a divine spark in a living being is capable of thinking, knowing and feeling. Each soul is infinite and retains its individuality since time immemorial; it is eternal and self-existing. Every soul is omniscient and full of consciousness. It is an embodiment of eternal knowledge, having infinite capacity to throw off the Karmas which bind it. Its true nature is true knowledge, true faith and true conduct. So long as the soul transmigrates, it passes through evolutions and involutions. The living (Chetana) and the non-sentient (The Jara) interact and cause diversities in the universe which cause evolution.

According to Jainism there are infinite number of living beings filling the entire space of the universe and are classed under two heads: (1) The freed Souls are those who have thrown off all bondage, are pure, translucent and have attained perfection. (2) The bound Souls are those who are bound down in the fetters of Karma. These fettered Souls are sub-divided into two classes: (a) "Sthavara" (Immobile) and (b) "Tras" (Mobile). The immobile Souls are those which are devoid of all power of locomotion and have only one organ of sense that of touch. Earth, water, fire, air and all that come within the range of the vegetable kingdom belong to this class (b). The mobile Souls are those which have power of locomotion and are grouped into four kinds according to the nature and number of sense-organs they possess. These are: (a) Those that have the organs of touch and taste (e.g. worms), (b) Those that have three organs such as touch, taste and smell (e.g. ants), (c) Those that have the organ of sight in addition to the above three organs (e.g. bees), (d) Those that have all the above four organs in addition to that of hearing (e.g. birds, animals and human beings).

There are according to Jainism five gateways of Knowledge which are: (1) 'Mati Jnana'—that form of knowledge by which a soul recognises an object through the operation of the sense-organs, (2) 'Sruti Jnana'—the clear knowledge formed on some verbal testimony of the omniscient, (3). 'Avadhi Jnana'—the knowledge in the form of recognition of particular physical occurrences that happened some time past, (4) 'Mana Paryaya Jnana'—the knowledge of what is in others thought, originating as it does from the removal of the hindrances to the formation of such knowledge, (5) 'Keval Jnana' —the pure, unimpeded knowledge which precedes the attainment of 'Nirvana'. It is characterised by omniscience, transcending all knowledge.

The Jainas consider that the foundation of true philosophy consists of nine principles. These nine principles are: (1) Soul, (2) Non-soul, (3) Merit, (4) Demerit, (5) The cause of merit or demerit, (6) Which stops in the inflow of foreign energies, (7) Bondage of soul with actions, (8) Destruction of action, (9) Freedom of soul from all actions.

The first of these nine principles is Jiva (Soul). The characteristics of a soul are described thus: "It performs different kinds of actions, it reaps the fruits of those actions, it circles round, returning again. These and none other are the characteristics of the Soul."

It has also been described as a conscious substance, capable of development, imperceptible to senses, an active agent, and as big as the body it animates. This conscious substance so long as it feels, undergoes continual reincarnations. The most perfectly advanced Soul possesses ten 'Pranas' (powers). The lowest type must possess at least four. Of these ten Pranas, five relate to the five senses. There are also three other powers known as bodily power, mind power and speech power. The ninth prana gives the power of respiration and the tenth prana is the possession of the allotted span of life.

The essence of Jiva (Living) is Chaitanya (consciousness) which has two manifestations. One is Darshana (Perception) and the other is Jnana (Intelligence); the former is simple knowledge and the latter is understanding knowledge. There is a fusion of pure Jnana and Darshana in a perfect soul. Perfect knowledge is free from all doubt, perversity and indefiniteness. All pure knowledge is in the Soul which manifests itself when the disturbing elements are annihilated. These elements are passions and emotions which cause the inflow of matter and prevent the soul from performing its natural functions in full capacity. Another impediment is the interest in the physical and outward conditions of life which imprisons our true knowledge. The unimpeded soul has the potentiality to know all things, past, present and future. In our daily life the purity of the soul is defiled by absorption of the unconscious substances. It is only when the opposing energies are completely annihilated, that the soul throbs with its natural music exercising its natural functions and spreading its glow. When the Soul is freed from the weight which keeps it down it rises up to the top of the universe. Deliverance can only be attained through suppression of the lower element by the higher spirit. Morality is absolutely necessary to shape man's nature and prevent the formation of new Karma. The path to Liberation is inner conversion.

The second principle is the non-soul (i.e. things inanimate). It is in all respects the opposite of soul. Until the soul is freed from one particular division (pudgala i.e. matter) of non-soul, it is impossible for it to progress towards freedom. The non-soul is divided into two classes (1) without form (Arupi) and (2) with form (Rupi). The Arupi has four great divisions and each of these is sub-divided into further divisions. The Rupi division of non-soul contain only 'Pudgalastikaya' or matter which possess colour, smell, taste, and form and is susceptible to touch. Pudgala can be consumed or destroyed or it may decay or alter its form.

The third principle is 'Punya' or merit. The actions which lead to the good Karma which bring peace to mind and soul are called Punya. Merit according to Jainism is not merely the knowledge of the good; it is also a love of the good. Love is not a blind impulse of sense and sensibility. It is the joy which is super-added to the idea of an object. The Jaina sages hold that in addition to love and knowledge there must be the supreme effort, an act of personal resolution without which merit (Punya) cannot be practised and completed. This will to do is known as 'Virya'. Punya is the moral strength consisting in wilfully practising the good with love and intelligence. It is by constant repetition of virtuous acts that one becomes virtuous in as much as this constant practice, transforms the Soul, providing it with a source of energy to rise higher. There are nine ways of performing these actions. These are giving food, supplying water, clothing the naked, sheltering a layman, providing beds or beddings, wishing well of everyone, rendering service to save life, speaking without offending and lastly by offering salutations. The Jainas believe that there are forty-two ways in which the reward of this merit can be reaped. From these principles it is evident that great emphasis is laid on selfless service. Service performed with sincerity not only opens the vision, enlarges the heart, and draws out the higher qualities of man; but also sets up such action-currents that would contribute to the higher evolution of the individual in the here-in-after.

The fourth principle is demerit or sin (Papa). As the Jainas hold that the Punya is the moral strength, so Papa is moral weakness. It is the result of the preponderance Passions of the senses. It is the dominance of the instincts and impulses. The chief factor which is found in Punya and Papa is the free will of the agent to perform it. A man has a free choice between the two alternatives. The Jainas give the eighteen forms of actions in and through which a being commits Papa by setting up action currents of injury and non-injury which acting on the soul retards its progress, blurs the vision and knowledge. According to Jaina tenets it is the most heinous of all offences to take life of any living creatures. The central thought of Jainism is not so much saving life as refraining from destroying it—that is non-violence. Destroy no living creature. This is the highest religion. The Jainas make a distinction between spiritual and actual killing. Spiritual killing is wishing death or desiring harm to any one. If one does not try to lift himself up mentally and intellectually also he is classed as spiritual murderer (or Bhava Himsa). The other killing is actually putting an end to life of any creature. Though violence is the greatest of offences the Jainas recognise seventeen others which are: (1) Untruthfulness, (2) Dishonesty, (3) Unchastity, (4) Courteousness, (5) Anger, (6) Conceit, (7) Maya which includes intrigue, cheating and attachment, (8) Avarice, (9) 'Kasaya' (this is the synthesis of the last four anger, conceit, intrigue and greed); prolongation of the last four in various degrees is also included in Kasaya. All these last four are called Kasaya or things which tie one down to this world. The Jainas sum up their teaching about these four sins by saying that when wrath is vanquished forgiveness enters, when conceit is vanquished humility comes, intrigues give place to simplicity and when avarice is vanquished contentment comes, (10) Overfondness or attachment (Asakti) for a person or thing is a sin, (11) Hatred or envy, (12) Quarrelsomeness, (13) Slander, (14) Back-biting, (15) Criticising, (16) Lack of Self-control, (17) Hypocrisy, which includes belief in a false religion or a false preceptor. Under the principle of sin the Jainas include the results that flow from it. They say that there are five ways in which sin can impede knowledge. Sin also can impede enjoyment. Sin has an evil effect on physical and spiritual sight. It impedes meditation. There are it is said eighty-two results which follow from sin.

The fifth principle is Karma (i.e. the accumulated result of action). 'Asrava' is the influx of the Karma particles into the soul. The influx of Karma is by virtue of certain powers through which the soul draws in matters from without. These are: (1) 'Mithyatya', i.e. subreption, (2) 'Averati', i.e. attachment, (3) 'Kashaya', i.e. propensity (4) Pramada', i.e. negligence, (5) 'Yoga', i.e. the functional activity of mind, speech and body. Just as water flows into a boat through a hole, so Karma flows into the soul through Asrava and impedes its progress. The easiest way for Karma to enter is through the sense organs. It may enter through emotions, namely anger, conceit, hypocrisy and greed. Karma also flows into the soul if one does not observe the five vows. Another channel through which it enters is through too much attachment to material objects through the agency of mind, body or speech. Besides these there are twenty-five minor ways by which Karma is acquired.

When Karma has flowed into the soul and coalesced with the same it is called Bandha i.e. bondage. This is the sixth principle. Bandha is classified into four kinds according to the nature and character in and through which it displays itself in the phenomena of life and thought. All our sorrows and afflictions are due to Asrava and Bandha caused by subreption. One should shake off all the Karma matter which works as a veil of ignorance and prevents the unfolding of right vision. Every chained soul is under the influence of nine kinds of Karmas: (1) The Karma which impedes the knowledge of Truth, (2) Perception, which impedes the Right insight, (3) Experiences of pleasure and pain, (4) That which impedes the adoption of right faith (false belief, prejudice, Bigotry), (5) which impedes the right path in practice (anger, pride, etc.), (6) Force which determines the duration of the association of soul with its physical body, (7) Forces which organise the body and limbs, (8) Forces which attract the soul into a new womb, and (9) Force which limits the powers of the soul.

The seventh principle is therefore the converse of the last one which consists in impeding the inflow of Karma into the soul. The Karma that has been acquired can be arrested to attain liberation. The Jainas consider this principle of 'Samvara' to be of great importance. says that there are fifty-seven ways of arresting Karma.

The first five ways refer to external behaviour. A man must exercise the greatest possible care in averting any injury to any living creature, even whilst walking, sitting or sleeping. He must also guard his speech which must be soft and kindly. He must be particular in matters of food, possession of things, be careful about the disposal of refuse. There are specified rules for controlling mind, speech and body. Mind can be controlled by not indulging in joy, anxiety, anger or grief; speech can be controlled by observing silence or speaking as little as possible and body can be controlled by restricting the movements. Since the inflow of Karma can be arrested by enduring hardship a man should learn to put up with hardships and endure hunger, thirst, cold, heat, sting of an insect; be content with any kind of clothes whether torn or rough; be indifferent to lodging; eschew the society of women. The monk must perform meditation either sitting or standing, keeping the limbs immovable; receive even beatings cheerfully and must look upon illness as a favour which would afford him an opportunity to check the inflow of Karma. When praised, he must receive it with indifference. He must faithfully perform his ten duties. The first of which is forgiveness; strive to control arrogance and cultivate humility. He must remain aloof from intrigues or deceits in speech and action and must cultivate simplicity; be free from greed, practise fasting and austerities; subdue and control his mind and be truthful, pure and clean. He must not look upon anything as his own, observe celibacy in nine specified ways. The inflow of Karma may also be arrested by observing the five rules of conduct which are giving up evil conduct and turning to good deeds, duty of repentance, to become bound to the world as loosely as possible and by keeping the twelve Great Reflections always in mind. The twelve great Reflections are that one must remember that earthly things and ties are transient, that there is no shelter in this world, keeping before him the vision of endlessness of rebirth, that we come single in the world and go likewise, that soul and body are different things, that Karma is constantly flowing in us through manifold channels and reflect how to arrest this Karma. He must remember that everything is easy in this world save the acquisition of the three Jewels. Right Faith, Right Knowledge and Right Conduct. The path to Nirvana lies through three Jewels, being Right Faith, Right Knowledge and Right Conduct. The belief that the Jaina Tirthankaras are the true Gods, the Jaina Sastras the true scriptures and the Jaina saints the true preceptors is called the Right Faith. Eschewing all sensual pleasures and considering them as a source of sin is known as Nishkankshita. To love the virtuous for their divine qualities irrespective of their divine bodies is called Nirvichikitsita. Not to recognise the false creeds and false beliefs is called Amudhadrishti Anga. It is a duty to remove the adverse criticism of the Jaina tenets. To intensify the faith of the wavering, to have love and respect for their co-religionists, to establish the glory of the Jaina Siddhanta by dispelling ignorance, is another duty cast upon them. Right faith leads to all kinds of prosperity and bliss.

Right knowledge reveals the nature of things as it is and with certainty. The soul which has acquired right knowledge begins to put into practice the rules of right conduct to attain the state of desirelessness by eradicating likes and dislikes.

Right conduct is of two kinds. The first is that which is followed by an ascetic which is stricter than the other which is practised by a layman. The chief feature of Jainism is Ahimsa (Non-injury) as understood in its double aspect, negative and positive. Fear of injury to any life governs the conduct of the Orthodox Jaina.

The eighth principle is 'Nirjara', i.e. destruction of Karma. Inspite of all precautions Karma goes on accumulating and one of the great categories of faith deals with its destruction. One of the chief ways is burning them up in the fire of austerities. These austerities are of two kinds exterior and interior. The bodily or exterior austerities are absolute fasting, partial fasting, taking limited food, abstaining from food which one likes. Then one may, subject the body to mortification, avoid temptation. The interior austerities are also six. Confession and penance rank first, then reverence, service to all mankind, study, meditation. The last is, becoming unmindful to the bodily needs and cravings.

The ninth principle is 'Moksha' (Liberation). When the soul is freed from bondage of Karma and has transcended the possibility of rebirth, it attains deliverance. A person who has attained deliverance is called Siddha, a perfected Soul. Jaina defines a Siddha as being "without caste, unaffected by smell, without sense of taste, without feeling, without form, without hunger, without pain, without sorrow, without joy, without birth, without old age, without death, without body, without Karma, enjoying an endless and unbroken calm."

It must have been seen from the brief summary of the nine principles of Jaina philosophy that Jainas attach enormous importance to Karma (energy accumulated by action). Karma is the key, according to Jaina philosophy, to the riddle of life. So long as the soul is fettered by the bonds of Karma, it must undergo rebirth. Karma is bound up with the soul and when the soul departs, it carries with it the accumulated force of Karma and is drawn to such state which is suitable to it. There are four sources of Karma, the first of which is attachment to the mundane things of life. An indiscriminate use of any of these things gives rise to Karma: The Jainas divide Karma according to its essence, nature, duration and content. "There are four parts of Karma; its nature, that is its character; its condition, that is the time it will last; its constitution, that is its essence; its scope or the whole of its content." The Jainas classify Karma into eight classes, which are: (i) that which veils the knowledge; (ii) that which veils the perception of true faith; (iii) that which excites the feelings of pleasure and displeasure, happiness and misery; (iv) 'Mohniya' Karma arises from mundane attachment an indulgence in passions; (v) the length of time for which the fettered soul must suffer the consequences of the Karma; (vi) the Karma which determines one's particular 'gati' (state); (vii) the Gotra Karma determines his caste that is to say of being high-born or low-born; (viii) the Karma that impedes one's volition or strength. In order to have deliverance from the bondage of Karma the Jainas believe that one should ascend the ladder of fourteen steps (Chavda Gunasthanaka), each of which represents a particular stage of development of the soul, following up from the quiescence, elimination or partial quiescence or partial elimination of certain energies of Karma. These fourteen steps can be epitomised into four only in the moral ascent of the soul. The first stage may be roughly called the stage of impulsive life, of lust and enjoyment when the soul is enveloped in darkness of ignorance as to its goal; the second is -the life of conscious selection and pursuit where the goal and the true path of realisation are misapprehended. The third is the life of conscience and faith. At this stage the Soul does not merely exercise a restraining influence, but gives an impetus to the right course of action. Some sort of harmony is attained but this harmony is incomplete because the deciding factor is mere reason. The fourth stage is the stage where all the conflicts disappear and the soul shines forth in its purity and omniscience. This is made possible after a clear intellectual discernment of what ought to be and of the right means of its realisation. The harmony at this stage is complete. To understand the principle underlying the arrangement of gunasthanas the first essentials are Right Perception, Right Knowledge, and Right Conduct. The successive stages through which the soul passes from bondage to deliverance are as follows: The first stage is false knowledge. The Soul at this stage is completely under the dominance of Karma and is therefore unable to perceive the true view of things. When a person is dissatisfied with the actuality of things of the world, he tries to speculate upon the state of the world and his relation to it which enables him to hold down in check the three kinds of energies. It has been said: "As a man blind from birth is not able to say what is ugly and what is beautiful; so a man in the Mithyatya stage cannot determine what is real and what is false." The second stage appears when the soul after a cycle of existence sheds some of its grossness and ignorance. The third stage is the stage of oscillation between knowledge and doubt. The fourth stage comes when the doubts are removed and is still unable to protect itself from the reaction of Karma. The soul attains five good qualities, In the fifth stage the soul realises the great importance of conduct and the person takes twelve vows which enable him to fight Karma. He observes the six rules of daily life, namely worship of God, serving the preceptor, study of the scriptures, controlling the senses, austerities and giving of alms. At the sixth stage some passions are controlled or destroyed and only a few 'Pramadas' linger which are pride, enjoyment of senses, (anger, conceit, intrigue and greed) and sleep. At the seventh stage anger is completely subdued and only greed, deceit and pride remain in a very slight degree. In the eighth stage the conduct becomes perfect, vows are observed and the heart is filled with joy. In the ninth stage pride is conquered altogether and the man rises above all the ideas of sex and devotes himself to meditation. In the tenth stage he loses all sense of humour, all aesthetic pleasure, all sense of sound or form and all perceptions of pain, grief, fear, disgust and smells. This stage is reached by an advanced ascetic who has renounced all worldly ambitions and all worldly cares and anxieties. The most critical period is the eleventh stage. If at this stage he is able to subdue the lingering tinge of greed and he passes to the twelfth stage at which stage there is no greed and he becomes free from all influence. In the thirteenth stage he shines in eternal wisdom and infinite delight. This stage is often known as 'Jivan Mukta'. The man having reached this stage forms a Tirtha' or order and subsequently becomes a Tirthankara. The last stage begins with all the influence of Karma has been entirely destroyed or successfully dissipated. The man at this stage attains Moksha and is called the self-realised. The self-realised do not merge themselves in an All-embracing one but remain in the region of the liberated as freed souls enjoying perfect freedom from every sort of bondage caused by Karma. The liberated sage has been described as "Omniscience, boundless vision, illimitable righteousness, infinite strength, perfect bliss, indestructibility, existence without form, a body that is neither light nor heavy, such are the characteristics of the Siddha."

A Jaina has to follow right conduct and for that purpose he has to take several vows, which help him to make progress towards deliverance. Before taking the vows he has first to renounce five faults. He must raise no doubts, he must not have a desire to adopt another faith, he must not question the reality of the fruits of Karma, undertake not to praise the hypocrites and not to associate with them. After renouncing the five faults he must take the first and the foremost vow of desisting from destroying or hurting any life either knowingly or intentionally, excepting offending lives living in his body. He shall not himself kill or cause the killing nor will he kill by mind, speech or body. The second vow is that of not uttering falsehood which includes rash speech, revealing secrets, speaking ill of ones spouse, giving bad advice. The third vow is of non-stealing as understood in its widest possible sense. The fourth vow is of chastity; the fifth is of non-possession. These five vows are called Anuvrata. If one keeps these vows in all its strictness and diversity of meanings, and interpretation, he can be rightly called a Sravaka.

These five vows are to be complemented by three Gunavrata which, assist one in keeping these vows. Eschewing of desires which curtail sin and therefore an individuals is exhorted to limit the circle of desires and must follow a strict and restricted conduct in all his doings. The Jaina believes that great advantages accrue from keeping the vows. By moderation he keeps his body in health and vigour and morally it frees the soul from attachment, animosity and the like. The Jaina aims in his life-time to bar all the channels through which he acquires Karma, and if he intends to tread a higher path he is advised to keep the eleven Pratima' which lead him gradually towards the attainment of his goal. To tread in the higher path he is advised to develop twenty-one virtues which are to be serious in demeanour, clean both as regards his garments and his person, good-tempered striving after popularity, merciful, afraid of sinning, straightforward, wise, modest, kind, moderate.

gentle, careful in speech, sociable, cautious, studious, reverent both to persons and to traditions, humble, grateful, benevolent and finally attentive to business.

All the Jaina ascetics have to take five great vows; which are to be more strictly observed than the vows of a layman. The first vow is of non-killing which runs thus: "Not to destroy life, either five, four, three or two-sensed or immovable (i.e. one-sensed) even through carelessness." He should respect the vow of non-killing -by exercising self-control, examining things taken, always maintaining the Five 'Samitis', and by inspecting things before he eats or drinks, and before he receives them. The second vow is against untruthfulness "undertaking to speak what is pleasant, wholesome and true is called the vow of truthfulness. Truth is untruth if it is not pleasant and wholesome." He should avoid jesting, greed, cowardice and anger and he must think before he speaks. The third vow is of non-stealing which consists in "not taking what is not given; wealth is the outward life of man, and if it is taken away the man is undone." The fourth vow is of chastity which is eighteen-fold. "One should have no dealings with Gods, human beings or animals of the opposite sex, should not encourage them or cause others to do so by speech, thought or deed." This vow is respected by not sitting on the seats previously occupied by women, female animals, or monarchs, and by not living in their vicinity, not participating in exciting conversation about women, not remembering former delights, not looking at woman's form, not decorating one's own person, not eating or drinking to excess or partaking of highly seasoned food. The last vow is of Aparigraha which consists in having no possessions, consists in relinquishing greed for anything, if we think that a particular thing is our own, the mind is agitated by greed." This vow is maintained by renouncing liking for pleasant touch, taste, smell, form or word and for all the objects of senses renouncing hatred, for unpleasant objects. An ideal ascetic, says a verse, possesses twenty-seven qualities. "The true ascetic should possess twenty-seven qualities, for, he must keep the five vows, never eat at night, protect all living things, control his five senses, renounce greed, practise forgiveness, possess high ideals and inspect everything he uses to make sure that no insect life is injured. He must also be self-denying and carefully keep the three Gupti, he must endure hardships in the twenty-two ways and bear suffering till death."

The quintessence of the Jaina philosophy lies not only in the fact that it has co-related ethical teachings with its metaphysical system, but also in the amazing knowledge of human nature which its ethics displays. It must have been seen from the above that very often the Jainas divide and sub-divide in a variety of ways the moral principles as to throw fresh light on them. In these subdivisions it seizes the essential truth of things.

In Jainism, God is not regarded as a creator, but it does recognise that there is a subtle essence pervading all things. This is termed as God. The perfected soul (Siddha) or the liberated soul is fit for worship as God. "He who is omniscient, free from all love of the world, and from all failings, he who is worshipped by the three worlds and who explains the inner meanings (of religion) as it exists; this adorable deity is the great God." "He is free from all faults, has destroyed all the Karmas and attained salvation. He is omniscient and is a teacher of Dharma. He is free from hunger, thirst, old age, disease, birth, death, fear, pride, attachment, aversion, infatuation, wrong conceit, hatred, uneasiness, sweat, sleep and surprise. It has been said that Jiva (Living) which being free from all relation to others and from alien thoughts through its own intrinsic nature of perception and understanding perceives and knows its own eternal nature to be such, is said to have conduct that is absolutely self-determined." Men thou art thine own friend, why wishest thou a friend beyond thyself. The only enemy of the soul is the vital force of its own Karmas (actions) but the soul has a capacity to destroy the Karma by becoming self-conscious. It would be evident that there is no absolute fatalism contained in Jaina tenets. For though the Karma is a vital force yet our present life has power and force to evade the effects of past Karmas.

SIKHISM

THE fifteenth century of the Christian era was a period of singular mental and political activity. In India and Europe people shook off the indolence and were awakened to the consciousness of intellectual and spiritual responsibility. All sacred learning had been monopolised by the priests which led to serious abuses and a gloom was cast on the religious aspirations of the people. During this period Martin Luther and Calvin in Europe warned men of the errors that had crept into Christianity and at the same time the Indian saints were denouncing priestcraft, hypocrisy and idolatry. A great movement was led to stamp out superstition and hypocrisy by forming new sects. Before the advent of Guru Nanak people thought that they possessed knowledge, but in reality were steeped in the darkness of ignorance. Men did what suited their fancy. Miracles and alchemy were professed, incantations, spells and witchcraft were practised. Men indulged in strife and murder. Out of one God they invented many. In the sphere of worship some worshipped the sun or moon, others propitiated the earth, the sky, the wind, the fire. Men divided themselves into high and low. Hindus divided themselves into innumerable castes, and Mohamedans divided themselves into several sects. The holy words of their prophets were forgotten. The great Sikh Sect, based on the concept of Unity of God, which was founded by Guru Nanak, was one of the most powerful of the sects which, from the beginning, rejected Hindu formalities and adopted an independent ethical system, ritual and standards which were totally opposed to the theological beliefs of Nanak's age. It forms a considerable section of the population of the Punjab, which is now scattered in all parts of India and in other countries. During the Mohamedan conquest of India in the middle ages, it became incumbent upon the Hindus to consider seriously their religious and spiritual life. Many Hindus, in order to avoid tyranny, or to obtain worldly advantages, adopted during that period Islam. Yet there were many others who sought safety from persecution in lonely forests and there were others who, in spite of the persecution, remained in search of religious truth.

Guru Nanak, the founder of the Sikh religion, was born at Talwandi in April-May in the year 1469 A.D. in the middle of the reign of Bahlol Khan Lodi. The town of Talwandi was governed by Rai Bular at the time of the birth and during the youth of Guru Nanak. Although the age was one of religious intolerance and persecution, Rai Bular was the reverse of a bigot and when he heard of Nanak's piety and learning he felt a mysterious interest in him. Nanak's father's name was Kalu, an accountant in the village of Talwandi in Punjab. His mother's name was Tripta. It is said that the astrologer who had come to write the child's horoscope, predicted regal grandeur and high dignity for the child whose name would be echoed in earth and heaven. It is said that at the precocious age of five Nanak began to talk of divine subjects. When Nanak was seven years of age he was sent to school where he surprised his school master with the innate learning which he possessed. To his father this precocious youth appeared to be insane, and he was distressed about his future. He sent him to herd buffaloes. At the age of 14 he was married to Sulakhmi. He continued to herd cattle, but he was indifferent to worldly affairs. He did not do any work for his livelihood and often his mother reproached him. He listened to no admonitions and did no other work than composing hymns. He became unsuited for all secular occupations. His father proposed that he should keep a shop or become a dealer in horses, so that he might earn his living. All attempts to draw him into secular life proved futile. With single-mindedness he devoted himself to praising God. Very little is known about his married life excepting that he had two sons, Shri Chand and Laxmidas. Nanak was induced to go to Sultanpur to join Jairam his brother-in-law. Jairam introduced him to Governor Daulat Khan who appointed him as a storekeeper. He performed his duties so well that everybody was gratified and congratulated him. Out of the provisions which Guru Nanak was allowed, he kept only a small portion for his own maintenance and distributed the rest to the poor. He used to spend his nights in composing and singing hymns in praise of God. One day after bathing Nanak disappeared in a forest and had a vision of God's presence. God said to him: "I am with thee, I have made thee happy and also those who shall take thy name. Practise the repetition of my name, pharity, ablutions, worship and meditation." He again heard "O Nanak, to him upon whom my look of kindness resteth, be thou merciful as II too shall be merciful. My name is God, the primal Brahma, and thou art the Divine Guru." Guru Nanak returned after three days from the forest. He went home and gave all that he had to the poor. A great crowd gathered and they all saw that the Guru's acts were the result of the abandonment of this world. After this he dressed in religious costume and formed associations with religious people. He remained silent for a day and next day he uttered the pregnant announcement: "There is no Hindu and no Musalman." The Sikhs generally interpret this to mean that both Hindus and Mohamedans had forgotten the precepts of their religion. Nanak's mind was filled with his mission. Thereafter, in company with Mardana, he moved (from one place to another in order to regenerate the human race. Guru Nanak travelled from East to West and from North to South. He visited Mecca and Madina where he vanquished the Mohamedan priests in arguments; when questioned by the high priest as to who he was, the Guru replied 'I have appeared in this age to indicate the way unto men. I reject all sects and only know one God whom I recognise on the earth, the heavens and in all directions." The Guru knowing that his end was approaching, appointed Angad as his Successor. When it became known that Guru Nanak was about to die people flocked to him and began to sing songs of mourning; the Guru fell into a trance and awoke after some time. The Guru drew over him a sheet, uttered "Wahguru," made obeisance to God, and blended his light with Guru Angad's. He breathed his last on the

10th Sud day of Aso Samvant Year 1595 (i.e. 1538 A.D.) at Kartarpur in the Punjab. The oldest authentic account of Guru Nanak was written by Bhai Guru Das who flourished at the end of the 16th and beginning of the 17th century. Janma Sakhi written by a Sikh in the year 1588 A.D. is the most trustworthy detailed record of the life of Guru Nanak. Guru Nanak was succeeded in turn by Guru Angad, Guru Amardas, Guru Ramdas, Guru Arjun, Guru Hargovind, Guru Har Rai, Guru Har Kishan, Guru Tej Bahadur and last, Guru Govind Singh. These are the ten Gurus of the Sikhs. All the Gurus kept up the ideal of simplicity in their lives. They maintained a middle path between asceticism and prosperity. Guru Nanak invented Gurmukhi language which is derived from Hindi. The Granth Saheb is in Gurmukhi language. His followers preached in colloquial language for expression of their ideas and precepts and avoided learned words and metaphysical subtleties. Guru Nanak spoke of himself as neither learned nor continent. He was the essence of humility. He preached with vehemence against idolatry, hypocrisy and distinctions of castes and creeds, but in so doing he never uttered a word which savoured of personal ambition, neither did he arrogate to himself the attributes of God.

Sikhism was meant for all castes and communities, and in the beginning converts were made from Mohamedans as well as the Hindus. Many outcastes and men of low castes were as acceptable as high class Hindus. In order to make no distinctions Guru Arjun included in the Granth the compositions of Kabir, of a Mohamedan saint Farid, of a shoe-maker Ravidas, Saina a Barber, and other such men. The Sikh Gurus declared the whole of humanity to be one, and said that a man was to be honoured not because of caste but because he is a man, —an emanation from God. All men are the same although they appear under different influence.

Having seen in short, the life of Guru Nanak we shall proceed to enumerate the cardinal doctrines of Sikhism established by him. The most fundamental doctrines of Sikhism are the oneness of God and the fellowship of man. The very basis of Sikhism is to love God, and the

Guru, the religious preceptor. All the Sikh Gurus who followed after Guru Nanak declare that the aim and end of life is not to attain heavenly abode but to develop the Essence that is in man, and thus merge himself in God. Guru Nanak and other Gurus have showed a way to attain this which is to worship the Name and believe in the Name. The Sikh scriptures have repeatedly emphasised that the repetition of the Name is the first essential of spiritual progress. "Remember God and banish neglect of Him from thy heart. Accursed the life of him in the world who breatheth without uttering the Name." "He who is dyed with God's praises never loveth the world and loseth his life in the game." God is described both as Personal (Sagun) and Absolute (Nirgun). To the Gurus God does not appear to be an abstract idea or a moral force but a Being capable of being loved and who is omnipresent and omniscient. He has no incarnations. "He lives in everything; He dwells in every heart. Yet He is not blended with anything. He is separate. He lives in all, is yet ever distinct. He abides with thee too. As fragrance dwells in a flower or reflection in a mirror, so does God dwell inside everything; seek him therefore in the heart." In Asa-di-war Guru Nanak in the first Stanza gives the belief about God. "There is but one God, whose name is true, the creator, devoid of fear and enmity, immortal, unborn, self-existent, great and beneficent." "God," says Guru Nanak, "is indivisibly one, above everything. He is the highest moral being who is inscribed in the hearts of all men with His Name and his moral Essence. To realise Him is very simple." "Make thy body the field, good works the seed, irrigate with God's name. Make thy heart the cultivator. God will germinate in thy heart and thou shalt thus obtain the dignity and reward of Nirvan."

Again Guru Nanak has said "Make attention thy service, faith in the name thy occupation. Make restraint of evil thine effort. . . . ." " He can be realised not through knowledge or performance of rites and ceremonies but through love and faith, singing His praises and meditating on His Name. The praise of God which he speaks of is not an idle mysticism but active, and untiring service, inspired by consuming desire to please Him. "Without pleasing God all actions are valueless therefore exert yourself in loving action, remember Him, leaving all pride of self. In the teachings off Guru Nanak one breathes the purest form of devotion. He adopts the Upanishad view that there is one Brahma without any second and he declares that creation is only the Maya (illusion) and all things spring into being through Maya. The individual Soul is in essence identical with the Supreme Being; man should therefore live in accordance with the will of God, resigning everything to His will, and approach God in a spirit of humility and self-surrender. Make the Divine will your own and obtain His grace through self-surrender. God must be worshipped with devotion and faith without which all attempts to realise Him will be in vain. The conception of God according to Sikhism is that He is one without any second. He was in the beginning and exists through all ages. He is beyond thought, and indefinable. His order cannot be described and all are subject to His order. None can describe His greatness and His deeds for in describing Him there would be no end. He is all seeing, omnipresent and omniscient. He is not established nor is created. He exists by Himself. His will is great and nothing is outside His Will. Though the Sikhs believe in a personal God, He is not in man's image. Guru Nanak calls him "Nirankar" that is formless. Gurudas speaks of him as "formless without equal, wonderful and not perceptible by the senses." All the Gurus have believed God to be diffused throughout creation. "Think upon the one" says Guru Nanak "who is contained in everything." Guru Govind Singh has forcefully said that God and His worshippers though two are in reality one as bubbles which are formed in water are again blended with it. As regards His Attributes it is said in Japji that they are described in endless words.

The word Sikh means a disciple. It is derived from the Sanskrit word "Shishya" or disciple. A Sikh is admitted to the community when he receives the Pahul (Baptism); when he is baptised, he adopts the five

"Kakas"—the "Kes" (uncut hair), the Kacha (short drawers), the "Kara" (iron bangle), the Kirpan (steel dagger), and the "Kangha" (small comb worn in the hair). Sikhism enjoins that obedience to the Guru brings release from future birth and attainment of eternal Bliss. It is said in the Japji that "under instructions of Guru, God's word is heard under the Guru's instruction its knowledge is acquired. Under Guru's instruction man learns that God is everywhere contained. The Guru is Shiv, the Guru is Vishnu and Brahma. The Guru is Parvati, Laxmi and Saraswati." The Sikhism is not merely a set of doctrines but a way of life. It has for its basis not a code of rules and forms, but it is based on discipleship. A Sikh is expected to rise early in the morning at about 3 a.m. and after taking bath to meditate on the name of God. He should recite the compositions of the Gurus as his daily prayers. At the end of certain recitations he must offer his daily prayer.

Service to fellowmen is an essential part of the duty of a Sikh. It is the practical expression of love. Those whom one is to serve must be obeyed. Service recognises no barrier of religion, caste, race or creed. The Gurudwaras afford opportunity to do service with love and devotion. The service in Gurudwaras takes the form of sweeping the floors, cleaning utensils, fetching water and service in the free kitchen (Guru-ka-Langar). This idea of service in Gurudwaras originated with Guru Nanak who intended to teach his disciples equality, fraternity and love between man and man. A Sikh is exhorted to perform acts of service with all in the same manner in which he performs it in the Gurudwaras. The Gurus have said the foundation of man's uplift is on man's own character as it is the character alone which helps one in moral crisis. Temptations seize a man unawares and he has to decide his action on the impulse of the moment. Therefore the Gurus have insisted that their followers must possess abundance of virtue so that they may not fall a prey to temptations.

The towering personality of the Guru assists the disciple in shaping his life towards divinity and forming a union with him. A man may possess much knowledge but without guide there would be utter darkness. The Guru forms the connecting link between God and man, and man and man. Guru Nanak has said "The true Guru must be such as to unite all men." In Asa-ki-War Guru Nanak has said "without the true Guru none has found God God has put Himself into the true Guru who has banished worldly love from him." Again we find "By meeting the true Guru who has removed pride from his heart and who preaches the Truest of the True, the True one is obtained." The Guru must be all perfect. Everybody else is subject to error, only the Guru and the God are without error. "True Guru possesses the sword of knowledge and fights with his heart, he knows the secrets of the ten organs of action and perception and the evil passions, he can unravel the divine knowledge and is free from pride and self-conceit, his heart is free from worldly desires, he is self-restraint, he sleeps little and takes scanty food, he keeps a guard over his saintly body, he is constant in devotion and penance, he utters divine knowledge day and night, he waketh in contemplation of God. He has effaced wrath, avarice, pride and greed. He cherishes holiness. He makes the body the vessel and remembrance of God his milk. He performs the work of God. He is humble, and contented. The Guru is sinless, he is above man's capacities. He is humble and humane. When a man is completely attuned to the Divine Will he is sanctified as a Guru and he becomes perfect and holy.

There is a lucid description given in Arjun's Sukhamani as regards the attainment of perfection by the Gurus.

"God does not die, nor do I fear death
He does not perish, nor do I grieve
He is not poor, nor do I have hunger
He has no pain, nor have (I any trouble
There is no destroyer but God
Who is my life and who gives me life
He has no bond, nor have I got any
He has no entanglement, nor have I any case

As He is stainless, so am I free from stain
As He is happy, so am I always rejoicing
He has no anxiety, nor have I any concern
As He is not defiled, so am I not polluted
As He has no craving, so do I covet nothing
He is pure, and I too match Him in this
I am nothing. He alone is everything
All around is the same He

Nanak, the Guru has destroyed all my superstitions and defects. And I have become uniformly one with Him."

Sikhism requires a close association with the Guru. A Sikh must merge himself with the Guru and be thus imbued with indestructible power and force. A true Sikh who with self-surrender follows the precepts of the Guru is enriched with spiritual force and his vital powers soar higher and higher and becomes a superman. Such a Sikh is called a "Khalsa" the personification of the Guru. "The Khalsa" says the Guru "is my order part, in Him I live and have my being." A single Sikh is only one, but when he takes Guru Govind Singh into his embrace the equation changes and he becomes "one lakh and a quarter." Such a change can only take place when his physical, mental and spiritual powers are reinforced. The Guru is responsible for elevating his character and increasing his force and energy. This is the individual reformation done by the Guru. Besides this individual reformation the Guru organises all of them into "Sangats" holi Assemblies and energize these organisations by putting his personality into them. This paved the way for the development of the influence of Gurus in institution. Guru Nanak had organised Sangat or holy fellowship. Local organisations were formed under authorised leaders called "Masands." Every Sikh was assumed to be a member of one of these organisations. The Guru was the priest of these organisations. Lehna was the Scion of Guru Nanak who was proclaimed his successor. "The wise being Guru Nanak descended in the form of Amardas. The common belief is that all the Gurus beginning with Guru Nanak and ending with

Guru Govind Singh the last of the Gurus are identical with Guru Nanak. Guru Govind Singh has said "The generality of men take them as different from one another. Very few recognise them as one spirit. But only those realise perfection who do recognise them as one." The silver link of love which subsists between the Guru and the Sikhs far surpasses mundane love.. "The Guru is Sikh and the Sikh who practices the Guru's word is at one with the Guru." "Vahe Guru" that is wonderful is Guru is the "mantra' which Sikhs repeat. The seat of the Guru is lower than the Holy Scriptures.

The prescribed form of worship is meditation on and singing of the hymns. The only way of worship with the Sikhs is that they read the hymns composed by their Gurus and sing them sweetly to the accompaniment with musical instruments. The Sikhs believe that the spirit of the Guru ever lived with them and helped the assemblies to acquire sanctity. In course of time these assemblies became the Panth which was regarded as an embodiment of the Guru. Thus after the death of Guru Govind Singh, the word and the personality were separated. The Panth bore the insignia of the Guru and the word became the Gyan Guru. It is evident from the history of the Sikhs that the community underwent a course of training at the hands of the ten Gurus and when it was found that the community was well developed the Guru merged his personality in the body of the nation. Thus we find that the Khalsa Panth was to be the Guru not by supplanting the former Gurus but in their place and in their name. It has to guide itself in accordance with the teachings contained in the Holy Granth. (It has been said "Let him that wishes to see me go to an assembly of Sikhs and approach them with faith and reverence and he will surely see me amongst them." By investing the Panth with the personality of the Guru, the Panth has become both unchanging and Progressive at one and the same time. It has been said above that the Guru does two things the first is Revelation of Truth through the word, which does not re - quire any change and secondly he guides to the practice of Truth, which function is properly fulfilled by the Panth, which because of it being evolving with the collective personality of the sect is ever progressing with the advance made in the evolution of intellect, feeling and moral sense.

Sikhism points out to men that there is one God primal and omnipresent. It places the king and the beggar on a spiritual equality and teaches them to respect each other. It preaches a religion of the heart as distinguished from a religion of external forms and ceremonies. It is chiefly based on the concept of the Unity of God; it rejected Hindu formulas and adopted an independent ethical system, ritual and standards which were totally opposed to the theological beliefs of Guru Nanak's age and country. Guru Nanak found that acts and austerities practised by professedly religious men of his age and country were without divine love or devotion. He declared that God, who has no form, cannot be found by wearing religious garb, but by humility; and if men rejected caste and worshipped God in spirit they would be received in His Court. The Guru examined all religious sects and found them all immersed and perishing in spiritual pride. He found Hindu and Mohamedan priests groping in the pit of superstition. The religious teachers possessed no knowledge and were in spiritual darkness. "Religion consisteth not in mere words. He who looks on all men as equal is religious.

"Religion consisteth not in wandering to tombs or places of cremation or sitting in attitudes of contemplation. Religion consisteth not in wandering in foreign countries or in bathing at places of pilgrimage.

"Abide pure in impurities of the world. Thus shalt thou find the way to religion."

The Holy scriptures of the Sikhs or the Holy Granths are two in number. The one was compiled by the 5th Guru, Arjun Dev. The other is a collection of miscellaneous hymns of the tenth Guru, Guru Govind Singh, and of translations of Sanskrit books made by various others under the orders of Guru Govind Singh.

The Holy Granth commonly known as Adi Granth contains hymns of the first five Gurus, with a few selections from the hymns of different contemporary saints.

These were all collected, arranged and formed into one Volume called Guru Granth Sahib by the 5th Guru. The teachings of Guru Nanak are contained in the Adi Granth. The hymns of the Gurus and saints are not arranged in the holy volume according to their authors but according to the thirty-one 'Rags' or musical measures to which they were composed. The first nine Gurus adopted the name of Guru Nanak as their pen-name and their compositions are distinguished by Mahallas or quarters. Thus the compositions of Guru Nanak are styled Mahalla one, the compositions of Guru Angad Mahalla two, and so on. After the hymns of the Gurus are found hymns of the "Bhagats" that is devotees under their musical measures.

Japji is considered by the Sikhs as a key to their sacred Volume and an epitome of its doctrines. It is the great morning prayer of the Sikhs. It is a collection of hymns composed by Guru Nanak. Sri Arjun Dev the 5th Guru arranged the hymns in their present form. It comprises the 38 Mool Mantras, 38 Pauris or rungs of a ladder and a Sloka which forms the epilogue. The Granth Sahib begins with Japji. The rest of the Granth Sahib is an exposition of the philosophical doctrines and teachings contained in t!he Japji. It guides the way to the realisation of God. In Japji Guru Nanak has given five stages through which an individual Soul must pass in order to attain eternal bliss. These are, (1) Dharam Khand, (2) Gian Khand, (3) Saran Khand, (4) Karam Khand, (5) Such Khand. The first Dharam Khand is the province of duty and action. Everyone will be judged by his deeds. His deeds will be the determining factor after his earthly existence. Therefore it is ordained that everyone should perform his duties well.

The second is Gian Khand. This is the realm of knowledge. Man's determination to perform his duties is reinforced by the knowledge that by performance of his duties he would, like great Souls Rama and Krishna, attain evelasting peace. From Gian Khand the Soul passes to Saran Khand, the Realm of Ecstasy. In this, duty comes to him naturally and spontaneously. It becomes a Part parcel of his nature and an ingrained habit.

From Saran Khand the Soul passes to Karam Khand, the realm of Power. His character is now built in the process of three former stages and he now acquires spiritual strength. He loses fear of death, and is freed from the round of births and deaths. He becomes invincible and powerful.

The Soul passes from Karam Khand to Such Khand, the abode of Truth. Here he finds the formless one. The individual is absorbed in the Divine Being and he attains God-hood.

For the realisation of the highest, the Gurus laid a great stress on building of man's character, which alone, in a moment of crisis assists him to make his judgment as to good and evil. The development of character or virtue must be such that it becomes a part of individual nature, a possession which shows itself at every moment of life. A simple method is shown for acquiring such a character, and that is by (1) singing and hearing the Name.

"By hearing the Name man becometh as Shiv or Brahma. By hearing the Name Truth, contentment and Divine knowledge is obtained.

"Hearing the Name is equal to bathing at sixty-eight places of pilgrimage. By hearing the Name the mind is composed and fixed on God.

"By hearing the name the depth of the sea of Virtue is sounded. By hearing the name a blind man findeth his way. The Second part of virtue is submission to the Will of God. An Absolute self-surrender in mind, body and spirit to the will of God.

"By obeying Him, wisdom and understanding enter the mind. Whoever obeys God knows the pleasure of it in his own heart.

"By obeying Him man attains the gate of Salvation. Whosoever obeys God knows the pleasure of it in his own heart."

Sikhism says that Man takes birth in this world with his past, and he inherits during his life his past character and the matrix of his family and race. The spirit of man is elevated by instilling a belief that he is not a helpless creature subjected to past tendencies and to an arbitrary will. He can shape his actions, character and destiny and is therefore responsible for them. With his will and through Guru's blessings his will can be attuned to Supreme force, which can assist him to transcend his past and determine his future conduct "Rebirth and Deliverance depend on thy will." According to Sikhism the ultimate source of all that is in us is God's alone "All virtues are thine O Lord, none are mine." An individual is exhorted to "Make contentment and modesty thine earnings, self-respect thy wallet, meditation the ashes to smear on thy body. Make the body, which is only a morsel for death, thy beggar's coat, and faith thy rule of life and thy staff. Make association with men thine Ai Panth (a sect of ascetics) and conquest of thy heart, the conquest of the world. Make divine knowledge thy food, compassion thy store-keeper and the voice which is in every heart, the pipe to call to repast."

"Make Him who has strung the whole world on His string, thy spiritual Lord. Let wealth and supernatural power be relishes for others."

"Union and separation is the law which regulateth the world. By destiny we receive our portion."

Sikhism teaches that the source of evil is none other than our own ego, which has been placed by God in human hearts. According as we surrender ourselves to God's will the ego turns out to be a boon or a curse. A man should not have an overwhelming sense of ego. As it grows it becomes a barrier between man and God and a man wallows from one sin to another. Man is clouded by ignorance and self-centredness and he thus misses the infinite which is within him. We must subject our tiny self to the great will of God and attain divine knowledge which is resplendent. "The True one is seated in the hearts of all men." Men are urged to practise the virtues and discipline themselves. "Make continence thy furnace, resignation thy gold, understanding anvil, divine knowledge thy tools, the fear of God thy bellows, austerities thy fire, Divine love thy crucible melt God's love therein." Sikhism, teaches us to perform good and virtuous actions because "According to men's acts some shall be near and others distant from

God." This solyes the problem of good and evil, which is nothing but union or disunion with God. Men must realise that all things are strung on God's will and as long as he is conscious of this he lives and moves in union with Him. But if he is led away by the sense of his tiny self he displaces himself from the Unity. "By the force of Union we meet God and enjoy Him even with this body."

And by force of disunion we break away from Him. But says Nanak it is possible to be united again. This gives hope to the erring.

The Sikh is enjoined to "put away from him lust, wrath and slander. Abandon Avarice and lovelessness and you shall be free from care. He who breaketh the chain of superstition shall be free and feel divine pleasure in his heart. Meet the True Guru and God Himself." A Sikh is exhorted to practise righteousness and rectitude. Continue to love God and you shall behold the unseen One pervading all three worlds. Sikhism preaches the fatherhood of God and Universal brotherhood of men. It urges men to work in good faith as a duty imposed upon by God, casting of fear of bad result, and giving hope of reward for good result. The Gurus lay great stress on the importance of prayer. As the conception of God is personal, so prayers are much in use. Guru Nanak says "Nanak, with the Lord it is prayer alone that succeeds, and not demands or commands." They say that nothing can be achieved by man without the grace of God. Through prayer and self surrender alone this divine grace descends. All religious and secular ceremonies are preceded by a prayer. It is not necessary to have the assistance of a priest for offering prayers. The composition of the prayers is one of the rarities of literature. The prayer is. communal in its language and subject matter. The Sikh is made to realise that he is a part of the corporate body called the Panth or the Khalsa. The Sikhs in their temples observe no elaborate ceremonies. The whole ceremony consists of nothing except reciting and singing sacred hymns. There is no preaching and no discussions or controversies are allowed.

The Sikh has to bring himself in a prayerful mood before he addresses himself to God. The Sikh prayer is an active yearning of the Soul to feel one with God. The object of prayer is to refresh our spirit and make us ready to do His Will.

Absorption in God is the supreme goal of human attainment. Certain Sikh Scholars maintain that Nirvana and "Such Khand" mentioned above are identical. The word Nirvana comes from "Nir" out and "Va" to blow which means the cessation of individual consciousness caused by the blending of the light of the Soul with the light of God. The Sikhs compare it to water blending with water.

> "As water blends with water, when
> Two streams their waves unite
> The light of human life doth blend
> With God's celestial light
> No transmigrations then avail
> The weary human Soul;
> It has attained its resting place
> Its peaceful crowning goal."

Nirvana is to be gained by meditating on God with devotion and Faith and by constant recitation of His Name and by following the teachings of the Gurus. Good works alone are not sufficient to gain Nirvana, but they must be performed with devout meditation and with mental absorption in God. If a man has done misdeeds or evil actions he must pass through countless transmigrations in order to attain the final reward of Nirvana.

ZOROASTRIANISM

HUNDREDS of years before Christ, there appeared a prophet—in the ancient home of the Aryans—whom the Greeks called Zoroastres and his own people called Zarathustra. He was much better known to the Greeks and Romans of the classical times than Moses and David. Legend tells us that his conception was divine. His guardian angel entered into a homa plant and passed with its juice into the body of a priest while he was offering divine service, at the same time a ray of heaven's glory entered the bosom of a maid of noble lineage; the priest married the maid and the imprisoned angel mingled with the imprisoned ray and Zoroastres took his earthly existence. As of Jesus, so it is said of him on the day of his birth he laughed aloud which drove away the evil spirits.

The place of his birth, and also the time of his existence have not been accurately determined. It is assumed that Zoroastres appeared and proclaimed the new teaching in the tenth Century before Christ in the reign of Kai Vishtasp. Modern historians place him between the sixth and tenth century before Christ. We find from some of the passages in the sacred books that Rhaga in Media was his birthplace but there are conflicting opinions and some say that Rhaga was his later residence. His main activity was in Bactria, East of Media, Iran and Persia. He died at a ripe old age, murdered at the hands of a horde of invading Turamians at Balk, after having firmly established his religion. The Avesta mentions his wife Hvovi and his three sons and three daughters. He chose to live in solitude and made his abode in mountains and lived on fruits and milk products. His incessant toil, untiring energy and boundless power of patience and perseverance betokened a healthy and robust constitution. From an early age he studied metaphysical questions and was eager to promote the physical and moral well being of his fellowmen. The religious system which he established gives ample proof of his broad intellect and his capacity for originality. He was intensely sensitive to nature and he watched and studied the objects of nature and their movements. He drew from the natural phenomena, spiritual lessons of high value and declared them to his people.

He was no less sensitive to human nature. He rejoiced in righteousness and truth. He was moved by compassion for the sorrows of the world. He had a loving nature and a tender heart. Even at the height of his spiritual power and glory he remained humble and made no false pretences. He never claimed himself to be God or to possess His powers. He always declared himself to be in constant search of Ahura Mazda—the Lord of Light. He unceasingly engaged himself in perfecting his character. It is said: "He was holiest in the holiness, he thought and acted according to law." He was not a mere recluse, meditative and inactive. In him we find a perfect harmony of the life of activity and the life of contemplation. He often declared that the highest spiritual life is the doing of active service to one's fellowmen. He teaches by his example and precept, that personal struggles, personal reformation, and personal purity are the only means for the attainment of the highest aim of life. It is said that in his youth he was tempted by evil spirits but he zealously and unwaveringly attached himself to his faith in Ahura Mazda, the Lord of Light. The Ahura Mazda appeared to him and gave into his hands the Avesta or the "Book of Knowledge and Wisdom" and exhorted him to spread the message to the World.

In the beginning he was ridiculed and persecuted. He fought against all opposition and he chose to suffer rather than disobey the voice. He had to fight against a host of evils, troubles and temptations and against sin, and ultimately he was victorious. He fought for the establishment of the kingdom of God and Truth in the world. He succeeded in establishing his religion and laying the foundation of material and moral welfare of mankind because of his kind and generous nature and persuasive and peaceful methods. He spoke in the common language of the people with sincerity of purpose and with fervour. He expressed his sayings in simple words with passionate feelings.

The religion of the Irano-Aryans after their separation from the Indo-Aryans was polytheistic nature-worship, but it was gradually tending towards monotheistic beliefs. When Zoroaster appeared, he found his people worshipping their ancestors, animals, the earth, air, sun, etc. Zoroastres was pained to find his people worshipping primitive deities. He revolted against it and proclaimed to the world one God, Ahura Mazda. He declared with vehemence that other gods were the manifestations of the divine attributes of Ahura Mazda. Kai Vishtasp, who flourished in the 10th century before Christ, was the first king of Iran who adopted the Zoroastrian religion and established it in his Kingdom. During the first half of the 8th Century before Christ, the Assyrians gradually established their supremacy over the whole of Iran. After an interval the Medes shook the Assyrian Yoke and in the seventh century before Christ Phraortes succeeded in forming an independent Median Kingdom. His son Cyaxares extended his rule over the Bactrians and other nations of eastern Iran. His successor proved to be a tyrannous ruler and the Median supremacy passed into the hands of the Persians under Cyrus the Achaemenian. Cyrus extended his empire to Babylon and Asia minor. Under Cyrus (559-529 B.C.) Persia rose to power and greatness. Zoroastrianism kept on spreading in eastern Iran under the Kayanians and even after their downfall continued to make progress. Under the later Achaemenian kings, the people seem to have adopted Zoroastrianism. The religion by this time had spread all over Persia. In 331 B.C., Alexander the Great attacked the Persian Empire and subjugated the last Achaemenian, Darius III. His rule, as also the rule of Seleucides and his successors, was oppressive; but in 250 B.C. the Parthians shook off the Greek yoke. The Parthians were tolerant, and in power and position ranked next to the Romans. Some of the Parthian kings became affiliated to Zoroastrian priests. During the Greek and Parthian Supremacy most of the people had fallen away from the belief in one God. They had become indifferent to Zoroastrian doctrines and customs. King Ardeshir I, the first Sassanian King (226-240 A.D.) was the most enthusiastic supporter of the Zoroastrian religion. He took strong measures, to eradicate idolatry and image worship. He reconstituted the code of Zoroastrian religion and re-united the scattered parts of the sacred Zoroastrian literature. After him, his son, Shapoor, I, remained faithful to the religion and maintained it in pristine purity. The ancient books were collected and were re-written. The Persians thus regained their old ascendancy, and for four centuries they were the rivals of Rome until the fierce invaders from Mohamedan Arabia who in 632 A.D. subjugated, vanquished and annihilated them and forced the rest of them to accept their faith or be exiled from the country. A few escaped to the mountain fastnesses of their conquered land and some of them came to Hindustan. These remnants of a great race, with their fragmentary literature and creed, ature "the only survival of the world renowned Persian people. They are called the Parsees. Their book, the "Zend Avesta" contains the last remains of their ancient doctrines, laws and customs. The early Aryans in Central Asia had a common religion, language and custom. We find a great similarity between the Vedic and the Zend Avesta language. The versification of Zend Avesta closely resembles that of the Vedas. The doctrines and ceremonials of the Zoroastrians have a remarkable similarity to those of the Vedas and the reason for this similarity is not far to seek. History informs us that one branch of the Aryan stock descended from the Himalayas and conquered and occupied the vast and wealthy regions of the Indus and the Ganges valleys, and the other branch of the family emigrated in the other direction to Iran, which was a less fertile region. Gradually these Iranians vanquished many countries on the west of the Himalayas and occupied the whole of Central Asia.

So we find Zoroastrianism and Hinduism had the same and had in part identical evolutions. The people separated from an identical stock having the same geographical and historical environment. In the initial stage the unfolding of both these creeds was similar, but later on, with the change in the physical, psychological and social atmosphere the differentiation became more and more evident and at last both stand as different religious creeds. It appears that Hinduism started with many gods, some having evil influences. Zoroaster also started with the admission of the principle of evil. It will be found on close scrutiny that both coincide in respecting monotheism and altruism as the noblest faith. Both these and the Buddhistic doctrines declare, in diverse languages that doing good to our fellowmen is the only way to universal happiness and improvement of the self. They proclaim that the highest homage to God and the shortest way to salvation is by doing good to our neighbour. In essence and in reality both Hinduism and Zoroastrianism are monotheistic, though ostensibly both appear to be polytheistic. On closer examination we find that the mythologies of India and Iran are identical. A Hindu ends by absorption in Brahma, a Zoroastrian with the victory of Ahura Mazda and the defeat of evil. In both, Soma Homa was the high form of worship, and 'Agni' (Fire) among the chief deities. Hinduism counted eight leading Gods and Zoroastrianism seven.

It is worthwhile to note that different doctrines and creeds which prevail at a time are not isolated phenomena and do not spring forth all of a sudden and from nothing. As time going on there is a constant development of moral and ethical thoughts and sentiments in different parts of the world. The history of religious thought has made it abundantly evident that each succeeding religious phase had its origin in its predecessor. Zoroastres did not claim to be a metaphysician or a philosopher. He was a prophet, who had a divine revelation. Zoroastrianism is a revealed religion of faith and devotion. It appears that Zoroastres has refined and reformed the former popular religion of the people. Instead of the former material pantheism, ancestor worship and deification of natural forces, he presented a new conception of the spirituality of Ahura Mazda the universal, all pervading, changeless, mighty, just, merciful, majestic, the holiest and the highest, the Lord of all that is. He personified and spiritualised the universe. He enthroned that principle in place of the worship of a multiple of deities. The idea of one God loomed large before him, dismissing the multiple bodies, agents, and powers.

He taught that the great object of religion or of state, or of society is the cultivation of morality. According to him the highest religious conception is purity of thought, word and deed. He assserted that Ahura Mazda has seven qualities : (1) Light, (2) Good mind, (3) Right, (4) Dominion, (5) Piety, (6) Well-being, and (7) Immortality. The good mind according to him is not any with human wisdom but one having divine wisdom. In addition to these holy spirits, there are guardian angels for every individual. These holy spirits and guardian angels help an individual to acquire a good mind. From his experience of disharmony, clashing elements vice and ill that prevailed in the world he concluded that besides these holy spirits and guardian angels there must be a third agency which he called evil spirits which hovered in the air, tempting an individual to crime and sin and arresting the progress of Ahura Mazda. These evil spirits were led by Angro-Mainyus or Ahriman, a replica of Satan, which was adopted by the Jews from Zoroastrianism, and bequeathed by it to Christianity. These two powers—Ahura Mazda and the Ahriman—are symbolised as genii of light and darkness respectively. Zoroastres defines the evil spirit as negation, destruction, lies, ignorance, vice, and the Holy spirit as veracity, honesty, purity in body and mind. The ideals of human life consisted in having purity of mind, body and spirit, and in following useful and productive activity.

There is an apparent dualism in this doctrine, but the dualism which he taught was both cosmic and ethical. The light denoted the power of goodness, happiness, truthfulness, etc. and darkness denoted the power of negation, lies, destruction, sin, etc. A virtuous human life remains unflinchingly in the service of light, subduring and extirpating evil. Evil or darkness is to be annihilated totally by light. In Yasna 3 it is stated: "At the beginning of things there existed two spirits Ahura Mazda and Angro-Mainyus; they represent good and evil. These two divine beings meet to create life and morality and all the world that was to be. The evil one was created for the wicked, for the pure and pious was created Ahura Mazda. The wicked chose the evil, the pure and the pious chose the good spirit."

It is further said: "Man is free in his choice; he can select the good or the bad; hence he is responsible for his actions." Ahura Mazda is the Supreme, all pervading, the protector, creator, sustainer, and the knower, 'changeless art thou, Ahura Mazda the same now and forever. Transcendant being art thou, unmoved amid moving things, unaffected in the midst of manifold changes.' All that is good and beneficial in the creation flow from him and everything that is opposite to him is the creation of Ahriman. He commands his followers to know God as one and to regard the prophet Zoroaster as his true messenger and to have perfect faith in the goodness of God and in the religion as propounded in Zend Avesta preached by Zoroaster, to shun evil actions and evil thoughts and to be engaged in virtuous ones.

By picturing a world in conflict between the good and the evil, Zoroastrianism established a stimulus and sanction for acquiring morality. The soul of an individual is represented as a battlefield of the good and the evil spirits and every individual is a warrior under the dominance of the power of light or of darkness. Every individual has a free choice and he may follow Light or Darkness.

From this general conception, Zoroaster has woven a detailed and simple code of morals. Man's duty, says Avesta, is three-fold: "To make him who is an enemy a friend, to make him who is wicked, righteous, and to make him who is ignorant, learned." The highest virtue is piety. The flesh in its numberless forms and colours divides and keeps apart and aloof man from man. But the spirit is one and the same in all. The twin sons of Fate, Ahura Mazda and Ahriman, will alternately predominate and remain in conflict for 12,000 years. It is declared that at the end of this time, this world will be annihilated.

It is generally supposed that the writings of Zoroaster were very numerous. He has left behind him nearly two million verses at least, in the form of hymns and meditations. Darmester thinks that it was at the time of Achaemenians at the latest that they were all and fully written. Tradition affirms that the sacred literature was written in golden letters upon one thousand two hundred cow-hides. It was left in the palace library at Persepolis, and destroyed by fire at the express command of Alexander. At any rate, upon the conquest of Persia by the Greeks these writings were either destroyed by fire or neglected and scattered and were lost. In the second epoch of the Persian empire under the Sassanian princes they were re-written in twenty-one volumes. With the last catastrophe brought by the Arabs on the Persian Empire in or about the year 632 A.D. this second edition of the sacred literature was again lost. In later years it was gradually re-written by the fugitive Magian priests from memory. It was in fragments and written most imperfectly. Those remnants of the great and glorious teachings form the present sacred book. Most of it consists of collections of later date but they do contain in essence the main features of Zoroastrianism. The Gatha and some of the well-known passages from 'Yasna' are genuine and contain the ideas, opinions and the words of Prophet. The Gathas are written in verse. The second part of Yasna contains prayers to the supreme Lord and other Deities. The Vendidard is a book for priests and has been preserved in its original form because it contains the code of practical religion. The Khordah Avesta or the Little Avesta contains Yashtas (invocations) and prayers for the layman. It is now universally admitted that the Gathas, the earliest portion of the original scripture, are an expression of personal experiences and the inmost sentiments of the human heart.

Dr. Mill says: "Everything in them is so simple, so sober, so rational and consistent as to leave no doubt that the authors were referring to contemporary persons and events." The Zend Avesta is a collection of sacred literature of different epochs, containing religious hymns, invocations, prayers, confessions, laws, precepts, myths and sacred reminiscences. Philologists have given different interpretations of the meaning of the words 'Zend Avesta' Fr. Spiegel explains it as denoting 'wisdom and knowledge'. The language and grammar and the mode of writing of the Avesta are imperfectly known and therefore it becomes necessary at times to guess the meaning. That is one of the reasons why the expounders are not always in agreement. The greatest difficulty is about the meaning of the technical words and figures of speech. The first part is Vendidard, which contains religious laws and mythical tales. The second part is Visparad which is a collection of litanies and invocations to be recited before other prayers. The third is Yasna. The Avesta contains direct communication between Zoroaster and Ahura Mazda, the Supreme Lord. The classification is unsystematic, containing an admixture of a variety of subjects, and composed over a long period of time. According to Spiegel and Hang they were composed or compiled at least one thousand years before Christ. Hang says: "Looking closely at the many and various fragments of the book and its doctrines... there are, besides, wide discrepancies in the language of the several parts of the book which witness to the diversity of hands, ages, and countries, the doctrine taught there too shows evident signs of slow development and of diverse stages requiring centuries for its successive formation. Thus the book cannot be the work of one person. To all appearance Zoroaster is not the originator of that Iranian religion but he has developed, shaped it and brought it into a high degree of perfection and spirituality." Hang goes on to say: "Now came the far-reaching reform of the great Zoroaster; his merit consisted in having reduced the many good spirits into one; and the many bad spirits also he reduced into unity. He spiritualised both these agents—Naturally he denominated the good principle of the universe, the holy spirit Spento-Mainyus as Supreme wisdom. Ahura, Mazda was his first born son or the great attribute. While the evil principle he called Angro Mainyus the wicked spirit of darkness, Drukh, lie, fraud, etc." Two independent and supreme powers are in the universe. They are involved in eternal antagonism, "Behold I have put before thee life with good and death with evil bidding thee to love God and walk in His ways that He may bless thee and thy country or if thou turnest to the evils then ruin and Joss of country will follow.... .Life and death, blessing and curse, I have placed before thee, choose thou life."

Avesta teaches that Ahura Mazda created twin powers of Good (Spenta-Mainyo) and Evil (Angra-Mainyu) in eternal struggle with each other. Thus in Zoroastrianism the Holy spirit was declared to be the Supreme God. Ahura Mazda is the Supreme Intelligence, Omniscience, the creator and progenitor of the truthful and all that is good. He is omnipotent, under whose command the universe stands. He has prescribed the orbits of the sun, moon and the stars. All the forces of nature are under his supreme control and guidance. He has created the earth and rules her and has surrendered her to man for his dominion and inheritance. Every good and noble thing proceeds from him. The Earth is his daughter, he procreates life, he is wisdom and intelligence. He is good conscience, piety and strength. The good are rewarded with happiness, the wicked are punished. He permits the wicked to exist but awaits their repentance.

One creation of Ahura Mazda, is the evil spirit Akomani or Drukh, the lie, the fraud, Angro Mainyus, the wicked, the harmful angry spirit commonly abbreviated into Ahriman, which is the later name for evil spirit. He is the creator of Devils, bad spirits, the murderer of life. Knowledge and wisdom are the means to put an end to his kingdom or influence. Ahriman is the living lie and every lie is his servant.

The court of Ahura Mazda is supported and graced by a council of 'Amesha-Spentas' the sanctified immortals (The archangels) who are seven in number. The first Vohumanu (good intentions); the second, Asha-Vahishta (purity and holiness); the third, Kshtraver (power and possession); the fourth, Spendarmad (love); the fifth, Hauravatat (health); the sixth, Amerelal (immortality); and Fire. Ahura Mazda sometimes figures as one of them. Spiegel thinks Ahura means master or Lord 'Maz' is great, and 'Da' is knowledge, thus the whole meaning is omniscient Master.

The thirty days of the Persian month are each presided over by a God, beginning with Ormazad. The six Amesha-Spentas, each preside over one of the first seven days of the month. For each of the thirty days, a God is declared as a special patron. There are thirty Shirozas or hymns for each day of the month, addressed to its respective patron Vohumanu, Mitra, etc.

The dignity of Yazatas, pervading the Avesta, corresponds to the just and righteous, the humble, the poor, the pious, the friend of God. In later myths, Zoroaster is shown to have become such a Yazata, the highest and the noblest on earth, a friend of Ahura. Some traces of ancestor-worship are found in some pages in Avesta. It is believed that the souls of distinguished persons continue their existence in Heaven. These souls are turned into Fravashis. By their vigilance and warnings they protect the present generation.

According to Avesta, Ahura created the universe in 365 days. He cautiously selected a time when Angro-Mainyus was careless, and did, not interfere with the good creation. The first man and woman are called Meshia and Meshiana.

A believer in Zoroastrianism can be distinguished by his dress. He wears a cap on his head, a 'Sadra' over his upper body with a pocket. He puts Pevun' over his face and the 'Kusti' with four mystic knots around his waist. He is recommended to sleep less, and to rise with the crowing of the cock. He has to offer his prayers in a prescribed manner five times during the day. He is enjoined to recount his actions and say his prayers before going to bed. Most of the laws on purity, prayers, and manners are in Vendidard. The priest belongs to a caste and claims to be of one origin and family. The caste is called Magi. A priest is designated there as Hathara, later as 'Mobed' or 'Dastoor'.

Belief in a future life is recognised. There is an earthly life and life in the far future. The future life is not life beyond the grave, but in a future period of bodily re-awakening. Zoroaster asked Ahura Mazda: "How shall I urge upon the godly men and women, as also the wicked,, that they have once to leave behind them the earth and all its wealth, and when are rewards given?" Ahura Mazda replied: "When a man is dead the hellish Deavas assail him, and when the third night is gone and morning appears and the sun rises upon the mountains then the friend, Vizaresha carries off in bond his soul. The soul then enters the way of time, the way boil, wicked and the righteous." It is believed that the soul of the dead hovers round the last resting place in the residence for four days. Thereafter it goes to the inter mediate world. Various ceremonials are therefore performed at his last resting place. On the morning of the fourth day the soul has to appear on the chivat bridge. For the righteous a beautiful madi awaits to welcome him and for him there is fragrance in the breeze. The soul then asks about the identity of the maiden and she replies: "'I am the embodiment of your pure thoughts, pure words, and pure deeds." He crosses the chivat bridge which is the seat of judgment, safely, and reaches heaven. The bridge offers an easy passage for the pious and the righteous. The soul passes to the golden seat, Ahura Mazda. In case of the impious soul there is a foul smelling breeze and a hideous old hag appears to receive him. The soul questions : "Who art thou Lady?" And she replies "I am the conscience of your own self, I am the embodiment of your own evil thoughts, evil words and evil deeds." He cannot cross the bridge and fells into Hell, the abode of torment. There he meets Mithra and his colleagues who pass summary judgment over the dead.

In heaven there are four grades. The grade of good thoughts, the grade of good words, the grade of good deeds, and the last and highest, the grade of endless light, In this last grade the soul enjoys the sight and companionship of Ahura Mazda.

Hell is also divided into four grades, that is the grade of evil thoughts, the grade of evil words, of evil deed» and lastly the grade of endless darkness where Angro-Mainyus dwells. Man will pass to such grades in accordance with what he has thought, what words he has. used and what deeds he has done.

The external cult of Zoroastrianism consists in the worship of Fire. Fire worship impersonated in God, Agni, is older than Magism. Fire is worshipped because it represents the most estimable, sacred and supreme symbol of God. It is believed to be the son of Ahura Mazda. The Prophet did not teach fire worship. He taught the worship of one supreme Lord of the universe, Ahura Mazda. Fire is the symbol of the Divine. In almost every religion fire is considered to be sacred and a symbol of the Lord. In Hinduism, Brahman is Fire. The Jews worshipped their God as a pillar of fire. Christians declare that their God is a consuming fire. Fire symbolises the brilliance of the Lord. In the Bible it is said "God is Light." Fire stands for effulgence, illumination and purity. Zoroaster himself held fire in great sanctity as a noble gift of God, Veneration for fire, if not worship, is to be found in all nations, sects, climes, and religions. There are in Zoroastrianism three types of fire temples: "Atash Behram, which is the highest and the best. Adarian, and Atash-Dadgah." The Jews first conceived the ideas of Heaven and hell, of angels and archangels, of Messiah, of the resurrection and the last day of Judgment from Zoroastrianism. These have laid the foundation of the doctrine of Christianity as also of Islam.

In the district of Baku on the Caspian Sea there still exists a shrine of the Zoroastrians, which was formerly a monastery, which has been preserved by the Russian Government as a relic. The Zoroastrians of Asia used to visit this Holy shrine. The temple as it is today consists of a large square courtyard surrounded by small chambers which used to be the cells of the monks, a square tower is in the centre from the four corners of which flames ascend from the crematorium where the remains of the faithful devotees were consumed. A large tower used to be the residence of the chief priests. Zoroastrianism does not recognise bloody sacrifices. The main sacrifices are Draonas and Haomo. The small round flat white flour cakes are called draonas; these are offered on frequent occasions and eaten by the priests. With these draonas was offered a sacrificial beverage which is called Haoma, which resembled soma juice. Sacrifice and image worship were discarded and worship of fire, as a symbol of the deity, was considered as the highest form of worship. There is no caste system. With such exalted ideas of God, the Zoroastrians established the idea of one human race, with one duty and one right; and pure morality for all mankind., Avesta expresses it thus, "Purity in thought, speech and deed" are the essence of their ethics. From thoughts emerge words and actions. But they alone are not the aim of man's life even though they be the noblest. It is action that is the supreme goal of man's life. Action is the highest perfection and drawing forth of the utmost power, vigour and activity of man's nature. Those who have thought pure thoughts can take the first step in heaven, those who have spoken pure words can take the second step, but the third, which is the sublimest, can be reached only by those who have done pure deeds in this world. Thus the reward of the pure deed ranks above the reward of virtuous words and of virtuous thoughts. The Gathas teach that from the beginning of time there existed two principles in the universe. One is the creation of Light Ahura Mazda and the other is of darkness Angro-Mainyus between which there is an eternal antagonism and an individual is exhorted to fight evil in any shape, form or nature. But it would be wrong to suppose that Zoroastrianism taught the worship of two gods. They did not worship Angro-Mainyus. They feared him, abhorred him and fought with him. They worshipped Ahura Mazda, the only God. For a follower of Zoroastrianism religion is to conquer his savage nature, the brutal in man. For him there is no despair or resignation but he acknowledges the prevalence of evil and declares it to be man's primary duty to annihilate it.

The earth is supremely holy. She is named Armait, a duty is laid upon all to keep her sacred and pure and that she should not be defiled with graves, useless debris, throwing of dead limbs and increasing the obnoxious matter. Obnoxious vermin, animals and insects are to be cleared off. by killing or otherwise, which is said to be a virtue and a sacred duty. The 'Baresma' or a bundle of sticks in the hands of a priest symbolises that duty. Another of man's sacred duties is to till the soil, cultivate and increase arable land, render it useful by irrigation, to dig wells and to clear forests.

In Avesta, the laws and ethics are couched in metaphorical and mystical language but the hidden kernel proves a high degree of rationality. Charity is made an essential part of religion and service of the poor is particularly emphasised. "Be diligent and moderate and eat of thy own regular industry. Offer a share of thine things to the needy and the good." Sins can be expiated by charitable acts. Charity is one of the cardinal virtues enjoined upon a Zoroastrian by his religion. He is taught to love God and to love man. "Love each other through righteousness." A Zoroastrian has to practise universal benevolence in thought, word and deed. "Let him have money who comes to you seeking for it, let him who desires to marry have a wife and let him be taught holy Mathra, who desire its knowledge. Virtues like truthfulness, honesty, hospitality, kindness to animals, chastity, obedience to parents, piousness and piety are enjoined. The priestly class should shun hypocricy, greed, slothfulness, negligence and unbelief in religion. 'The essence of religion is Truth, the essence of Law is virtue.' It is said righteousness is the best acquisition of man, the world's highest riches. All the world is but dust but righteousness ends not for it is deathless." The warrior should avoid oppression, violence, breach of promise arrogance, vanity, insolence, encouragement of evil, etc. Agriculturists should give up jealousy, malice, rudeness and slander. The key note of Zoroastrian morality is perfect purity in every action of personal life: to do good actions, to be pure in thought, speech and deed, to have a pure heart, to wish good of others, to speak the truth, to do charity, to be kind and humble, to acquire knowledge, to control anger, to be pious, respectful to parents, teachers, the old and the aged, to utter sweet and pleasant words, to be patient, to be friendly towards all, to be content, and to be ashamed of forbidden acts. "Be not enamoured of respect and reverence; shun them, they hinder spiritual progress." "Truth knows no racial or geographical boundary. Truth is the same for all. Truth always triumphs and conquers falsehood. Truth blinds falsehood as the dazzling sun blinds the owl." Avesta attaches supreme importance to mind and will. It insists upon acquiring intellectual discernment and prudence. It exhorts man to fix his choice not upon base things but on good things. Men are taught to bring out the highest and the noblest in them. It urges men to acquire knowledge and wisdom for they are allied to holiness. Sraosha signifies obedience to law, and to remain in constant service of God and His creatures. Men are urged to devote themselves in such service altogether with their body and soul. Avesta enjoins on men to live hopefully and cheerfully. It asks them to seek eagerly, acquire virtuously and to use rightly all powers, intellectual, material and spiritual. Time' it says 'is life, and time ill-spent is life wasted away; time is more precious than the most valuable thing in the world. Time can neither be bought nor borrowed.' Therefore do not trifle away time but seek eagerly. The Avesta preaches that labour is divine and that man's food, his power and riches must come through his industry, patience, perseverance and courage. This religion condemns the quest after material welfare alone "Form no covetous desires, for the demon of greediness will grip thee and blind thee to the beauty and purity of the world, and make the spirit unperceived." It exhorts man not to acquire the riches of the material world at the cost of the spirit, for he who destroys the spiritual world in order to obtain the riches of the material world shall possess neither the celestial light nor the paradise of Ahura Mazda. The Avesta shows the dignity and position, the end and aim, the duties and obligations of man on earth. It says that after man is created, he depends every moment of his existence upon Ahura Mazda. Every good act which he does is the combination of the act emanating from God and his own will. He alone is responsible for his own conduct. His is the delegated spiritual strength on earth and it is his duty to maintain Righteous order. Ahura elevates man to the highest order. It says that the highest aim of man is perfect happiness, which consists, firstly, in making his life perfect and secondly in enjoyment of the companionship of Ahura Mazda. "Do thou, O Ahura, bless my corporeal life with peacefulness of mind, righteousness and excellent power and prosperity."

It is evident that acquisition of perfect happiness is the final goal of life and means to attain it is 'Asha' the holiness which is to know God's will and strive to do it. 'Asha' is the soul and substance of Avesta philosophy. One would find in Avesta ethical precepts and wise moral exhortations in abundance. The Avesta forcibly impresses upon men that this is a world of trial and tribulations. The life of man is a perpetual struggle in which he has to receive his physical, intellectual and moral training. He has to defend himself against his enemies from within, which appear in the form of evil thoughts, evil feelings, evil inclinations, tastes and tendencies. He has also to combat external evil influences which conspire to destroy him. It will be seen that that there is an absence of a fatalistic tone in the Avesta.

The Zoroastrian confession of faith runs thus: "I believe in the purity of the good Mazdayasnian faith, in the creator Ormazd, in Amshaspands, in furthering of righteousness, in the resurrection off the new body as Ormazd has imparted it to Zartush, his successor and Dastoors have brought it down to us." The Zoroastrian confession runs thus: "My sins, which I have committed against father, mother, sister, brother, wife, child, relation, friend, if I have broken the whispered prayer, or eaten without prayer, if I have gone without kusti or defiled my feet or practised deception, contempt, idol worship, told lies, etc. I repent with 'Palet' Pardon."

The Avesta prayers express a loving relation between man and God. In them he acknowledges the Creator's power, His mercy, His glories. He implores his assistance and thanks Him for granting it. In them He gives expression to his humility and dependence. He confesses his sins, repents and asks for forgiveness. "Give me a cultivated mind, and active soul and a continually developing understanding and long-lasting virility." Of all the

Avesta prayers Ashen-Vohu and Yatha-Ahu-Vairyo are important. Ashen-Vohu runs thus: "Purity or holiness is good. Purity is the best of all good. Purity is happiness. Happiness is for him who observes purity for the sake of attaining the highest. The will of God is the law of holiness. The riches of Vohu-Manu (good-thought) will be given to him who works in the world for Mazda and wields in accordance with the will of Ahura. He gave him to relieve the poor." Holiness is claimed to be the final aim of Zoroastrianism. Holiness is practical holiness for the good is practical good. Holiness means purity of body and of mind. That purity is procured by the law of Mazda to him who cleanses his own self and fills it with good thoughts, words and deeds. "And they shall thenceforth in their doings walk after the way of holiness, after the word of holiness, and after the ordinance of holiness." The Avesta preaches ideal morality. It lays great stress on Asha which means holiness. It comprises all the internal and external, visible and invisible acts of men. Zoroastrianism is purely and simply rationalism without the liveries of mysticism.

When it is asked "who rejoiceth the earth with the greatest of joy?" The answer is "He who fills up holes, cultivates the fruits of trees and grass on the fields, provideth for water, tills the ground, etc. He promotes Mazda Yasnian law." In common parlance according to Zoroastrianism, virtue is simply to do good, to be useful to his fellowmen, to create things for the comfort of humanity, such a man is dear to God and God looks after his wants. A dog is the constant companion of man and his guardian. Dog is counted upon next in holiness to man and has the same rights and privileges as man. In the Avesta it performs an important role. A dog is brought into the room where the? dead body lies. Then the ceremony called 'Sydid' is performed. It is believed that the evil spirit called "Nasu" who was about to take hold of the corpse is frrightened away to hell at the sight of a dog. To kill him is worse than murdering a man. The cock is considered to be a holy bird. The Bull is also considered to be holy. The primeval bull was created by Mazda and killed by Ahriman. The bull is oftentimes invoked in Zoroastrian literature. It represents nature's wealth and productiveness. Persia has everywhere many venerable trees which are superstitiously worshipped by the people. Amerilat is the goddess of plants.

The Magian custom was to expose the dead body to be devoured by beasts and birds. They did not bury their dead, because they believed that a grave contaminates the soil. The dead cannot be cremated by fire nor buried in earth or thrown in sea as all these elements are holy and are not to be defiled by the contact of the dead, which belongs to Ahriman.

In Vendidard, it is asked "Creator, when a woman is affected with blood marks, how to act," and the answer is that she must be removed away from trees made for firewood to some dry hill, isolated from fire, water, baresma and pious people. Her food is reached out to her. She is not to take flesh meat for three days. Her food must be simple and plain. The cause of her isolation is stated to be that she is under the influence of the evil spirit but the real reason is hygiene.

Ahura is asked "Which is the most deadly deed, whereby a man increases the power of the Daevas?" Ahura answers: "It is when a man combing his hair or paring off his nails drops them from which unclean creatures are produced." Zoroaster asked Ahura: "Who is it that grieves thee with the sorest grief" and he answered, "It is the Gahi (woman of lust) who goes whoring after the faithful and the unfaithful, after the wicked and the righteous, when such a one yields her body to these men, she is guilty of death. Her looks dry up the mighty mountain floods and withers the golden hued plants, her touch withers the faithful's thought, his strength, and his holiness."

The Kustee symbolises the bond of the faithful with Ormazd. It is the badge of the faithful. It consists of 72 filaments and goes three times around the waist. It is worn both by males and females; the four knots symbolise the belief in Ahura Mazda, in his worship. in Zoroaster its prophet, and in the demand to keep God's commandments.

It is injudicious and unjust either to sublimate or to hold up to ridicule injunctions of a religion as to outward symbols. We must take such practices for what they were really intended, as means or symbols of edification, and a constant reminder to men to perform their duties.

Ahura Mazda created sixteen good-lands or regions which were counteracted or destroyed by Angro-Mainyus. These sixteen lands are simply the Iranian countries known Zoroaster.

Zoroaster sitting on the mountain by the Darega River, praying to the Amesha-Spentas asked: "O Ahura! how shall I make the world free from that Drugh the evil-doer, Angro-Mainyus? How drive away the Nasu (Impurity of the dead?) How cleanse?" The faithful Ahura replied: "Invoke Amesha-Spentas, boundless time and Vayu the powerful wind and Spenta Armaite." Zoroaster asked: "With what manner of sacrifice shall I worship and forward Ahura's creation?" Ahura answered "Let the faithful cut off a twig of Baresma as long as a ploughshare thick as barleycorn, the faithful, holding it in his left hand,shall not leave off keeping his eyes upon it while he is offering up the sacrifice."

This symbolises the struggle of Mazda worshipper against Ahriman. According to Zoroastrianism human virtues did not mean only prayer, meditation, sacrifices or rituals, but it meant a great deal more, and that is fighting evil, making efforts for good and assisting the activity of Ahura-Mazda. This is a religion of deeds and doings. It teaches that there is an enternal delight in leading a righteous life that there is a joy in desiring and in striving to do one's duty, that there is delight in death and delight hereafter. Death may alter a man's present abode but cannot alter his character. If a man is good and pure before death he would remain so after death.

JUDAISM

IT is believed by the Jews that the people of Abraham came from Ur in Sumeria and had settled in Palestine (c 2200 B.C.) and that Cannan, being their promised land, was conquered by them. It appears that later, Palestine was ravaged by Egyptian armies. No date can be fixed as to when the Jews entered Egypt, but it is certain that they were in great numbers in Egypt at the time of Moses. The Biblical stories and Rabbinical legends give us a picture of Moses who imparted to the Jews the divine revelation received by him on Mount Sinai. The Bible tells us that he was of Jewish parentage and was adopted by Pharaoh's daughter. From an early age he was wont to visit the lowly and the outcaste. He was once informed by these people that their father Abraham, who had left Ur in search of freedom found it in the new land of Cannan which flowed with milk and honey. For a number of years they had settled there till their spirit of adventure made them leave the place, and at last they came to the land of Pharaoh where they were ground down in poverty and yoked to servitude. Moses was captivated by the history of these people. Once, outraged at the merciless whipping of one of these men by an Egyptian, he in anger killed him, which obliged him to flee from Egypt and to take shelter in the desert. It was the serenity of the life in the desert that gave him knowledge of God. But all through these years he could not forget those slaves and he pined to restore the Jews to their native home, to unite them into a free nation and to give them a religion and a God. He entered Egypt and urged the slaves to revolt; he unsuccessfully petitioned the Pharaoh on their behalf to give amnesty to the slaves. Pharaoh hardened his heart and issued inhuman orders for punishment of the slaves, if they failed to produce a certain fixed quota of grains. It is said that Jahovah, to rescue his children, visited upon Egypt the ten plagues. Moses took the Jews out of

Egypt. He was fired with a desire to organise them, to breathe a living soul into them and to give them a new code of morals and a new standard of life. For this purpose he selected Mount Sinai. Here he delivered to his people the following Ten Commandments.

(1) I am the Lord, thy God which have brought thee out of the land of Egypt, out of the house of bondage.

(2) Thou shalt have no other Gods before me. Thou shalt not make unto thee any graven image or any likeness of anything that is in heaven above or that is in the earth beneath or that is in the water under the earth; thou shalt not bow down thyself to them, nor serve them for I, the Lord thy God, am a jealous God, visiting the iniquity of the fathers upon the children unto the third and fourth generation of them that hate me and showing mercy unto thousands of them that love me and keep my Commandments.

(3) Thou shalt not take the name of the Lord, thy God, in vain for the Lord will not hold him guiltless that taketh his name in vain.

(4) Remember the Sabbath day, to keep it holy. Six days shalt thou labour and do all thy work; but the seventh day is the Sabbath of the Lord thy God; in it thou shalt not do any work, thou, nor thy son, nor thy daughter, thy man-servant, nor thy maid-servant, nor thy cattle nor thy stranger that is within thy gates; for in six days the Lord made heaven and earth, the sea and all that in them is, and rested on the seventh day; wherefore the Lord blessed the Sabbath day and hallowed it.

(5) Honour thy father and thy mother; that thy day may be long upon the land which the Lord thy God giveth thee.

(6) Thou shalt not kill.

(7) Thou shalt not commit adultery.

(8) Thou shalt not steal.

(9) Thou shalt not bear false witness against thy neighbour.

(10) Thou shalt not covet thy neighbour's house, thou shalt not covet thy neighbour's wife, nor his man-serv-

ants, nor his maid-servants nor his ox, nor his ass nor anything that is thy neighbour's.

These positive Commandments given by Moses have retained their place at the core of the Jewish religion and have influenced it. These Commandments give a simple, pure worship of one God, establish family order, justice and self-restraint between man and man. Moses may be assigned the position of a great religious leader. He created a nation out of an enslaved and lost people and he did it by imparting to them an elevated conception of the Divine nature. The sublime conception of a people ruled by God was given by him to his people. Moses taught that religion did not consist in offerings and formal rituals, and ceremonies but it consisted in simple worship and reverence to God, and obedience to Divine precepts.

As regards the racial origin of the Jews one can assert they were Semites. They remained for a long time as independent tribes governed by the principle of the patriarchal system. Their first king was Saul, who was succeeded by David and after him, his son Solomon. During the reign of Solomon he increased the wealth of Jerusalem. It was he who adorned the City with a temple dedicated to Yahveh. In the epic of the Jews the building of the Temple was the most important event. It raised the ancient religion from primitive polytheism to a faith of a creative creed. In primitive times the Jews worshipped rocks, cattle, sheep, the spirit of caves and hills, the serpent, the golden calf, etc. It was bv a slow process that out of this multifarious pantheons they conceived of Yahveh as the one national God, who established the Jewish faith, unity and simplicity. Shortly after the death of Solomon, the Pharaoh of Egypt captured Jerusalem and looted all its wealth. It was at this time of religious degeneration and political downfall, that Prophets appeared on the arena of the religious life of the people and became the critics of their age. Isaiah was filled with scorn for those who were fleecing the people. Though he was bitter in his attacks, he gave them Messianic hope. He was the source of the early Jewish conception of a Messiah who will re-establish the temporal power of the Jews. He undertook the task of transforming the God of Hosts into the God of Love. The writings of the Bible during this time exercised a very great influence. The Prophets had predicted the fall of the Jewish nation; and it came to pass that after the subjugation by Egypt they came under Babylon.

The successors of Josiah made an unsuccessful attempt to liberate themselves from the Babylonian rule; but ultimately Jerusalem was captured, burned to the ground, and the temple destroyed. Even at this period of time, prophets like Jeremiah and Ezekiel preached against moral depravity and fiercely attached idolatry and corruption that had set in the Jewish life.

It was an unknown author who completed the book of Isaiah, and thus restored the religion of Israel. He announced the first clear revelations of monotheism and offered to the Jews a new aspect of God infinitely richer in loving kindness and tender mercy than the awe-inspiring Yahveh.

It was a turning point in the history of Israel when at last Cyrus the Persian Emperor entered Babylon as a world conqueror and gave the Jews full freedom to return to Jerusalem. Slowly Jerusalem became a Jewish city where a new temple was built.

About the year 444 B.C. Ezra, a learned priest read to the Jews "The Book of the law of Moses." People pledged themselves to accept this Code of laws as their constitution and to obey it forever. The books which Josiah and Ezra caused to be read to the people formulated that Mosaic Code on which all later Jewish life has been built.

The primary source of Jewish religion is the first five books of the Old Testament. They are called Pentateuch (which means five Rolls). The Old Testament is not only law, it is history, poetry and philosophy of the highest order. It commences with the story of Creation and brings us down to the period of Ezra and his reformation. The first book of the Pentateuch, commonly termed Genesis, describes every act of creation, as directly the work of Elohim and this is the predominant note of the narrative. This narrative is a popular explanation adapted to .a simple uneducated people and it must be remembered that it is not a scientific explanation of the act of creation. We have a series of pictures ending with the creation of man, Adam and Eve, male and female on the sixth day and a conclusion, which gives a foundation and sanction for the Sabbath as observed by the Jews, by attributing to the Creator rest on the seventh day. The book of Judges, Samuel and Kings have been put together as a collection of national traditions. The stories of Saul, David and Solomon display a richness in style and frame. The enchanting romances found in the story of Ruth and the tales of Isaac and Rebecca, Jacob and Rachel, Joseph and Benjamin and Samson and Delilah have been woven into the fabric of history and philosophy. The Song of Moses and the Song of Deborah are given in poetic and inspiring language. The final culmination or quintessence of lyrical poetry is reached in the Psalms. Regarding the Psalms, Edward Irving has said: "For pure pathos and tenderness of heart, for sublime imagination, for touching pictures of natural scenery and genial sympathy with nature's various moods; for patriotism, whether in national weal or national woe, for beautiful imagery whether derived from the relationship of human life or forms of the Created universe, and for the illustration by their help of spiritual conditions — moreover for those rapid transitions in which the lyrical muse delighteth, her lightsome graces at one time, her deep and full inspiration at another, her exuberance of joy and her lowest falls of grief and for every other form of the natural Soul which is wont to be shadowed forth by this kind of composition, we challenge anything to be produced from the literature of all ages and countries, worthy to be compared with what we find in the English version of the Book of Psalms."

The Psalms are distinguished by their directness of appeal to God. In the midst of trouble, life is associated with God in such a way that the human and the Divine meet each other. Divine greatness and majesty developed in some of the Psalms contain the sublimest poetic expression. They are to him who sings them a mirror wherein he may see himself and his soul. In the old

Testament we have the Book of Job. The book of Job is unique in its poetic grandeur and in its philosophy. "I call it" says Caryle "one Of the grandest things ever written with a pen... A noble book; all men's book. It is our first, oldest statement of the never ending problem-man's destiny, and God's ways with him here on this earth...." The book may be regarded as a statement of the most painful problems in the government of the world, the physical and mental trials of the righteous and the justification of God's dealings with good men. "The book shows in a most tragic and pathetic way that good no less than wicked men lie open to the most cruel losses and sorrows, that these losses and sorrows are not always signs of the Divine anger against sin, that they are intended to correct and perfect the righteousness of the righteous." Its higher intention is to show that man is capable of loving right simply because it is right and of hating wrong purely because it is wrong even though he would not gain by it but lose.

The Bible is the basis of the Jewish Creed. It teaches the relation of God with man and the laws to be followed. Within the Bible, there are other writings namely the Prophets and the Psalms. These elucidate the teachings which Moses imparted to Israel. By the side of the written law as contained in the Law and Prophets there has been from the beginning the unwritten law which has its continuous development in the words "for the precept which I command thee is not in heaven... but it is very night unto thee in thy mouth and in thy heart." These words invest the unwritten Law with the authority of the Mosaic Revelation. Tradition plays an important part in Judaism. Tradition is defined as "The developing Power which contains in Judaism, as an invincible creative agent, as a certain ennobling something that never obtains its full expression, but ever continues to work, transform and create. Tradition is like revelation, a spiritual energy that ever continues to work, a higher power that does not proceed from man, but is an emanation from the Divine spirit, a power that works in the community, chooses its own ministers, manifests itself by its ever purer and riper fruits and thus preserves vitality and existence itself."

In the treatise of the Mishna known as "The Ethics of the Father" there is a passage which says that Moses received the Law on Sinai, and handed it to Joshua, Joshua to the Elders, and Elders to the Prophets, and Prophets to the men of the Great Synagogue. In this is indicated what is known as the chain of tradition. According to tradition the scribes were the teachers of the taw, Ezra being the first, Simon the just being the last. Many acts are ascribed to these scribes. They introduced a scientific method of interpretation.

The Bible can be divided under three broad headings, (a) Law, (b) Prophets, and (c) Writings. The Law comprises five books of Moses with the story of the Creation of the world till the death of the Law Giver. This is the Torah which forms the basis of Judaism. It is the written Law containing 613 precepts covering the whole sphere of man's life. The Prophets comprise both the historical books and the writings of the Prophets. They are sub-divided into two. The former prophets which include the books of Joshua, Judges, Kings and the latter prophets by which are meant the great prophets Isaiah, Jeremiah and Ezekiel. There are twelve other minor prophets. The third division is the "the writings" which include everything not comprised under the two former heads and which are the Psalms, Proverbs, Job, Song of Solomon, Ruth, Lamentations, Ecclesiates Ester, Daniel, Ezra, Nehemiah and the two books of the chronicle.

The Bible is a treasury of the most sublime thoughts. It is a compendium of moral and ethical laws, it gives a scheme of life, it points the way to goodness to establish fellowship with God. The responsibility of human life is laid down as a fundamental obligation resting upon man's brotherhood and his relation to God as being made in His image. The pivot of the teachings lies in the Supreme idea of Faith in God. One of the Rabbis has summed up as follows:-

The 613 precepts communicated to Moses were compressed by the writers of the Psalms into eleven. Isaiah compressed them still further into three which is "To do justice, love mercy, and walk humbly with God" and Habakuk condensed them into one "The Righteous shall live by Faith." Faith is not enjoined as a Commandment but it lays emphasis on knowledge through which one comes to Belief. "Know therefore and consider this day in thy heart that the Lord, He is God there is none other." The first article of Faith therefore is belief in God as One alone wihout a partner. The serving of other Gods is the gravest offence against God. Judaism has an abhorrence of idolatry. Isaiah, in strong words denounces the fashioning of the so called gods and contrasts the helplessness and unreality of a figure cut from wood or stone with the grandeur and illimitability of the power of one God. Closely allied to the belief in the Unity of God is the love of God: "And thou shalt love the Lord thy God with all thy heart, with all thy soul and with all thy might." Love is made reciprocal. God has selected (Israel for special grace and to witness the truth of revelation. He cares for His people and guides them. This is the covenant between God and the people of Israel. Love demands allegiance. To the Jews the ideal to strive for is following the example of God. The standard that is set before the nation is not the human ideal but a divine one, which made the nation to belong to one household united by one thought, one worship and one God. The Laws enjoy great sanction among the Jewish people for they are believed to have emanated directly from God. Belief in God and love of God lead to a noble life. The chief conception of Judaism is that the earthly doings are taken in the light of Divine purpose. It is this conception that gives a meaning to the human struggles. With the conception of God as the Lord is blended the conception of His omnipotence. God according to Judaism is the source and essence of all strength. He is the Creator and Ruler of the Universe. All that exists is created by Him and all that happens is His achievement. His powers are limited only by His own Will. "He does what He willeth." The idea of the omnipotence of God is coupled with that of His omniscience. He is the all seeing, all hearing and all knowing God. He is eternal and not limited in space or time. His omniscience and omnipotence are interlocked with His omnipresence and eternity.

"For my thoughts are not your thoughts, neither are your ways my ways saith the Lord; For, as the heavens are higher than the earth, so are my ways higher than your ways and my thoughts than your thoughts." He transcends the changes and conditions of time. His Eternity establishes that His purpose however thwarted or delayed will prevail and His omniscience carries with it a conviction that no machinations whether in thought, word or deed can arrest the realization of His purpose. Judaism recognises two distinct types of divine attributes. The one is that God is represented as a transcendental Being who passes our comprehension and the other is His Holiness which invests Him with moral perfection, and He thus becomes the ideal and pattern for the loftiest morality. "Be ye Holy for I, the Lord your God, am Holy." This is the Cardinal idea of the Jewish Law. This divine attribute of holiness has a two-fold meaning. The first is one of spiritual eminence transcending everything temporal and sensual. This is the purifying power of God. In the second place it indicates the condescending mercy of God. The Soul after being purified from evil influences, endows man with the power of perfecting himself. The contemplation of divine holiness is to inspire man with the fear of the bog of sin and to exert himself towards perfection. The fullest disclosure of the spiritual and moral character of God was revealed to Moses as a "Merciful being gracious, slow to anger, abundant in loving kindness and Truth, keeping loving kindness to a thousand generations, forgiving, iniquity, transgression, and sin, but who will by no means clear the guilty."

These attributes constitute the holiness of God. They are related to His dealings and actions with man and have been communicated as rules of conduct to man. Man stands in special relationship to God. This is expressed in "God made man in His own image." Man is exalted and is recognised as possessing a God-given spirit. This forms a personal relationship with Him. God has provided man with earthly and spiritual qualities and he is asked to participate in fulfilling the purpose of God, both with his physical and spiritual faculties. God created the world and all that is but He has entrusted its development to man. And God blessed them and said unto them, "Be fruitful and multiply and replenish the earth and subdue it." Man has not been called to fulfil a material purpose alone; he has also been entrusted with a spiritual task and is exhorted "Ye shall be holy for 'I, the Lord Your God, am Holy." The holiness that is demanded of man is not external but inner holiness. He is urged to practise all the positive virtues with which holiness is associated in the Bible which finds expression in service and duty, exercise of charity and love of man. Man is exhorted to attempt to realise the divine pattern of holiness. To the Jews, the real ideal to strive for is the imitation of God. God is in good, righteous, just, and merciful. So should man be good, righteous, just and merciful. From birth till death every action, every thought should be modelled on the example of God. Judaism is not an intellectual or philosophical system, but is in essence a religious belief in the holiness, righteousness and mercy of God. As the Rabbis express it, "The Torah commences with a loving act of God. "He made them garments, and closes with a loving act, 'He buried him' (Moses) just as God clothes the naked and buries the dead so do ye Israelites likewise." Judaism does not teach a superficial conduct of life but it teaches the expression of life manifested in love and echoed in love and harmony all round. Belief in God and love of God lead to the goal and therefore all actions and thoughts must be Godlike. The idea of holiness attached to God and man created in His image should inspire him to conform to the divine example set before him. "As he is gracious so be thou gracious, as he is merciful so be thou merciful." Life according to Judaism is a moral striving and man has to become a coworker with God in His Divine Scheme by becoming in likeness to Him, through the knowledge of Him the knowledge of the way of Lord, to do righteousness and justice. God must penetrate and control his life. The true aim of human existence according to Judaism is holiness emulating God striving to do good for the sake of good without expectation of recompense and to desist from evil because it is evil and not from fear of punishment. The strength in the idea of holiness lies exactly in its negative character. There is no comparison of higher of lesser degree possible between man's imperfections and God's perfect goodness. Instead there is an absolute contrast between mankind which even in the noblest types must wrestle with the power of evil and God in whom nothing can be imagined which would even suggest the possibility of any moral shortcoming or imperfection. As the prophet says: "Thou art too pure of eyes to look complacently upon evil" and according to the Psalmist "Who shall ascend into the mountain of the Lord and who shall stand in His Holy place? He that hath clean hands and a pure heart." God's holiness is manifested in his indignation at falsehood and violence, slander and hatred. His hatred of wrong and wrong-doing. God is wrathful, because He desires the purification of the human Soul. He is displeased with wickedness and is provoked at any violation of His law and He is kindled with anger when the poor and the weak are oppressed. But His anger says the Psalmist is but for a moment. His favour is for a lifetime. Even in His wrath he remembers compassion. He docs not delight in the death of the sinner, but His delight is in the return of the sinner from his waywardness and evil. God is long-suffering. His aim is to elevate man and to lead him to a higher life. He does not desire to annihilate the sinner but he wants to exterminate sin. Since He is long-suffering, He waits for the erring man till he, by his struggles, attains a higher state of purity and divine conduct. According to Judaism, God's Government of the world is seasoned with Mercy and Justice. "The Judge of all the earth cannot act unjustly and Righteousness and Justice are the foundations of thy throne." Man is incapable of understanding divine justice. "Thy Righteousness is like the mighty mountain. Thy judgments are like the great deep." Right and Justice belong to God who is the protector of the helpless and the weak, the lowly and the lost, "Who executes the judgment of the fatherless and the widow who regardeth not persons, nor taketh bribes." Thus every violation of justice is the violation of God's cause and every vindication of justice is the triumph of God, "He will judge the world with righteousness and the people with equity." His ideal of justice is to be established not in any future world but in the present— in the existing life. The love of fellow-man is an integral part of the law in Torah. Hillel on being asked by a non-Jew to be taught the whole law replied : "What is hateful to thee, do not, to thy fellow-men. This is the whole law and the rest is the explanation thereof. Go learn it." To hate one's fellow-man is to hate God. The injunction to love one's fellow-man is all-embracing, irrespective of any creed or race. "If thy brother be waxen, poor and fallen in decay with thee, then thou shalt relieve him, yes though he be a stranger or a sojourner that he may live with thee." The elevation of Judaism is markedly shown in the treatment of strangers. At the root of all Jewish ethics lies holiness from which streams of precepts flow such as "Love thy neighbour as thyself," "hate not thy brother," "avenge not," "bear no grudge," "Love the stranger." To love one's neighbour is to eradicate all hatred from one's self. Thus it is said "thou shalt not hate thy brother in thy heart." Hatred can be exterminated by believing in the brotherhood of man, all men being the sons of one father. To love one's neighbour is doing justice. This is summed up in two maxims. Let the property of thy fellow be as dear to thee as thine own. Let the honour of thy fellow as dear as thine own. Man is urged not to wrong his neighbour even by words. Man is asked not to insist his right, but he is asked to act "within the margin of judgment." Righteousness fulfils itself in the love of one's neighbour. Any kind of personal service of affectionate sympathy to fellow-man is an act of righteousness. Judaism lays down the Code of actions that shall govern the intercourse of man with man. Respect for human life, regard for neighbour's property, care for his honour, honesty, chastity, truthfulness, fidelity, etc. are some of the concomitants of the belief in the Holiness of God. Man has been shown the right way to live and is accountable for his conduct. The sins which Judaism condemns are intemperance and luxury, oppression of the poor and the weak, of widows and of orphans, unjust appropriation of another's goods, dishonesty in trade, the sorbid pursuit of gain, harshness towards debtors and the like. "He has shown thee, O Man, what is good, what does the Lord thy God require of thee, except to do justice, love mercy, and walk humbly with God." According to Jewish view, mercy and love are the milder aspects of God and they cannot counteract or replace God's justice. A deep rooted sympathy for the oppressed and the down-trodden is echoed at many places in the Bible. "When he crieth unto me I shall hear, for I am gracious." God calls himself, "the judge of the widow," "the father of the fatherless." He calls the poor "my people." His tender mercy is over all his works, says a verse in a Psalm. "Whosoever has compassion on his fellow-creatures on him God will have compassion." Love must be guided by justice or else it would be unworthy. Love of good must be accompanied by hate of evil. "God's love must needs unfold His perfection and beauty and reveal itself in His creatures, and love for these creatures must again elevate an imperfect world to His own perfection. Thus is engendered in man that yearning for love with which he endeavours to emulate the divine perfection." In the end, right doing will inevitably be blessed. The sorrows and sufferings of the righteous are not without consolation.

God is the everlasting Truth and therefore hypocrisy and insincerity, deception and guile, untruthfulness and lying, perfidy and cunning, simulations and pretence in whatever form or shape are most loathsome to Him. "Truth is the seal of God. Man is exhorted to walk in His way and it is truthfulness that puts on man the divine pattern. Truth demands not only the eschewing falsehood but any kind of insincerity of speech which includes flattery and cajolery, hypocrisy and blandishment with intention to deceive, 'To steal man's mind by false pretences is like stealing the mind of God." "Let therefore your yes be righteous and your no be righteous."

Peace and harmony occupy a predominant place in Judaism. Peace is the soul of the Divine attributes, the symbol of human perfection. The greatest ideal set before man is to bring harmony between man and his fellow-man. "Seek peace and pursue it." "It heralds the Messianic age." "Righteousness and peace kiss each other."

God is near to man "ready to hear his sighs, answer his supplication, count his tears and relieve his wants When his own power fails." God's greatness consists in His condescension and in humility. Wherever man seeks Him, there He is and therefore a Psalmist says "thy condescension hath made me great." God bends low to raise him up to Himself.

In the ethics of the Father it is asked who is the hero? Who is rich? The reply is : "He who is satisfied with his lot." Contentment is a great virtue for it implies surrender to Divine Will. Contentment must be coupled with humility. One must surrender oneself to the Divine will humbly in fear of God rather than in fear of His punishment. God lifts up him who humiliates himself and he who raises himself will be humiliated by him. "Be thou cursed, not he who curses, be of them that are persecuted, not of them that persecute. He who sacrifices a whole offering shall be rewarded for a whole offering, he who offers a burnt offering shall have the reward of the burnt offering, he who offers humility unto God and man shall be rewarded with a reward as if he has offered all the sacrifices in the world." "To walk humbly with the Lord together with the doing of justice and loving kindness." These are the three qualities which God requires of a man to acquire.

Man is made in the image of God and is created after His likeness. He can reach his goal by striving and eschewing the sensuous and the sensual. He has to unfold the powers that are latent in him. In the eighth Psalm it is expressed:

"What is man, that thou art mindful of him?
And the son of man, that Thou thinkest of him?
Yet thou hast made him but little lower than the godly beings.
And hast crowned him with glory and honour.
Thou madest him to have dominion over the works of thy hands.
Thou hast put all things under his feet."

Both the physical and spiritual powers of man are divine and the choice is left in man's own hand to attain his goal. If a man attempts to fulfil the divine purpose he will have all things under his feet, if not he will descend to the lowest level of brute creation. The body and soul of man possess an innate potentiality of a nobler life. Man has a will of his own and he should exert his own will and power to reach the highest. God is the ideal and pattern of all morality, and man in order to attain this has to "walk in the ways of God to be righteous and just" as He is. To express it in familiar words: "It has been told thee, O man, what is good and what the Lord doth require of thee. Only to do justly and to love mercy and to walk humbly with thy God."

But to Judaism, God is not an implacable Judge. The relationship between man and God is that of father and son. The truly religious man is he who seeks to find grace in the eyes of God and of man. Judaism lays down a code of laws that shall govern the relationship between man and his neighbour. It is incumbent upon each man to observe the laws. The principles set down in the code are to be translated into concrete actions in daily life. Man is urged to conquer unholy desires and impure passions and to resist temptations of every kind. Self-control and self-abnegation are the first stages of human development through which self-perfection is attained. The highest form of self-control is that which is exhibited in the cause of God. Every act of self-restraint, self-abnegation and self-sacrifice in the service of God or of fellow-man leads to perfection. The true spirit of Judaism does not teach man to run away from the world and to be an ascetic. Life is not considered curse. Its motto is "God established the earth. He created it not in vain. He formed it to be inhabited. God has communicated to mankind a simple set of rules by observing which every individual will become a co-partner with God in fulfilment of the Divine purpose. These are abstention from: (1) idolatry, (2) blasphemy, (3) incest, (4) murder, (5) theft, (6) eating of limb torn from a living animal and (7) to do justice. A man would attain righteousness if he puts them in practice. The struggle for perfection does not require the suppression of the rightful use of the body, but it requires its cultivation and restraint. When asked "who is the hero" it is replied "He who controls his inclinations." Sobriety and moderation tinged with cheerfulness and delight are the key-notes of Judaism.

Judaism is a religion willed by God for the foundation of divine order, fulfilment of divine purpose on earth and establishment of the kingdom of heaven. The Torah was given to Israel to fulfil this divine purpose. It is the means to that great end. By following the law as laid down in the Torah individual and social life was to be brought in harmony with the Divine scheme and for fulfilling the holy will of God. It aims at idealising the temporal life. "The Torah has been given to ennoble mankind." It is true that the Torah has been revealed by God but man is made the pivot, who is urged by its means to improve and perfect his life on the divine pattern. In the Torah one finds an interweaving of morality and religion. It transmutes the moral laws into religion and religion into moral life. The Torah embraces the whole life of man. It is a collection of commands and precepts comprised in the five books of Moses. They had been from the beginning an unwritten Torah handed down from generation to generation which the prophets sought to engrave on the hearts of the People. The written as well as the unwritten laws guide the Jewish people. Every Jew is charged with the task of studying the Torah and he recites as his daily prayer Grant us our portion in Thy Torah." The essence of Judaism lies in its ethics which is expressed in the verse "Ye shall be holy for (I the Lord your God am holy."

God is the ideal, of morality and perfection which gives to the Jew a motive power and an inspiration for attaining perfection and to lead a nobler life. Having conceived God as holy, and man being asked to walk in His way the Jew becomes a co-worker with God in the work of creation. To sum up Jewish ethics provide for self-elevation under the elevating power of a holy God. Man should emulate God and "walk in the ways of God." The human life must be in imitation of Divine goodness and holiness. The man who has "clean hands and a pure heart, who has not lifted up his soul unto falsehood nor sworn deceitfully." Can stand in His holy place. An epitome of Jewish ethics is contained in the famous three sentences of Hillel. "If I am not for myself, who will be for me? But if I am for myself alone what am I? And if not now when then?" This gives three phases of duty which are towards one's self, towards others and towards the life before us. Accordingly self-preservation self-reformation and self-perfection are the primary duties, of every Jew. In regard to our moral and spiritual self the maxim is "Beautify thyself first and then beautify others." The Psalm verse, "There shall be no strange God in thee" is interpreted to mean that neither anger, nor passion, nor evil desire, nor pride shall assume mastery over thee. Not only one's life is to be maintained amidst all trials and tribulations as a sacred trust but also one's individuality, freedom and rights are also to be guarded. One should not become a handmaid of others. For it is said "they are my servants and not servants to servants." Accordinng to Judaism one can forgive one's enemy but cannot love him. The real meaning given by Rabbis to the command "Love thy neighbour as thyself" is "put thyself in his place and act accordingly." Love without justice leads to abuses. Therefore justice in the eyes of Judaism is the all inclusive principle of human conduct. Justice that is required is not only the action but in thought and spirit. This implies that man is required to be honest in intention, upright in speech and mien and must maintain perfect rectitude; that is, he should neither take advantage of ignorance nor abuse confidence. Righteousness includes charity and benevolence. "He who prevents the poor from reaping the corners of the field or the gleanings of the harvest or in any way withholds that which has been assigned by the law of Moses is a robber." According to Judaism, charity is not condescending love but a duty. Those who refuse to give the poor their share abuse the divine trust. Justice includes social justice. "Woe unto them that join house to house, that lay field to field, till there be no room." This condemns the persons who in their greed and avarice deprive and dispossess the poor and oppress them. Judaism teaches a robust morality and perfect conduct. Life is a struggle for God, for right against every sort of injustice, for truth against falsehood, purity against impiety. It is a religion of virtues, of meekness, submission and resignation, kindness and consideration to animals, peaceableness, harmony and modesty. "For the righteous, there is no rest, neither in this world nor in the next, for they go from host to host, from striving to striving and they will see God." The Jewish ideal or holiness is an aim to sanctify every pursuit and every effort to purify all relations and activities and to instil a pure motive and disinterested conduct. "As one follows the divine pattern of holiness, all that he is and all that he has body and soul, weal and woe, wealth and want, pain and pleasure, life and death become stepping stones on the road to holiness and godliness." The kingdom of God for whose approach the Jews yearn from the beginning until the end does not rest in a world beyond the grave, but in a complete moral order on earth, the reign of truth, justice, righteousness and holiness among all men and nations.

Sin, according to Judaism, is inherent in human nature. It rejects the idea that there is an inclination in man to sin. It is contrary to the idea of holiness. Sin is no illusion. "Sin dieth at the door. Thou shalt rule over it." Sin is a straying from the path of God. Sin issues from the impurity of human mind and it lies in wrong thinking and planning. Sin engenders a feeling of disunion with God. It forms a barrier between man and God. Every sinful act causes an estrangement from God and it strains the relationship between man and God. "But your iniquities have separated you and your God and your sins have hid His face from you." But the divine relationship is not indestructible, and forgiveness of the true penitent sinner is asserted, and the assistance of God's holy spirit is besought in efforts after righteousness. "Ye are children of Lord, your God, even if you sin you are still his children." Divine reconciliation with man can be effected only by returning to the right path and doing justice. God dispensing His justice does not desire to punish the Sinner but he desires the sinner to return to Him. "Return ye and turn yourself from all your transgressions, so shall they not be a stumbling block of iniquity to you. Cast away from you all your transgressions, wherein you have transgressed; and make you a new heart and new spirit, for why will you die, house of Israel? For I have no pleasure in the death of him that dieth, saith the Lord God; wherefore turn yourself and live." The same thought has been expressed in "Return unto Me and I shall return unto you." Man, through his penitence and confession makes for himself a new heart and a new spirit and then can hope to be reconciled with God who in His kindness and mercy forgives him. The belief that God grants prayers and forgives sinners is founded on a mutual relation between man and God. "Like as a father hath compassion on his children, so hath the Lord compassion upon them that fear Him." It is prayer that bridges the wide gulf between the human Soul and God. Divine mercy can be hastened by prayers. Through prayer a man confides in Him alt his fears and yearnings to attain peace. As a Psalmist has said "My Soul thirsteth for God; for the living God." The decree of God can be altered through prayer of the pious. "God longs for the prayer of the pious." Every genuine prayer lifts man up towards God. It gives him power to conquer fate, sin. misery and death. "The Lord is nigh to all of them that call upon Him in Truth." All the Jewish 'saints have laid a great stress on the efficacy and power of repentance. Man's fate depends upon repentance and prayer. The aim and end of all wisdom is repentance. The gate of repentance is never closed. Even the righteous shall not attain to so high a place in heaven as the truly repentant. Even a part of a day spent in repentance gives more joy to the angels than a life-time of righteousness. It is said that even if the gates of heaven are shut to prayers, they are open to tears. What is needed is the tearful heart of the penitent.

The Jews believe in resurrection and in angels. They believe that every man's actions will be weighed on the day of judgment and men will have to pass after their resurrection along the bridge of Hell. The simile of the seed of corn which is sown in earth and which shoots out in countless blades is often instanced as a proof of the resurrection. When the seed which was buried in the earth springs up in the manifold clothings of blade how much more will the virtuous who have been interred rise again? The Jews believe in future life and in Heaven and Hell.

Judaism is often said to be a religion of ceremonial and lacking in spiritual worth. This opinion is erroneous, for, the prophets have in no uncertain terms condemned performance of ceremonials and observances divorced from truly sincere and religious heart. "For I desire mercy and not sacrifice and the knowledge of God rather than burnt offerings." Isaiah spoke in a similar vein, "To what purpose is the multitude of your sacrifices, saith the Lord; I am full of burnt offerings of rams, and the fat of fed beasts; I delight not in the blood of bullocks nor lambs or of he-goats... wash you, make you clean, put away the evil of your doings from before Mine eyes. Cease to do evil, learn to do well. Seek justice, relieve the oppressed, judge the fatherless, plead for the widow." The great prophets have in scathing words denounced sacrifice and have said that it is out of harmony with the true spirit of Judaism. However ceremonial has played a large part in Jewish life; from the Bible come the observance of the Sabbath, the institution of festivals and the origin of innumerable rituals and customs which are the outward expressions religion. The Sabbath is the day of rest. The festivals are divinely ordained to commemorate the great events in the people's history. The Passover recalls the

Exodus and the events that led up to it. Pentecost in early summer is associated with the giving of the law. Tabernacles in the autumn are associated with the tents in which Israelites dwelt in wilderness. The Day of Re-. membrance or New Year is an occasion for solemn introspection over the year that has gone. The day of atonement is set apart as a day of fasting and prayer whereby if a man is penitent he can obtain God's pardon. The Prophets have repeatedly said that ceremonial law was meant to tie them up together and to bind the nation together.

CHRISTIANITY

IN the Chapter on Judaism we saw how the prophets began to cherish the idea of a new relation between God and man. God, they declared, was preparing a new epoch, in which He would receive man in a more intimate communion than before. They declared that man would be directed along the right path, not by covenants and laws, but by constant inspiration of a present deity. The new approach would be one which would be shared by all nations.

But instead of becoming broader, to realise its universal destiny, Judaism grew narrower and sophisticated. Though it was enriched in its inner consciousness by the teachings of the prophets, it maintained its earlier semi-heathenish forms of worship, adding only touches of new stateliness and significance, and garbed itself in the hard shell of public rituals and personal observances. The Jews separated the, lot of humanity from that of their little race and cultivated an exclusive pride. Though under the Maccabees they displayed a heroic tenacity, amid the towering influence of Hellenism, it is noticeable that in succeeding periods many signs appeared which showed that their religion was losing its inner gusto. The priests and scribes extended their power, and tradition and observance seized the imagination of the people. The sense of the divine presence grew faint and multitudes of spirits filled the air and oppressed human life with a sense of uncertainty and doubt. "Sometimes the righteous were to await resurrection; sometimes they were to be received at the moment of death into Abraham's bosom; sometimes resurrection was to be general; sometimes it was to be reserved for the faithful; sometimes it supposed a renewed earth and a new Jerusalem; and sometimes it supposed a previous annihilation of the Universe." Such was the condition of the religion of the Jews at the advent of Jesus.

Jesus was born at Nazareth, a small town of Galilee This enchanted' place, smiling and majestic, the cradle of Nature, was for years the environment of Jesus, which from childhood gave a large scope to his vivid imagination and which helped his education. The precise date of his birth is not known. He was born in the reign of Augustus. His foster-father Joseph and his mother Mary were people in humble circumstances, artisans living by their labour, who lived a simple life. Jesus spent the first years of life at Nazareth. Before Jesus had taken any part in public life Joseph, his father, died. Mary remained the head of the family and that is why he is referred to as the son of Mary. He followed the trade of his father which was that of a carpenter. Jesus never married, his love centred upon his celestial vocation. He learned to read and write by rote. From his infancy he used to visit annually the feast at Jerusalem, where people assembled and exchanged ideas; this afforded Jesus an opportunity for making himself conversant with the ideas of his countrymen. It inspired him with a lively antipathy for the shortcomings of the. official representatives of Judaism. The mother-tongue of Jesus was a Syrian dialect mixed with Hebrew. Jesus was inspired and influenced by the principles expounded by Hillel. The allegories and Psalms contained in the Old Testament filled him with inspiration. The advent of the Messiah with his glories and his terrors—the nations falling down one after another, the cataclysm of Heaven and earth, were familiar to him and enriched his imagination. Jesus had heard of John the Baptist who had a reputation throughout Palestine. He was a young man full of zeal and enthusiasm and led a solitary and ascetic life. He was possessed with Messianic hope and wielded a vast influence. Jesus was impelled by a desire to meet the man whose teachings had so much in common with his. Jesus went to John and John felt in Jesus a spirit akin to his own. The great thing which Jesus learnt from John was lessons in preaching and popular action. The feature which distinguished Jesus from his contemporaries was his perfect idealism.

Jesus, as soon as he began to think, was infused with such an atmosphere. These ideas loomed large and did not belong to any one school of thought. Jesus was untroubled by doubts and by the political events of his time. He was free from selfishness and he thought of his mission and of humanity in general.

The teaching of Jesus was principally oral. The chief sources of information, respecting Jesus and the time in which he lived, are the five great collections of writings. The first are the Gospels and the writings of the New Testament; the second are compositions called Apocrypha; the third are the works of Philo; the writings of Philo have the great advantage of showing us ideas which, in the time of Jesus, fermented in the minds of those who were engaged with questions of religion. The writings of Josephus are polemical in character, being meant for the pagan reader. The Apocryphal books of the Old Testament, especially the Jewish portion, the book of Enoch and the book of Daniel, have primary importance inasmuch as they present the development of Messianic theories. They are also useful for understanding the conceptions of Jesus regarding the kingdom of God. The book of Enoch gives us a key to the expression "Son of man" used by Jesus. Some critics are of the opinion that the true understanding of the circumstances which surrounded the development of Jesus are found in th compilations of Talmud.

The Gospels were composed in the second half of the 1st Century A.D. They are full of miracles and of supernatural allusions. Each of the four Gospels is headed by the name of a personage. The formulae, "according to Matthew," "according to Mark," "according to Luke," "according to John," "according to the most ancient opinion," do not necessarily imply that they were written by those under whose name they are entitled. They may signify that these were the traditions proceeding from each of these Apostles. These Gospels have a very high value. Amongst these, the Gospel of Luke is a regular composition based on past documents. It is written with great care after proper selection and pruning, and the narrative is nature. The Gospels of Matthew and Mark do not possess that singular individuality and personal touch. The writing of Mark is an interpretation of Apostle Peter, which is brief and incomplete, but it is much firmer, more precise than that of Luke. These three Gospels are called Synoptics. The fourth is of John. In this there are discourses which are different from that of Matthew. One finds in these discourses some admirable gleams which truly are of Jesus but the mystic tone does not correspond to the eloquence of the Master.

Jesus did not owe the high conception of divinity to Judaism. It was the creation of the vastness of his mind and the greatness of his soul, which formed the fountain-head of all his power. He realised the Divine within himself. He felt himself imbued with God and he drew from his heart all he said of God his father. He lived in the constant presence of God and directly communicated with him. He understood him and felt Him. He never claimed himself to be God. He preached his oneness with God and said of himself that he was the son of God. He did not claim to be a theologian or a philosopher nor did he claim to establish a dogma nor a system. The theology consists in simply realising God as father. This is the great departure of Christianity from the ideas common to the times. The God of Christianity is the God of humanity and the establishment of universal fatherhood of God. The revolution which Jesus intended to usher into the world was expressed by his favourite phrase "The kingdom of God" which would suddenly renovate the world. And when he was asked the external signs of its approach he frequently used to say that the kingdom of God which he intended to establish was within all. The true kingdom of God according to the Christian doctrine is the kingdom of the meek and the humble, the universal brotherhood of men as sons of one father. As a result of the sublime consciousness of God as father, several other consequences are deduced. Jesus expressed himself in singularly concise aphorisms and in a significant form. Some of these aphorisms have their roots in the books of the Old Testament and some were the thoughts of the sages of the age. Jesus adopted some of the teachings but imbued them with a superior spirit and expressed them in excellent form. All the virtues such as humility, forgiveness, charity, abnegation and self-denial and all other virtues have acquired the name and are included in the word Christian. As to justice the well known axiom of the Christian faith is "whatever ye would that men should do unto you do ye even unto them." We find that this did not satisfy him and he expressed- it in even stronger terms "whosoever shall smite thee on thy right cheek turn to him the other also...."

The morality of the Gospels reminds us of one of the highestcreationsofthehu10.2manconscience,inwhichone finds as beautiful a code of perfect life, as any moralist can trace. Jesus saw the imperfections and incompleteness of the Mosaic law but did not speak against it. He repeatedly exhorted men to go beyond what has been commanded by the sages of old. Throughout the Gospels the Commandments of Jesus and their fulfilment are spoken of. In Matthew v. 21-26 it is said "you have heard that it was said by them of old time, thou shalt not kill but I say unto you that whoever is angry with his brother shall be in danger of the judgment; and whosoever shall say to his brother Raca shall be in danger of the Council If therefore thou art offering thy gift at the altar and there rememberest that thy brother has aught against thee, leave thy gift before the altar and go thy way first to be reconciled to thy brother and then come and offer thy gift. Agree with thine adversary quickly...." Christian doctrine teaches us to live at peace with all men, and not to justify our anger towards anyone, nor should we consider another's anger against us as causeless. Men are exhorted to remove from their minds the stigma of hostile feelings, and the flame of anger which destroys us must be quenched at its source. The second Commandment is stated in Matt. v. 27-30 thus: "You have heard that it was said by them of old times, thou shalt not commit adultery. But I say unto you that whosoever looketh on a woman to lust after her hath committed adultery with her in his heart. And if thy right eye causeth thee to stumble, pluck it out and cast it from thee for it is profitable for thee that one of thy members should perish and not the whole body be cast into Hell." As in the first Commandment so here — Jesus says that adultery arises from the fact that women and men hold each other as the objects of their desire. Therefore one must eschew all that arouses lust. This Commandment removes all the evils that flow from sexual desires of men.

After the second Commandment follows the third which is (Matt. v. 33-37): "Again ye have heard that it has been said by them of old time, thou shalt not forswear thyself but I say unto you Swear not at all...." This injunction follows from Jesus's teaching that one should always submit to the will of God. Then follows that fourth Commandment (Matt, v. 38-42) : "You have heard that it was said an eye for an eye and a tooth for a tooth; but I say unto you Resist not him that is evil; but whosoever smiteth thee on thy right cheek turn to him the other also. And if any man would go to law with thee, and take away thy coat let him have thy cloak also. And whosoever shall compel thee to go one mile go with him twain. Give to him that asketh thee, and from him that would borrow of thee turn not thou away."

A Christian's love should be like God's love which must flow unrestrained, and uncurbed and is limitless. This Commandment is very simple and clear. It says never resist the evil-doer by force, do not meet violence with counter-violence. Endure the wrongs, renounce revenge, yield up possessions and surrender and suffer for it is nobler to give than to receive. This Commandment express the Truth with clarity and exactitude. The fifth Commandment says (Matt. v. 43-48) : "Ye have heard that it was said thou shalt love thy neighbour and hate thine enemy; but I say unto you love your enemies, bless them that curse you, do good to them that hate you and pray for them that despise you; that ye may be sons of your Father which is in Heaven, for He maketh his sun to rise on the evil and the good and sendeth rain on the just and the unjust....Ye therefore shall be perfect, as your heavenly Father is perfect."

It will be seen that this Commandment is replete with meaning. It says that men must aspire to be perfect like God and this perfection can be achieved by practising His attributes. God does not make any distinctions between man and man but He showers His blessings upon all and therefore one should be like God. One must love all men and do good to all alike; one should not make distinction between man and man.

It will be noted that before each of his injunctions Jesus has quoted the worlds of the ancient law and contrasted those words with his own doctrines. By contrasting, Jesus has placed before men the correct doctrine. The doctrine which Jesus intends to instil into us is that revenge is a most degrading animal passion and that violence is not merely a shameful thing but is derogatory to the truc happiness of man and that the highest respect is merited not by him who takes and preserves what is his from others but by him who gives up the most and serves others.

The fulfilment of Jesus's teachings expressed in the five Commandments would establish the kingdom of God which will bring peace, happiness and plenty to all men. Peace among men is the highest blessing attainable by man on earth. All five Commandments have but one aim and that is establishing everlasting peace upon earth. In all his sermons Jesus speaks only of the things that divide men and hinder them from establishing peace and entering the kingdom of God. All the parables are but a description of what the kingdom of God is, and they explain and exhort that it is only by loving each other with strong brotherhood that one can enter the kingdom of God. Further on Jesus goes on to say that if real peace is established men will beat their swords into Ploughshares and their spears into pruning hooks.

The centre of gravity of the whole thought lies in the words "Resist not him that is evil" and the other ideas, °f presenting the other cheek, giving up the cloak, submitting to be beaten and persecuted follow as an explanation. In this and in all the Gospels everything confirms the same teaching that is non-resistance to evil. Jesus has repeatedly said that only he can be His disciple who takes up His cross and abandons everything, that is only he who is ready to suffer all consequences, which are the outcome of the fulfilment of the law of non-violence to evil. To His disciples Jesus says: "Be beggars, be ready without resisting evil, to accept persecution, suffering and death." To say "turn your cheek, love your enemies" is to express the essence of Christianity. The motive upon which He rested these maxims was always the same: 'That ye may be the children of your Father which is in Heaven, for He maketh the sun to rise on evil and the good."

It is a religion of pure worship without external observances, a religion based on the heart and imitation of Godhood and the establishment of a direct communion of conscience with God. God only sees the heart and therefore external purifications of the body have no significance. Sincerity is placed on a higher level than tradition, which was held sacred by the Jews. Jesus was disgusted with the hypocrisy of the Pharasees who in praying turned their heads to see if they were observed, who gave alms with ostentation and put marks upon their garments that they might be recognised as pious persons. He had an aversion for grimaces of false devotion. "They have their recompense" said he "but thou when thou doest thy alms let not thy left hand know what thy right hand doth, that thy alms may be in secret and thy Father which seeth in secret Himself shall reward thee openly; and when thou prayest thou shalt not be as the hypocrites are for they love to pray in the synagogues in the corners of the street that they may be seen by man. Verily I say unto you they have their reward; but when thou prayest enter into thy closet and when thou hast shut thy door pray to thy Father which is in secret and thy Father which seeth in secret shall reward thee openly. But when ye pray use not vain repetitions as the heathens do for they think that they shall be heard for their much speaking. Your Father knoweth what things ye have need of before ye ask him." He was opposed to the display of any external signs of asceticism. Prayer and meditation upon the mountains and in solitary places where men have always sought God satisfied him. This sublime conception of the relationship of man with God is summed up in a prayer which he taught his disciples.

"Our Father which art in Heaven
Hallowed be Thy name
Thy kingdom come: Thy will be done
On earth as it is in Heaven.
Give us this day our daily bread
Forgive us our trespasses as we
Forgive them who trespass against us.
Lead us not into temptation but
Deliver us from the evil one—Amen."

Jesus insistently worked upon the idea that Heavenly Father knows better than we, what we need and that we almost sin against Him in asking Him for this or that. Jesus effectively and strikingly proclaimed these principles. He was opposed to all forms which stifled religion. He laid the true and eternal foundation of true religion. He established an entirely new idea ofworship which is based on purity of heart and conscience and on human brotherhood and establishment othekingdom of God upon earth.

His ingenuity in expressing his aphorisms in a more lively way and making them sterner is remarkable. He possessed great skill in contrasting the old law with the new which he imparted. Popular proverbs and sayings were imbued with a richer spirit. He made happy use of popular proverbs. "How wilt thou say of thine brother let me pull out the mote out of thine eye and behold a beam in thine eye. Thou hypocrite first cast out the beam out of thine own eye and then thou shalt see clearly to cast out the mote out of thy brother's eye."

Jesus declared that the world is the enemy of God and His saints; but God will avenge His saints and the world of evil will be swept off. He proclaimed the advent of the new order which shall govern humanity. He was to establish the Kingdom of God upon earth. He took no part in politics and submitted to the established authority without any protest and had no desire to rise in revolt against the Roman Empire. He declared that since right and justice were not of this world why should one trouble oneself with vain anxieties. Condemning the world, he took refuge in the ideal Kingdom of Heaven. "My kingdom is not of this world" he said. It was a moral revolution which he intended to usher in for every man. The doctrine of the liberty of soul which he preached and which he proclaimed will always remain enshrined in the hearts of men by the sentence "Render unto Caesar the things which are of Caesar and unto God things which are God's." He created, — apart from politics, — a refuse for souls in the midst of brute force.

One of the most exceptional things we find in the teachings of Jesus is the all-pervading idea of triumph over brute force by self-suffering, — a detachment of spirit, resignation and purity of heart. He taught men to annihilate riches and power by voluntary suffering and surrender. His dream was to bring about a great social revolution in which rank will be overturned and authority in whatever form or feature will be humiliated. The word 'Christian' has been made the antithesis of what is 'wordly'. Christianity teaches the love of goodness and truth which lies in the soul of man. Man's inner struggle to shed light on life's phenomena and to attain the spiritual life is all important. The success of the teachings was decisive. A group of men and women who adhered to him believed him to be a Messiah, but the name which he preferred for himself was the son of man.

The teachings of Jesus are the teachings of the son of man that is present in all of us. It is the teaching of the strivings of all men after what is good and of the reason, shared by all, which illuminates that striving. His teachings of the son of man — or son of God which form the basis of all the Gospels, is expressed most simply and clearly in his conversation with Nicodemus.

"Each man besides being conscious of his physical personal life cannot but be conscious of his birth from above (John iii. 5-6-7). That of which man is conscious of in himself as free is that which is born of the eternal that which we call God. That which is born of God (the son of God in man) we should exalt in ourselves in order to attain true life. He who exalts in himself that son of God above all else, he who believes that life dwells only in that, will not be in discord with life. Discord with life results only because people do not believe in the light within themselves" (John v.v. 18-21).

Jesus teaches us to exalt the son of man within who is the son of God. He says: "When you exalt the son of man you will know that J speak nothing of myself." The Jews did not understand his teachings and asked "who is this son of man that must be lifted up?" (John xii. 34). And to this question he replies: "Yet a little while is the light in you, walk while ye have light, that darkness overtake you not; he that walketh in darkness knoweth not whither he goeth."

To the question what is meant by "lift up the son of man" Jesus replies "Live in light that is in man." According to Jesus the son of man is that light in which men ought to walk by while they may have light within them." "Look therefore whether the light that is in thee be not darkness" (Luke xi. 35).

It is said in (Matt. vi. 23) "If the light that is in thee be darkness how great is the darkness." Jesus says that light dwells in every human heart.

Jesus for a long time communicated his ideas to a select few who were secretly but sincerely devoted to him. In those days each town had its synagogue or place of meeting. In the synagogue of the town of Capernaum he was offered a book to read, which he read and explained to them in conformity with his own thinking, which gave a new force and spirit and they admired and encouraged him. The charm of his person and speech captivated the imagination of the people and the sphere of his influence considerably widened. It was here that two brothers, Simon surnamed Peter and Andrew, became his devoted disciples. The brothers continued to ply their trade of fisherman and Jesus who liked playing upon words told them that he would make them fishers of men. Another family named Zebedee had two sons, James the elder and John who played a very prominent part. Salome the wife of Zebedee was much devoted to Jesus and followed him until his death. Women in fact received him with eagerness. One of them, Mary of Magdala, was of a very pious disposition and was very much attached to him. Jesus had twelve disciples. Many others followed him and recognised him as their Master.

Jesus also had his favourite or inner circle in his group of followers. James and John were first in rank. The affection of Jesus for Peter was very strong. Peter was upright, sincere and impulsive. John was youthful and possessed a tenderness of heart and had a lively imagination. His nature was powerful and profound. Among his disciples there was no hierarchy. They were to call each other "brothers." Jesus denounced titles of superiority and the greatest title one could covert was to become the servant of servants. All these disciples began their career as fishermen and only Matthew (or Levi) was a publican.

The ignorance of the people was extreme, their intelligence feeble; they believed in apparitions and spirits. They had very little Jewish instructions but their hearts overflowed with faith. Sometimes Jesus instructed his followers who crowded upon the shore from a boat; sometimes he sat upon the mountains which bordered the lake. They saw in the floating clouds, in the germinating seed, or in the ripening corn the sign of the approach of the Kingdom of God. They believed that they were about to commune with God. They believed that the dawn of universal consolation would soon approach. That His preaching was gentle and pleasing and overflowing from a plane superior to that of humanity appears from the Sermon on the Mount."

"Blessed are the poor in spirit for theirs is the kingdom of God.

Blessed are they that mourn for they shall be comforted.

"Blessed are the meek for they shall inherit theearth.

"Blessed are they which do hunger and thirst after righteousness for they shall be filled.

"Blessed are the merciful for they shall receivmercy.

"Blessed are the pure in heart for they shall see God.

"Blessed are the peace-makers for they shall be called children of God.

"Blessed are they which are persecuted for righteousness' sake, for theirs is the kingdom of God."

In their simplicity and sonorous tone these assertions are exquisite and penetrate the heart. They carry with them hope and faith.

Contempt for the worldly life inspired Jesus with charming apologues. "Lay not up for yourself treasures upon earth where moth and dust doth corrupt and where thieves break through and steal, but lay up for yourselves treasures in Heaven where neither moth nor dust corrupt and where thieves do not break through nor steal for where your treasure is there will your heart be also. No one can serve two masters for cither he will hate the one and love the other or else he will hold to the one and despise the other; you cannot serve God and Mammon. Therefore I say unto you take no thought for your life what ye shall eat or what ye shall drink nor yet for your body what ye shall put on. Is not life more than meat and body than raiment. Behold the fowls of the air yet your Heavenly Father feedeth them; are ye not much better than they. Which of you by taking thought can add one cubit unto his stature. And why take ye thought for raiment, consider the lilies of the field how they grow; they toil not, neither do they spin and yet I say unto you that even Solomon in all his glory was not arrayed like one of these. Wherefore, if God so clothe the grass of the field which today is and tomorrow is cast into the oven, shall he not much more clothe you, O, Ye of little faith? Therefore take no thought saying what shall we eat or what shall we drink or wherewithal shall we be clothed, for all these things do the Gentiles seek; for your Heavenly Father knoweth that ye have need of all these things. But seek ye first the Kingdom of God and his righteousness and all things shall be added unto you. Take therefore no thought for the morrow for the morrow shall take thought of the tilings of itself. Sufficient unto the day is the evil thereof."

This essentially Galilean sentiment had a great influence on the destiny of the infant creed. In effect such preaching calls upon men to rely on their heavenly Father with hope and faith for the satisfaction of their wants and to regard the anxieties of life as an evil Again Jesus has more forcefully said: "Sell that ye have and give alms. Provide yourself bags which wax not old a treasure in the heaven that faileth not."

As an example of human folly Jesus loved to cite the case of a man who after having enlarged his barns and hoarded wealth for long years, died before having enjoyed it. Our societies are founded upon very rigorous ideas of property and possession. The poor and the downtrodden have really no place under the sun. Jesus expressed himself firmly on the sin of covetousness, which is the very basis of Christian morality. The teaching of Jesus redeems men from the ruinous life people live. The folly of men consists in considering their present life as a real thing, something that is within their grasp. Jesus has by a series of parables and discourses showed to mankind that they have no right to life till they accept the true life by rejecting the shadow of life. In order to understand his teachings rightly one has to convince oneself that one's individual and personal life is senseless and meaningless and is a mockery of one's reason and of the good in man. Jesus, in the beginning of his teachings, says: "Repent, or ye shall perish." He says (Luke xii. 54-47): "When ye see a cloud rising in the West straightway ye say there cometh a shower....Ye hypocrites ye know how to interpret the face of the earth and the heaven....And why even concerning yourselves Judge ye not what is right."

In simple words "why do you not bethink yourself?"

However you may strive against death, at last it will be death that will conquer you; therefore is it not better not to devote your life to what will certainly perish: not to concern yourself about your body and raiment, and in vain you try to safeguard your life with posses sions? Jesus says that the meaning of life cannot consist in what we possess and acquire. In the parable of the virgins awaiting the bridegroom, and of the end of the days and the day of Judgment, Jesus besides relating the end of the world also shows that death stands before us at every moment. He who labours personally and accumulates riches knows that one thing is awaiting him and that is — death. Therefore life for oneself can have no meaning. If one wants to live a true life one must live in such a way that death cannot destroy one's life. Jesus shows such a way. Man living an isolated and individual life has forgotten or wishes to forget all that was done for him before his birth, and all that is being done while he is alive, and that something is therefore expected of him. According to his teaching we should understand, feel and realise from our birth till our death that we are overwhelmingly in debt to others, to those who lived before us, to those now living with us, and to those who will live and to that which was, which is and which will be— the source of all things.

Each moment of our life is an obligation. We must forgo our own will and live according to the will of our Father and His will is not that we should live an isolated and personal life but the life of the son of man dwelling within each of us; and therefore a man preserves his life only when he accepts his life as a loan, a talent entrusted to him by the Father for the service of the life of all. We must enter into communion with the ever-living God, Jesus, replying to the question of a young man and of a lawyer how to enter eternal life, said: "Eternal life continues in the son of man and what is needed to preserve it is the observance of the commandments which express God's will for the whole humanity."

According to Jesus, service of God is a service of the God of all mankind. One should therefore renounce the illusory personal life and transfer it into the life of the whole humanity. The first condition of becoming a disciple of Jesus was to sell one's property and to give the price of it to the poor and the needy. Jesus often repeats that he who has found the Kingdom of God ought to buy it at the price of all his goods, and in so doing he makes an advantageous bargain.

Jesus does not make it compulsory to sell one's goods and give them to the poor, except as a suggestion towards greater perfection. But sometimes he makes a strong declaration: "It is easier for a camel to go through the eye of a needle than for a rich man to enter the Kingdom of God." Be it noted, however, that by rich. Jesus meant those who were inordinately attached to wordly possessions. He conceives the Kingdom of God as an inheritance of the poor, the lowly and the lost.

With perfect insight Jesus realised that man's inattention, want of Faith, and lack of morality were born of the distractions which he permits himself and the cares which occupy him, which a growing civilisation multiplies beyond measure. The weariness of an ordinary life can find the most efficient solace in the Gospel. It gives a potent diversion from the anxieties of the world and gives, a right direction for attaining perfection.

Jesus had no prepossession and he sensed that the official world and the aristocrats may not accept his teachings. He formed his resolution with extreme boldness and sought the simple, the humble and the outcaste and left those of sterile hearts and piquant prejudices to themselves. He declared very often that the Kingdom of God was made first for children and those who came near them, second for the outcastes of the world, victims of social injustice; thirdly for heretics, publicans, pagans etc. In simple words, the doctrine of Jesus proclaimed that the pure alone shall be saved and that the advent of the reign of the poor is approaching. "Woe, unto you that are rich for ye have received your consolation. Woe unto you that are full, for ye shall hunger. Woe unto you that laugh now, for ye shall mourn and weep."

It will be found from every page of the Old Testament that God will vindicate the poor and the weak. The prophets with one voice have incessantly expressed their feelings against the great and the glorious and have established a close relation between the words rich, impious, violent, wicked and on the other hand between the words poor, gentle, humble and pious. For the true followers of Jesus, poverty remained an ideal. To possess nothing was true faith and mendicancy became a virtue, a holy condition. "To have made poverty an object of love and desire, to have raised the beggar to the altar and to have sanctified the coat of the poor man was a master stroke which political economy may not appreciate, but in the presence of which the true moralist cannot remain indifferent. Humanity in order to bear its burden needs to believe that it is not paid entirely by wages. The greatest service which can be rendered to it is to repeat often that it lives not by bread alone."

Jesus gave subtle answers which exasperated the Pharasees. "The son of man is come to save that which was lost, I am not come to call the righteous but sinners to perfection." Lastly that delightful parable of the prodigal son in which he said that he who is fallen is represented as having a kind of privilege of love above him who has always been righteous. Weak and fallen women, realising for the first time the attractions of contact with virtue, approached Him freely and He shared their miseries. He appreciated conditions of soul only in proportion to the love which was mixed together with it. Women with tearful hearts and regret for their sins were nearer his Kingdom than the others.

In a dignified manner He showed His contempt for the 'world.' He had no external affection for austerity. He did not fly from pleasure. He willingly went to a marriage feast. Jesus liked the gay and animated aspect of life and drew parables from it. Women came to pour oil upon His head and perfume His feet. His disciples sometimes repulsed them, but Jesus who loved ancient usages and all that indicated simplicity of heart, repaired the ill done by His too zealous friends. He protected those who wished to honour Him. He thus gained the adoration of women and children. The new religion which He preached in many respects became a movement of women and children. Whenever He got an opportunity He used to repeat that children are sacred beings, that the Kingdom of God belongs to them, that if we want to enter the Kingdom we must transform ourselves into children and should receive it as a child. He said that God hides His secrets from the wise and reveals them to children. The idea of the disciple is to His mind almost synonymous with that of children.

Jesus almost every year went to Jerusalem for the feast of the passover. While at Jerusalem Jesus passed His days in the temple. The period of the feast brought a concourse of people to the City. He felt Himself in a hostile world where He was looked upon with scorn and hatred. He felt repulsed at everything He saw there. The temple did not present an ennobling spectacle. The accessories of worship presented repulsive details of mercantile operations. Shops were established within its sacred precincts. Beasts and birds were sold there for sacrifice. There were tables for the exchange of money. This profanity in the sacred place wounded the religious spirit of Jesus. He said that they had made the house of prayer into a den of thieves. One day, carried away by emotion, He scourged the sellers with a "Scourge of small cords" and over-turned their tables. In general, he had little love for the temples. The worship of his father which He preached had nothing in common with scenes of butchery.

He was greatly disgusted with the impious and the haughty priesthood, sacrifices and all other forms of worship which then prevailed, and from thenceforward He concluded that nothing can be achieved without the destruction of Judaism.

On this subject He used striking comparisons. "No man putteth a piece of new cloth into an old garment, neither do men put new wine into the old bottle." The pride of blood appeared to him a great enemy which was to be combated. Jesus was a revolutionery. He called all men without exception to a worship founded solely on the fact of their being children of God. He proclaimed with vehemence, the rights of men and not the rights of a particular caste or creed. He taught the religion of man and not the religion of the Jews. He desired the deliverance of all men and not of the Jews alone. He wanted to found the religion of humanity which was to be founded not upon distinctions of blood but in the hearts of men. And for these purposes he found the temple to be useless and he condemned it. Jesus disregarded all religion which did not flow from the heart. He vigorously despised the ostentatious practices ol devotees, the outward formalities for attaining perfection. He cared little for fasting. He preferred forgiveness to sacrifice. He taught the love of God, the practice of charity with mind and heart and mutual forgiveness. Jesus did not teach any religious rites and ceremonies. Prayer to be real must flow from the recesses of the heart. Mere good-will was no alternative to genuine love of goodness. His religion consists in persistently doing good in spite of evil. He vehemently opposed the numberless outward observances which were based on traditions and were supposed to be law. "There is nothing from without a man that entering into him can defile him but things which come out of him those are that defile the man." "Blind leaders of the blind take care lest ye also fall into the ditch." "Oh generation of vipers how can ye, being evil speak good things? For out of the abundance of the heart that mouth speaketh." Those aphorisms show how much Jesus cared for inner purity. It is trite to observe that in His teachings there is absence of pedantry and declamations against idolatry. That which struck his imagination was not idolatry, but men's servility to traditions and formalities. He says with vehemence that true brotherhood can be established amongst men by charity and love and not by creeds. In his estimation the "neighbour" was the man who has pity on his kind without distinction of class or sect. His teachings are replete with the establishment of human brotherhood in its widest sense.

The contemporaries of Jesus believed that for the establishment of a supernatural mission, miracles and the fulfilment of prophecies were necessary. Jesus and his disciples employed these methods and thus complied with the spirit of the times. Healing was considered a moral expedient, and Jesus, who wielded moral power, believed in his fitness to heal. The healing of the sick was considered to be one of the signs of the Kingdom of God which emancipated the poor. He performed his miracles with a degree of reluctance.

From the very inception, the chief idea of Jesus was the establishment of the Kingdom of God which has been interpreted in diverse ways. At times he desired only the triumph of the poor and disinherited, at others the fulfilment of the apocalyptic visions of Daniel and Enoch; and lastly the approaching deliverance of the spirit. It will be seen from the reading of the Gospel that all these conceptions existed at the same time in the mind of Jesus. As a democratic leader desiring the triumph of the lowly and the lost, ushering in a temporal revolution, does not seem to have impressed him much. It was not in accord with his sentiments to regard earth or the riches of the earth or material welfare as worth pursuing. He did not care for worldly ambitions. He never appears to have desired to forego his religious mission for social uplift. He had a religious mission to fulfil and subordinated everything else to this divine mission. Full of heavenly ideals he never abandoned his poverty. Jesus appears to hold the other two conceptions simultaneously.

The apocalyptic ideas of Jesus may be summed up thus. The present condition of humanity is approaching its end. This end will be full of anguish and there will be a revolution of new faith. The revolution will be preceded by calamities and heralded by unimaginable phenomena. The Messiah will appear in clouds, clothed in glory and majesty, the dead will rise and Messiah will proceed to pass judgment. At this judgment men will be divided into two classes according to their deeds. The angels will be the executors of the sentences. The chosen ones will enter the delightful mansions clothed with light. The rest will depart into Gehenna, which is a gloomy, filthy valley full of fire. When Jesus was asked about the time of the advent, he refused to reply; he declared once that the date of this great day was known only to his Father. By the side of this false, cold and impossible idea of an ostentatious advent of the real city of God. he presented the Sermon on the Mount, the apotheosis of the weak, the love of the people, regard for the poor, humble, true and simple.

If Jesus were convinced of the prevalent idea that the end of the world was nigh, then the main tenets of his teaching would have been to detach oneself by slow degrees from the present life and to aspire to the Kingdom about to come. But this was not so. The teachings of Jesus have a different aspect and an ampler sphere. He proposed to create a new state of humanity. He often declared that the Kingdom of God had already begun and that it was borne by every man within his heart and he can partake of it by silently converting the heart. The Kingdom of God is only the highest form of good and noble. It establishes the reign of justice, liberty of the soul, something analogous to the Buddhist Nirvana, It was the separation of the soul from matter and union with the Divine Essence. The Kingdom of God was the Kingdom of the soul—founded on liberty and on filial sentiment which the virtuous man feels when resting on the bosom of the Father. "It established a pure religion, without forms, without temple and without priests; it was the moral judgment of the world delegated to the conscience of the just man and to the arm of the people."

Jesus taught that men, when they associated together in the union of love, found that their souls were brought together and they became powerful. He further declared that whenever men assembled in his name he would be in their midst. Whenever we love one another and mutually depend upon one another we establish oneness. He did not preach war against nature and ask men to have an entire severance from ties of blood unless they interfered with their duties. The anxieties, troubles and cares of life draw a man downwards and Jesus required from his associates a complete detachment from the earth and devotion to his work. They must practise absolute poverty, live on alms and hospitality. "Freely ye have received, freely give." He predicted for his followers severe persecutions and the hatred of mankind. He sent them forth as lambs in the midst of wolves; they would be scourged in the Synagogues and dragged to prison. "The disciple is not above his master nor the servant above his Lord." "Fear not them which kill the body but are not able to kill the soul." His requirements had no longer any bounds. "If any man come to me and hate not his father, mother and wife and children and brethren and sister and his own life also, he cannot be my disciple." Employing still more emphatic words he said "If any man will come after me let him deny himself, take up his cross and follow me. He that loveth father or mother more than me is not worthy of me and he that loveth son or daughter more than me is not worthy of me. He that findeth his life shall lose it and he that loseth his life for my sake and the Gospels shall find it. What is a man profited if he shall gain the world and lose his own soul."

He said "come unto me all ye that labour and are heavy laden and I will give you rest. Take my yoke upon you and learn of me; for I am meek and lowly in heart and ye shall find rest unto your souls, for my yoke is easy and my burden is light." Men's happiness he says cannot depend upon property and possession. By detachment from life, the bond of life was severed. The state, the law, common to all, stood in sharp contrast to the Kingdom of God. Perfection was placed beyond the ordinary conditions of society." According to the teaching of Christ, each individual will be leading a true life if he understands that his vocation is not to consume the works of others, but to devote his own life to working for others and to give his life as a ransom for many. A man who acts thus is worthy of his subsistence. This thought is expressed in His own words. "The labourer is worthy of his meal."

In (James ii. 14-22) it is said: "What does it profit, my brethren" says James "if a man say he has faith and has not works? Can that faith save him. If a brother or sister be naked, and in lack of daily food. and one of you say unto them, go in peace, be ye warmed and filled and yet ye give them not the things needful to the body what does it profit? Even so faith, if it have not works is dead in itself...." It teaches that the only signs of Faith are the works which flow from it and therefore that Faith from which no works flow is a matter of mere words and is therefore no faith. The Faith which is demanded must be capable of promoting deeds. Again Faith rests on truth and Jesus demands Faith in Truth. When Jesus was asked by Peter to confirm his Faith by promising a reward Jesus replied with the parable of the labourers hired at different times and receiving identical payment. To the identical question of James he answered that James had not understood his teachings which consisted in the renunciation of personal life and he was asking for personal fame and personal reward. He has repeatedly said that the meaning of human life does not lie in personal gain, but in serving all. Man lives not to be served but himself to serve and give up his life as a ransom. Only conversion of heart would satisfy him and nothing less than that would fulfil his mission.

Jesus was not unmindful of the dangers with which he was surrounded. The orthodox Pharisees created great obstacles. They were staunch Jews, narrow-minded and cared much for formalities. This created a breach between them and Jesus. He was pressed to go to the feast of Tabernacles. He suspected foul play and at first refused, but he changed his mind and secretly set out. It was the last farewell which he bade to Galilee. Surrounded by snares and difficulties he was incessantly pursued by the ill-will of the Pharisees. The arrogance of the priests and their opulence caused him disgust. He criticised everything which he observed in Jerusalem and praised the poor and the outcast. One day to embarrass him they brought before him an adulteress and asked him what was to be done to her. He said: "He that is without sin among you let him first cast a stone at her". Jesus pierced hypocrisy to the heart. He plainly repudiated all external authority and urged that man must not Judge because he is himself guilty. This very thought has been expressed several times saying that with dirt in one's eye one cannot see the dirt in another's eye and that the blind cannot lead the blind. He bids all men to forgive others that they may be forgiven their own sins. One of the most constant efforts of the Pharisees was to involve Jesus in discussions on political questions. They asked; Is it lawful to give tribute to Caesar or not?" His reply was admirable "Render unto Caesar the things which are Caesar's and unto God the things which are God's." These words establish separation between matters spiritual and temporal. His powerful eloquence always burst forth when contending with hypocrisy: "Woe unto you Scribes and Pharisees, hypocrites for ye make clean the outside of the cup and of the platter but within they are full of extortion and excess. Ye blind Pharisees clean first that which is within the cup and platter that the outside of them may be clean also."

The last episode of the life of Jesus is most illuminating as it casts a glow around his life and teachings and it is necessary to relate the same, though briefly. At the end of the month of December at Jerusalem he celebrated a feast called the Feast of lights because during the eight days of the feast lamps were kept lighted in the houses. At Bethany he performed the miracle of raising of Lazarus. This contributed to hasten his death. The enemies of Jesus were much irritated at his fame. It was Annas who was the principal actor of the terrible drama and killed Jesus. He used to say "Better the death of one man than the ruin of a people." The death of Jesus was thus resolved upon from the month of February. Jesus set out with his disciples to see once more and for the last time the unbelieving city of Jerusalem. Jesus spoke to his disciples of his approaching end and the sufferings he would have to undergo. He felt the visions of his death.

Jesus was praying at nightfall at the mount of Olives. His disciples were sleeping near him when an armed troop appeared with an order from the high priest to arrest him. Judas headed the troops. Jesus surrendered himself. The disciples took to flight. Peter and John alone did not lose sight of their master. Jesus was charged with the crime of corruption. His enemies had planned to convict him and condemn him to death on the testimony of witnesses and by his own avowals of blasphemy and of outrage against the Mosaic religion. Annas questioned Jesus as to his doctrine and his disciples. Jesus refused to be dragged into dicussions about his followers. Regarding his teachings he declared that he had taught in public and never held any secret doctrine. Annas had not the power to pronounce judgment upon Jesus so he went to his son-in-law Kaiaphas who acted as his instrument. The fatal sentence which Jesus had really uttered: "I am able to destroy the temple of God and to build it in three days" was cited though the assembly knew that Jesus referred to his own resurrection. Jesus confessed and proclaimed before the assembly. The assembly declared him guilty. During the night he was ill-treated. They had to get the sentence ratified by Pilate. On the morning of Friday, April 3, Jesus was bound and led to the Judgment hall. Pilate displayed his displeasure at being mixed up with this affair. The dignified and calm attitude of Jesus impressed him and he desired to save him. "My kingdom is not of this world" Jesus explained the nature of his kingdom, declaring that it consisted in the possession and proclamation of truth. This idealism was beyond thc understanding of Pilate. To him Jesus appeared to be a harmless dreamer. Pilate knowing that Jesus was arrested in consequence of the jealousy of the priests tried to obtain for him the benefit of the custom of handing over a prisoner to the people at the time of the Passover. Pilate however did not want to compromise his position by becoming indulgent; he therefore caused him to be scourged. Scourging was in general a preliminary to crucifixion. Then took place a revolting scene. He was led in front of the people. Soldiers filed past him, others spat upon him. The tumult increased, the cry 'Crucify him" was raised from all sides. The Jews told Pilate: "We have a law and by our law he ought to die because he has made himself the son of God." The motive for the death of Jesus was entirely religious. Pilate, fearing an uprising of the people, passed the death sentence on Jesus, after declaring that he was "innocent of the blood of this just man." The scene of execution was Golgotha. He was divested of his garments and fastened to the cross by driving nails into his hands and feet Jesus felt these horrors in all their atrocities. A burning thirst devoured him and he asked for a drink. A soldier dipped a sponge and raised it to his lips, he sucked at it. Jesus made one last prayer: "Father forthem for they know not what they do." John and Mary, the mother of Jesus, were at the foot of the cross and Jesus seeing' his mother and disciple together said to the one "Behold thy mother" and to the other "Be. hold thy son."

He saw only the ingratitude of men and exclaimed: "My God why hast thou forsaken me?"

The death of Jesus occurred in the year 33 of the Christian era. Jesus created around him a circle of disciples whom he inspired with boundless affection and in whom he had planted the seeds of his doctrine.

"To have made himself beloved to a degree that after his death they ceased not to love him was the great work of Jesus and that which most struck his contemporaries. His doctrine was so little dogmatic that he never thought of writing or causing it to be written. Jesus was not a founder of dogma or a maker of a creed; he infused into the world a new spirit. To follow Jesus in expectation of the Kingdom of God was all that was implied by being Christian. The Kingdom of God as we conceive it, differs notably from the supernatural apparition which the first Christians hoped to see appear in the clouds. But the sentiment introduced by Jesus into the world is ours. His perfect idealism is the highest rule of the unblemished and virtuous life. He has created a Heaven of pure souls, where is found what we seek for in vain on earth, the perfect nobility of the children of God, absolute purity, the total removal of the stains of the world; in fine, liberty which society excludes as an impossibility and which exists in all its amplitude only in the domain of thought. He was the first to proclaim the royalty of the mind: "My Kingdom is not of this World."

His creeds are not of fixed dogma but images susceptible of indefinite interpretations. We should seek in vain for a theological proposition in the Gospel. Jesus will ever be a creator of the pure spirit of religion. The Sermon on the Mount will never be surpassed. Unreservedly devoted to his mission he subordinated everything to it to such a degree that towards the end of his life the universe no longer existed for him."

ISLAM

BEFORE the advent of Islam in Arabia, the principal religions of the Arabs ranged from rank polytheism and gross idolatry to rigid atheism. Amongst these idolatrous Arabs, there were some who had embraced Magism, Christianity and Judaism. There were many in Mecca who could read the Bible in Hebrew, and Medina had become a stronghold of Judaism. The stories of the Old Testament were known to the common people. The idolatry of the Arabs consisted in the worship of planets, fixed stars, angels and their images. At the time of sacrifices and other ceremonials, they sought the intercession of the idols as mediators with God. The ancient Arabs had seven celebrated temples dedicated to the seven planets. Besides these deities each tribe had one or more peculiar object of worship. These idols were in the form of large rough stones which they carried with them on emigration. They had several superstitious rites and customs. But in their worship of idols there was an under-current of a distinct belief in the existence of an omnipotent and supreme God whom they called Allah, who transcended all the idols and who was supposed to be the creator of the world. But the influence of religion on the social or individual life of the people was negligible and there was an absence of cultural life among the people. Human sacrifices were offered to the idols. The normal social polity was without any restraint. Fratricidal and internecine wars were waged on the slightest pretext. Life was lewd and undisciplined; drinking and gambling were rife. Daughters at a certain age were thrown down from a precipice and were thus murdered, and incest was a common occurrence. The Arabs were divided amongst themselves but possessed some remnants of power in the province of Yaman, where they had set up the four last kings prior to Mohamed. But the Greeks under Heraclius attacked them and they not only lost their new conquests but lost a part of their old dominions. It was only after the Arabs were united under Islam that they totally subdued the Greeks. In the time of Mohamed, the Grecian Empire was weak and declining but Arabia was strong and flowering. It was peopled at the expense of the Grecian Empire whence many had come to seek refuge in a free country, on account of the violence of the domineering sects, consequently they poured themselves into Arabia, which was at that time a free country, where they found a secure retreat. The Arabians were unacquainted with the luxuries and delicacies of the Greeks and the Persians and were inured to hardships of all sorts. They led a simple life. They had become accomplished cliefly in eloquence and skill in expression, horsemanship and in wielding arms and in hospitality. They were also known for their liberality. The chief occupations of the Arabs were two. Those who dwelt in towns and cities had for their vocation tilling, cultivation, breeding camels, trade and commerce. The occupation of the Arabs who lived in tents was pasturage. The tribe of Koreish to which Mohamed belonged had much to do with trade and commerce. At the time of Mohamed, the Arabs were divided into multiple, independent tribes which made it possible for Mohamed to propagate his new religion. But once they embraced his religion there was a resultant union of tribes.

This in short was the state of the ancient Arabs. Mohamed had to reclaim his countrymen from such gross idolatry, teach them the ethics of life, nobility of conduct, and had to establish the sole worship of one God.

Mohamed (means the praised one) was the son of Abdulla by his wife Amna and was born at Mecca on the 20th April 571 A.D. He came of the tribe of Koreish, a tribe which was highly esteemed in the whole of Arabia. His father, Abdullah, was the son of Abdul Matlib, and died very young leaving his widow and an infant son in very bad circumstances. When Mohamed was six years of age his mother on her way back to Mecca from Medina died, and Abdul Matlib was obliged to take care of his grandson which he did during his lifetime. At the time of his death Abdul Matlib left

Mohamed to the care of his son Abu Talib who was Mohamed's uncle. At about the age of ten or twelve Mohamed herded goats for some time.

Abu Talib affectionately provided for young Mohamed and instructed him in the business of a merchant. At the age of twelve Mohamed accompanied his uncle Abu Talib to Syria on a commercial expedition. It was at this time that he met a Christian monk Buhera who, on seeing Mohamed, saw in him the future prophet. The chief vocation of Koreish was that of trade and commerce. Mohamed followed this profession. In his younger days he often accompanied his uncle. He was a man of extraordinary part and address. He gained a reputation for honesty and fairness. He was truthful, faithful and trustworthy. During his travels as a merchant he acquainted himself with the political and religious state of his time. He had the art of making the best of every incident and turning the dubious and dangerous to his advantage. When he attained the age of 25 he had established a high position in business and had taken part in public life. His fame attracted the notice of a very rich widow who was about 40 years of age named Khadija. She entrusted him with her merchandize to be taken to Syria. After his return from his journey she proposed to marry him. Mohamed consented and the marriage was celebrated This advantageous match gave Mohamed a life of comfort and ease and raised him to equality with the richest in Mecca.

It is said that during all these years, Mohamed never offered any worship to the idols nor did he ever take part in the ceremonies of worship of the idols.

He intended to destroy the gross idolatry into which the generality of the people of his time had fallen. He intended to replant a new religion in place of the ancient one professed by Adam, Noah, Abraham, Moses and Jesus and other prophets. He desired to weed out the corruptions and superstitions, which were introduced by the ancient religions. He Intended to replace these by the worship of one God and to purify religion. He was burning with passion to bring to the pagan Arabs the knowledge of one true God. He had a deep-rooted conviction of the unity of God to which he was chiefly attached. All his other doctrines were a corollary to this main conviction. He believed that mankind had totally violated the faith in one God and he thought that it was his sacred duty to rescue the world from gross ignorance and superstition. His warm enthusiasm made him suppose that Providence had destined him to effect the reformation. In pursuing his mission he showed high prudence and wise conduct. He declared himself to be a messenger of God to guide mankind to know His Will.

Mohamed began to lose interest in the life which was then led by him and his kinsmen. He often used to retire to a cave called Hira and used to spend his time in contemplation and prayer. He was thus preparing himself for the message which he was to deliver to the world.

As regards the beginning of the revelations Ayesha, one of Mohamed's wives, says: "The first revelations which the Prophet received were in true dreams, and he never dreamt, but it came like the dawn of day." After this the Prophet became fond of retirement and used to seclude himself in a cave in Mount Hira and worship there day and night till one day an Angel came to him and said "Read" but the Prophet said "I am not a reader," Then, said Mohamed, he took hold of me and squeezed me as much as I could bear and he then let me go and again said "Read" and I said "I am not a reader." Then he took hold of me a second time and squeezed me as much as I could bear and then let me go and said "Read" and I said "I am not a reader." Then he took hold of me a third time and squeezed me as much as I could bear and said, "Read in the name of thy Lord who generated man from a clot of blood. Read for thy. Lord is the most beneficent. He hath taught the use of the pen. He has taught man that which he knoweth not." After this first appearance of the Angel tradition says that the revelations stopped for some time, which made him so sad that he determined to commit suicide; but when he was about to carry out his intention, the Angel appeared to him and said, "O, Mohamed, verily thou art the Prophet of God in Truth." At this words he was comforted and at ease. He returned home, and informed his wife Khadija of the miraculous appearance of an angel. She acclaimed the news with great joy, and she was the first person who professed her faith in him. Among the first set of converts were Ali and Abu Bakr. Abu Bakr was rich and influential and exercised great authority amongst the Koreish tribe and it was Abu Bakr who by persuasion prevailed upon the principal men of Mecca to follow his example. The persons who came within Mohamed's fold were those of a gentle and pious nature, who had felt disgust for idolatry In a space of three years, persons from all classes of society embraced the new religion and used to offer their prayers in secret. Thereafter Mohamed made his mission no more a secret and proceeded to achieve his object by persuasion. Soon he began to preach in public to the people. He openly rebuked them for their idolatry and other perversities. One day the prophet went to Kaaba and declared that there was no God but Allah. This infuriated the idol worshippers and they attacked the Prophet and it was with great difficulty that he was saved. The Koreish were powerful. They derived their influence and power from the offices they held at Kaaba. They feared that with the end of idolatry their influence too would end. They did not desire to change their course of immoral life and their crude and sensual pleasures. The Koreish were enraged and resorted to persecution. Mohamed and his followers were the targets of the cruelties and persecutions of the Koreish. Mohamed permitted some of his followers to seek refuge elsewhere. The methods of proselytization and preaching of the new faith which Mohamed adopted were simple. He fell into no controversies. His high personality, character and patience contributed in a high degree to the spreading of his message.

In the fifth year of his mission some of his followers fled to Ethiopia and were received kindly by the Ethiopian king. In the sixth year of his mission his party was strengthened by the conversion of his uncle Hamza, a man of great valour and courage. (It is said that great progress was achieved amongst the Arab tribes In the tenth year of his mission Mohamed told his uncle Abu Talib that God had showed his disapprobation of the league which Koreish had formed against them by sending a worm to eat away every word of the instrument except the name of God. On inspection the Koreish found that it was true and dissolved the league. In the same year Abu Talib died and a few days after his death, Khadija, Mohamed's wife also died. On the death of these two the Koreish began to be more troublesome than ever to the Prophet and he was obliged to seek shelter sixty miles away from Mecca where he was coldly received, and he returned to Mecca. In the twelfth year of his mission Mohamed gave out that he had made his night journey from Mecca to Jerusalem and from thence to Heaven. This story was not believed by some of his followers but Abu Bakr vouched for its veracity. This incident increased Mohamed's standing. He called this year the "accepted year." A few persons came from Medina to Mecca and took an oath of fidelity to Mohamed. Mohamed sent one of his disciples named Masab to instruct the people to Medina to perform the ceremonies of the new religion more perfectly. In the thirteenth year of his mission Masab returned to Mecca accompanied by seventy-three men and two women of Medina who were converted and who vowed allegiance to the new religion. It must be admitted that hitherto Mohamed had propagated his religion by gentle means. The success before his flight to Medina was due to pursuasion. He has affirmed at several places in the Quran that his business was only to preach and that he had no authority to compel any person to embrace his religion. His followers were strictly instructed not to use force and they were asked to bear injuries patiently. When he was persecuted he chose to quit the place of his birth and retire to Medina. But it seems that passiveness and non-resistance were due to want of adequate force and no sooner was he confident of the assistance which he could procure from Medina than he fought his enemies and declared that God had allowed him and his followers to defend themselves against attacks and persecution of the infidels. When his forces increased he declared he had divine sanction to attack the infidels and to destroy idolatry and to set up the true faith. In the twenty-second chapter of the Quran there appears a passage which gave him permission to defend himself by arms. Similar passages are scattered here and there in the Quran.

In order to secure his ground Mohamed formed a league with the people of Medina. This caused fear in the Koreish. They therefore resolved to prevent Mohamed from going to Medina and hatched a plot to kill him. The conspiracy came to the knowledge of Mohamed and to amuse his enemies Mohamed directed Ali to lie down in his place covered with a green cloak. Mohamed safely escaped and returned to Medina three days later. After settling in Medina in safety he began to make reprisals on the Koreish. The battle of Bedr which was fought in the second year of the Hijra (that is the flight from Mecca which is the Mohamedan year which dates from 16th July 622 A.D.) laid the foundation on which he built his succeeding greatness. Some reckon no less than 27 expeditions in which Mohamed was personally present. His forces were maintained by contributions from his followers which he called ZAKAT. By the success of his arms, he, in a few years, raised his prestige and power. By the sixth year of the Hijra people began to show veneration and respect for him. It has been said that he was held in great veneration, which the kings and princes of his time lacked. In the seventh year of Hijra he thought of propagating and spreading his religion beyond Arabia and sent messengers to the neighbouring princes with a request that they should embrace Islam: This attempt was not without success. The eighth year of Hijra was a very fortunate year. In the beginning of that year Syria and other countries were converted and later Egypt also embraced Islam. In this year Mohamed took the city of Mecca and the battle with the Grecians was won. The latter part of this year was devoted to the destruction of the idols in and around Mecca. The ninth year of the Hijra is known as the "year of the embraces;" during this year the Koreish saw that it was beyond their capacity to resist Mohamed and so flocked to his fold in large numbers. In the tenth year of the Hijra, Ali was sent to Yaman to propagate his religion and the whole tribe was converted. Thus was Islam established and idolatry uprooted even in the life-time of Mohamed throughout all Arabia except only Yamania. A year later Mohamed breathed his last.

If the people of his time had treated him with kind generosity, and had not obliged him through persecutions to 'seek refuge in outside territories, and to take up arms against them in his own defence and in defence of his followers, he would have contented himself with the respect and adoration due to his prophetic mission; but, encouraged by success and persecution, his aspirations rose higher and he found it difficult to circumscribe the spreading of the new cult. His personal qualifications greatly helped him to accomplish his undertakings. Without high qualities he would never have succeeded to such high eminence. He was sagacious and well-versed in all the arts of persuasion. He possessed excellent judgment and a keen memory. He was a man of few words, of cheerful disposition, pleasant in conversation, in offensive in behaviour and showed great consideration towards his inferiors. In his manners he was comely and agreeable and polite in address. He had no higher education than was customary in his tribe. The absence of learning did not impede his progress but assisted him, for he believed that the writings which he produced were direct revelations from God.It is really amazing that with so little learning, he could compose a book of such excellent merit in such unsurpassed style.

The prophet never posed as a world teacher. When he reached Medina, the Arabs, the Christians and the Jews asked him, "What is it that you wish to teach us." The prophet replied, "I want to teach you to believe in God, to believe in the divinity and the truth of God, of divine revelations that have been handed down to mankind by God. I want you to believe, that every messenger and prophet of God always brought true message. I do not want you to regard me as God. I am a man like any one of you. I am fallible. I want you to be kind to the poor and the weak. I want you to be pure in your thoughts and conduct."

The name given to the religion founded by Mohamed is 'Islam'. It means submission to the Will of God. It is a religion of self-surrender, acceptance of the revelations and following the commands of God. 'Islam establishes a universal brotherhood of man. The cardinal tenet of Islam is "There is no God but Allah and Mohamed is his Prophet." Traces of Zoroastrian and Judaic influences are found in Islam. The religion is plain, simple and practical. It is said that "No man is true believer unless he desireth for his brother that which he desires for himself. God will not be affectionate to that man who is not affectionate to God's creatures. He is the most favoured of God from whom the greatest good comes to His creatures. The best of man is he from whom good accrueth to all humanity. All God's creatures are his family. He is most beloved by God who trieth to do more good to God's creatures. Feed the hungry and visit the sick and free the captive if he is unjustly confined. Assist any oppressed person. Love thy fellow-beings first." Islam preaches and establishes a strong brotherhood of man. Islam is a religion of service—The service and worship of God. In Islam people are taught more of ethics than of deep philosophy. It teaches that its followers should acquire the manifold attributes of God. Islam forbids fighting. It says that "you shall not take up arms except in the cause of self-defence." If you tyrannise over people, if you are cruel to them, you shall be punished. "Fear thee the prayer of the wronged, for verily there is no veil between him and God." Jihad is exerting oneself for the cause of religion. Islam strictly prohibits application of force for its observance. It teaches that God has sent prophets to mankind to bring them on the path of goodness.

The ideals preached by Islam are numerous, and can be usefully practised in our daily life. When someone asked "O Prophet of God. teach me something," the prophet replied: "Abuse no one and despise not anything good, and speak to the brother with an open countenance verily, that is of good acts and kindness; and if a man revile thee and reproach thee for what he knows in thee then reproach not him for what thou knowest ill of him, so that thou mayest have the reward thereof and the sin be against him,"

Abuse, anger, avarice, back-biting, blood-shedding, bribery, calumny, dishonesty, drinking, envy, flattery, greed, hypocrisy, lying, miserliness, pride, slandering, suicide, usury, violence, wickedness, warfare, wrong doings, are all deprecated and virtues like brotherhood, charity, cleanliness, chastity, forgiveness, friendship, gratitude, humility, justice, kindness, labour, liberality, love, mercy, moderation, modesty, neighbourliness, purity of heart, righteousness, steadfastness, truth and trust are all enjoined.

When the prophet was asked, "What man is the most excellent?" The prophet replied: "Every clean-hearted true-tongued man" and when he was asked "what is the clean-hearted man?" he said "He is pure, the pious in whom there is no sin and no transgression, and no grudge and no envy."

"Whom do you imagine to be strong or powerful?" the prophet asked of his disciples. The disciples answered, "He who throws people down." Nay, replied the Prophet, "It is he who masters himself when angry."

As regards prayer, the Prophet has said: "Nothing keeps away the decree of God except prayer and nothing increases the life of man except goodness."

"He who humbles himself for the sake of God, him will God exalt verily; modesty and faith are related to each other, when one of them is taken away, the other also is taken away." As regards liberality it is said "The upper hand is better than the lower hand; the upper hand bestows and the lower begs."

Mercy is an offshoot of the merciful God. The prophet was asked about the best part of Faith and he said: "That thou love for God and hate for God and make thy tongue act in mentioning God, and that thou love for men what thou lovest for thyself, and hate for them what thou hatest for thyself."

The Prophet exhorted his followers to "Seize the five opportunities before the five calamities; thy youth before the weakness from old age; thy health before thy sickness; thy riches before poverty; thy leisure before thy business; thy life before thy death."

As regards purity of heart the Prophet has said "Purify my heart from all hypocrisy and my work from all show and my tongue from all falsehood and my eyes from all deception for verily thou knowest the deceitful of eyes and what men's breasts do hide." About truth the prophet has said "Verily, truth is goodness and goodness leads to Paradise and verily, lying is wickedness and wickedness leads to fire of hell." The doctrines from which the precepts of Islam are derived are the following:— (1) The Quran, (2) The Sunna, (3) The Ijma, (4) The Qias,

The Quran, the chief foundation of Islam, is the book which contains the revelations Mohamed received from time to time, as a divine message and is therefore called the Word of God. It is asserted that everything contained in the Quran rests on direct revelation from God, communicated to Mohamed in a miraculous manner. The chief modes of divine inspiration were the following:—• (1) By mediation of an angel coming to the Prophet with a peculiar sound like the tinkling of bells, (2) By instilling in the heart of the Prophet, (3) By mediation of an angel in human shape, (4) By the appearance of an angel to the Prophet while asleep, (5) By direct communication from God to the Prophet in his waking or sleeping state.

The Quran is said to have been extant in the highest heaven from eternity, near the throne of God; from thence it has been sent down to the lowest heaven in the month of Ramadan in the night of Al Qadr and stored up there in the Temple of Majesty, from whence it was revealed to Mohamed in smaller or longer portions in the course of twenty-three years. Mohamed did not collect or systematically arrange his revelations in one book. This task was undertaken by Abu Bakr who was the Khalif at the time. Notwithstanding the attempt of Abu Bakr to systematize and arrange the texts of the Quran, differences in reading the Quran continued,andin order to remove the confusion thus caused, the Khalif "Uthman" was pursuaded to have a new recension of the Quran made, which was to be accepted as the authorised text of the Holy Book. The Quran has one hundred and fourteen chapters of unequal length called Suras. These are divided into verses. Each of the Suras is headed by a special title. Some of these chapters have been revealed by stages during a period of twenty-three years over which the revelations of the whole book are spread. Mohamed passed thirteen years in Mecca and ten years in Medina. Every Chapter is sub-divided into smaller portions which are called "Ayat" which signifies wonders. There are seven principal editions or ancient copies of Quran; two of these were published and used at Medina, the third at Mecca, the fourth at Cufa, fifth at Basra, the sixth at Syria and the seventh is called the common edition. There is a variation in the number of verses ranging from six thousand to six thousand six hundred and sixty-six. Next after the title at the head of every Chaper (except the ninth) is prefixed "Bismillah" that is, "in the name of the most Merciful God." The Quran has been universally accepted as written with purity of language and in an elegant style. It is a masterpiece of literary production: It is admirable in its concept of divine nature, its fervent trust is the power of one God, and its deep moral earnestness and its sententious wisdom. It is a standard of the Arabic language. 'Its style is beautiful and fluent, and when prophesying it soars higher. It is concise in form, though at times it is obscure. At times it is enlivened with florid language and it becomes sublime and magnificent when describing the majesty and attributes of God.

The general design of the Quran is to unify the different religious practices prevailing in Arabia, , and to establish the worship and knowledge of one God which Mohamed declared to be his chief aim. He taught that whenever religion became neglected or corrupted God through his prophets, re-informs, and corrects mankind. He declared himself to be the last of such prophets. He admonished his people to listen to him,a otherwise God would inflict punishment upon those who reject and decry His messengers.

The Sunna, the second foundation of Islam is held next in importance to the Quran. The term signifies usage, habit, tradition of the Prophet. It designates the modes of action, the sayings and declarations under different circumstances of the life of Mohamed. It is also called Hadith, that is, narrative, or the story and record of the doings and sayings of the Prophet. The science of traditions is considered the noblest and most excellent. Traditions have been divided into various classes according to the degree of authenticity they possess.

The third source book of Islam is Ijma, that is the unanimous agreement of the Muslim nation, or rather of the Mujtahidin or the great doctors of the nation.

The fourth source is the Qias, by which is meant the reasoning by analogy of the. learned doctors of Islam, with regard to certain doubtful questions of doctrine or practice.

The foundation upon which Mohamed built his religion is, that from the beginning to the end of the world there has been, and there will be one belief; acknowledging one God and obeying such messengers as He would, from time to time, send to manifest His Will to mankind. There are two general divisions under which the various doctrines and practices of Islam can be treated. The first is theoretical which deals with creeds, articles of faith, called the. roots of religion. This part is called Iman . Every true Muslim must necessarily believe in these articles of Faith. They are comprised in the formula of the Creed: "There is no God but God, and Mohamed is the apostle of God." The following are the articles of Faith referred to: (1) Belief in God, (2) Belief in His Angels, (3) Belief in His scriptures, (4) Belief in His Apostles, (5) Belief in the Resurrection and Day of Judgment, (6) Belief in God's absolute decree and predestination both of good and evil. The second or the practical part (called Din) consists of precepts and Commandments to be obeyed, rules and customs to be observed and duties to be fulfilled. It is generally called "Fiqh," that is, knowledge, and treats of the following subjects;' Prayer, Almsgiving, Fasting and Pilgrimage to Mecca. "Islam is," says Sharastani, "built up on five foundations: the confession that there is no God but God, and that Mohamed is His Apostle, the performing of Prayer, the giving of Alms, the keeping of the Fast, of Ramadan, and the performance of the Pilgrimage, where there is the possibility of doing so." Before we proceed to treat the several articles of Faith it is of importance to know what is the exact meaning of Faith and its relation to Islam. "The Orthodox doctrine of faith now generally accepted is that it is a belief of the heart or mind of the articles of Creed. The intellectual conviction of the truth is quite irrespective of the tongue or the performance of good works. A man therefore may be a believer, though he neither confesses his faith nor performs any good work; but on the contrary, be an evil doer. This is the faith of the lowest degree, but still it is true faith and he who possesses it, is a real believer. He, however, who combines belief with confession and good works has reached perfection in faith." The doctrine concerning God, "Allah", His Unity, His essence, His attributes and His works forms a very important part of Quran which speaks in many passages of His Absolute Sovereignty and Majesty. Mr. Peacock, in his book on the life of Mohamed, has, in a masterly way, summarised the conception of God according to Mohamed which runs thus:—

"Praise be to God, the creator and restorer of all things, who does whatever He pleases, who is the master of the glorious throne, and mighty force, and directs His sincere servants into right path, and straight way, who favoureth them, who have once borne testimony to the unity by preserving their confessions from darkness of doubt and hesitations; who directs them to follow His chosen apostle upon whom He has showered the blessing and peace of God; and to go after His most honourable companions to whom He has vouchsafed His assistance and direction which is revealed to them in His essence and operations by the excellencies of his attributes to the knowledge whereof no man attains but He that has been taught by hearing. To these as touching His essence he maketh known that He is one and hath no partner, singular, without anything like Him, uniform having no contrary, separate having no equal. He is ancient having no first, eternal having no beginning, remaining forever having no end, continuing to eternity without any termination. He persists without ceasing to be, remains without falling and never did cease, nor ever shall cease, nor is subject to any decree so as to be determined by any precise limits or set times but is the first and the last and is within and without. What God is not He is not a body endued with form nor a substance circumscribed with limits or determined by measure neither does He resemble bodies as they are capable of being measured or divined. Neither is He a substance, neither do substances exist in Him. Neither is He accident nor do accidents exist in Him. Neither is He like to anything that exists, neither is He anything like to Him; nor is He determinate in quality nor comprehended by bounds nor circumscribed by the difference of situations nor contained in the heavens. He sits upon His throne which He himself has described and in that same sense which He himself means; which sitting is far removed from any notion of contact or resting upon or local situation but both the Throne in itself and whatever is upon it are sustained by the goodness of His power and are subject to the grasp of His hands. But he is above the throne and above all things even to the utmost end but so above as at the same time not to be a whit nearer the Throne and Heaven, since he is exalted by infinite degrees above the Throne no less than He is exalted above the earth and at the same time is near to everything that has a being, nay, nearer to man than their veins and is witness to everything though his nearness is not like heaviness of bodies, neither is His essence like the essence of bodies. Neither doth He exist in anything neither doth anything exist in Him but He is too high to be contained in any place and too holy to be determined by time; for He was before time and place were created, and is after the same manner as He always was. He is also distinct from the creatures by His attributes;

neither is there anything beside Himself in His essence nor is His essence in any other besides Him. He is too holy to be subject to change or any local motion neither do any contingencies befall Him, but He abides through all generations with His glorious attributes from all danger of dissolution. As to the attributes of perfection, He wants no addition of His perfection as to His being He is known to exist by the apprehension of the understanding and He is seen as He is by an ocular intuition which will be vouchsafed by His mercy and grace to the Holy in the eternal mansion completing their joy by the vision of His glorious Presence.

"As to His power, it is living, powerful, mighty, omnipotent, not liable to any defect or impotence, neither slumbering nor sleeping nor being obnoxious to decay or death. To him belong the Kingdom and the power and the might. His is the dominion and the excellency and the creat›on and the command thereof. The Heavens are folded up in His right hand and all creatures are couched in His grasp. His excellency consists in creating and producing and His unity in communicating existence and a beginning of being. He created men and their works and measured out their maintenance and determined time. Nothing that is possible can escape His grasp nor can vicissitudes of things elude His power. The effects of His might are innumerable and the objects of his knowledge infinite. Nothing passes in the empire nor the Kingdom neither littie nor much more nor small, nor great, nor good nor evil, nor profitable nor hurtful, nor faith nor infidelity nor knowledge nor ignorance, nor increase nor decrease nor obedience nor rebellion but by His determinate and counsel and decree and His definite sentence and Will nor doth the wink of Him that seeth nor the subtlety of Him that thinketh exceed the bounds of His Will, but it is He who gave all things their beginning. He is the creator and restorer, the sole operator of what He pleases; there is no reversing His decree nor delaying what He has determined nor is there any refuge to man from his rebellion against Him but only His help and mercy, nor hath any man any power to perform and any duty towards Him but through His Will and Love."

It is quite evident from the above that Mohamed had a true notion of God and his attributes.

It is essential to believe in the existence of the angels and their purity and he would be reckoned as an infidel who denies their existence or in their high personalities. The angels are beings endowed with subtle bodies, created of light, who neither eat nor drink, in whom there is no distinction of sexes and who therefore do not propagate their race. Their chief characteristic is complete obedience to the Will of God, their dwelling place as a rule is heaven; their chief work consists in praising God day and night and in executing his orders. The four Archangels towards whom God is favourably disposed are Gabriel, called also the Angel of Revelation, who is God's messenger; Michael (friend and protector of the Jews), Asra'fil (whose duty is to sound the trumpet at the resurrection), Azrael the angel of death, (who separates man's soul from the body). There are two other guardian angels who observe and write down the actions of every man. Mohamed is reported to have said that every man has ten angels, who have charge over him by day and night from the very beginning of his life to the moment of his death. Angels intercede for man, but their intercession is of no avail unless God is pleased to accept their intercession; they also assist believers against infidels. The devil whom Mohamed named "EBLIS" was once one of those who are nearest to God's presence but fell for refusing to pay homage to Adam at the command of God. Besides the angels and devil the Muslims are taught by the Quran to believe in the existence of the intermediate order of creatures which they call "Jin," some of these are supposed to be good and some evil

As human reason is insufficient to guide man to the knowledge of Truth, God has from time to time sent his servants, the Prophets and Apostles in order to guide and teach men, and it is the duty of every Muslim to believe in such messengers of God. Besides, Muslims are taught by the Quran that God in diverse ages of the World Save revelations of His Will in writing to several prophets and it becomes incumbent upon every believer to believe in every word of it. According to Mohamed the sacred books are hundred and four in number, of which the last four the Pentateuch, the Psalms, the Gospel and the Quran, were given respectively to Moses, David, Jesus and Mohamed; the last being the seal of the prophets, these revelations close with the Quran and no more are to be expected. The next article of faith declared by the Quran is belief in a general resurrection and future judgment. Mohamed taught that though man's body will be consumed by the earth yet one part of it will remain uncorrupted till the last day. Muslims are taught that after death there is an intermediate state both of body and the soul. When a corpse is laid in the grave he is received by an angel who gives him notice of the two examiners named Munkir and Nakir, who will examine him concerning his faith as to the unity of God and the mission of Mohamed. If he answers rightly he is permitted to rest in peace, if not they will beat him till he roars in anguish. The angel of death separates the soul of the dead. He does this with great ease and gentleness towards the good and with violence towards the wicked. It enters a state which is called Berzakh or the interval between death and resurrection. The time of resurrection is a perfect secret to all but God, but the approach of that day may be known from certain signs which are to precede it. Resurrection will be general and will extend to all creatures. Everyone will be examined then, concerning his deeds and words done and uttered during his lifetime. There will be a balance in which all things will be weighed, after which mutual retaliation will follow, every creature taking vengeance on another. The manner of giving satisfaction will be by taking away a part of the good works of those who offered injury. After this if there is a balance of good deeds God will double it and allow him to enter Paradise, but if there remains evil only, God will order an equal weight of sin and he will be punished. After the closure of the trial those admitted to Paradise will turn to the right and those destined to Hell-fire will turn to the left, but both shall have to pass over a bridge called

"AL SIRAT" over which the good will pass, and the wicked will fall. The Magians also believe that mankind will have to pass over a bridge called "Chinwad." As to the punishment of the wicked, Hell is divided into seven parts, the various torments of hell which the wicked will have to suffer have been described in the Quran. The Infidels will be liable to eternal damnation, whereas the believers in Mohamed's faith will be delivered, on their expiating their sins.

The righteous, having safely passed the bridge, will at last enter Paradise and in its heavenly garden will enjoy all kinds of delights, bodily as well as spiritual. The Quran gives a detailed description of these delights. The Paradise is a shady place full of sweet perfumes and no one there suffers from fatigue. In it there arc delicious fruits. The Paradise is situated above the seventh heaven, next under the throne of God. The Quran gives a graphic description of Paradise. There will be a remarkable tree called Tuba. It is fabled that it stands in the palace of Mohamed, but its branches will spread over the believers. Quran often speaks of rivers of Paradise as a chief ornament, some flowing with water, some with milk and some with milk and honey, all springing from the root of Tuba tree. To the godly are promised magnificent garments of finest silk and brocade, with silver and gold bracelets on their arms, and crowns of inlaid jewels and shining pearls on their heads. They "will rest on beds of silk. They will enjoy a perpetual youth. Their ears will be entertained with divine music. The happiness of the blessed will consist not solely of corporal enjoyments but includes spiritual enjoyments also. The highest spiritual delight the blessed will enjoy consists in seeing the face of God. The possibility and reality of God being seen by his faithful servants in Paradise is an article of faith which must be believed by every Muslim, as it is supported by the Quran, Traditions and the Ijma.

The important point of Faith which the Muslims are taught by the Quran is the belief in God's absolute decree, and predestination of both good and evil and that God has from eternity predetermined and decreed everything good, as well as bad, belief and unbelief, and that everything that has been or will be depends entirely on His fore-knowledge and sovereign Will. The Prophet has said: "There is not one amongst you whose place is not written by God whether in fire or in Paradise." Thereupon the Companions of Mohamed said "O, Prophet, since God has appointed our places, may we confide in this and abandon our religious and moral duties?" He said "No; because the righteous will do good works and the wicked will do bad works." Though good and evil are predetermined and decreed by God, yet man may not use this doctrine as an encouragement to commit sin. Again the doctrine of predestination must not prevent man from asking God in prayer and supplication what he is in need of, for his praying and obtaining in answer to prayer what he is in need are also predetermined.

A great importance is attached to prayer. This important duty is frequently enjoined in the Quran: "Glorify God when it is evening and morning and to him be praise in heavens and the earth and at afternoon and at noon tide." Under this practice purifications are necessary. There are two degrees of purifications. "WAZU" that is ordinary ablutions are essential before prayer. In extraordinary cases total immersion in water is required. Mohamed is said to have declared that the practice of religion is founded on cleanliness, which is one half of faith and the key of Prayer. Four degrees of purification are recognised: firstly cleaning of body from all pollution, dirt and filth; secondly cleaning of all the parts of body from all wickedness and unjust actions: thirdly purifying the heart from blamable inclinations and from all vices; and fourthlv purging of all affections from everything except God. Other acts of cleanliness which are recognised are combing of hair, cutting of beard, paring nails, removing the hair from armpits, and circumcision.

Mohamed obliged his followers to pray five times in a day. Mohamed used to savs: "Five prayers has God prescribed for his servants. God has promised that he will cause him who performs them to enter Paradise. There are set intervals of Prayers, (a) before sunrise, (b) when noon is past, (c) in the afternoon before sunset (d) in the evening after sunset, (e) after the close of the day. At the time of the prayer the face must be turned towards the West, that is towards Mecca. There must be an inward submission of head and heart. They must put aside their costly apparels. Certain postures are prescribed during prayers. The total of these various postures with their respective prayers and praises constitutes what is called a Rak'a. Each full prayer-service consists of a number of such Rak'as. The worshipper, having completed the first Rak'a, now performs the second in the same manner as the first beginning however with the Fatiha. At the end of every two Rak'as as also after the last one, instead of rising from his last kneeling, half sitting posture, he remains sitting on his left foot and placing his hands above his knees he says, "Praise be to God and prayers and good works. Peace be on thee O, Prophet with the Mercy of God and His blessings." This is called the salutation. Then raising the first finger of the right hand he recites the confession: "I testify that there is no god but God and I testify that Mohamed is the apostle of God." At the end of all the Rak'as he asks for blessings on Mohamed and his descendants saying: "O God, have mercy on Mohamed and his descendants, Thou art to be praised, and Thou art great. O, God. bless Mohamed and his descendants as Thou didst have mercy on Abraham and his descendants; Thou art to be praised and Thou art great." This is called the Blessings. Then Salutation is said, "Peace be on you and Mercy of God." At the close of the prayer, the worshipper raises his hand as high as his chest with the palms towards heaven and offers up a supplication and when this is done he draws his hands over his face as if to convey the blessing received from above to every part of the body. Women are not admitted in public for prayer; they must perform the devotions at home; or if they visit a mosque they must do it when men are not there.

Giving of alms is another fundamental ground of religious practice next in importance to prayer "Perform the Prayer and give the alms." They are of two sorts.

legal and voluntary. The legal cannot be dispensed with, but voluntary alms depend upon the will of the giver. They are taught the virtue of liberality and to free the soul from avarice and greed. "Verily greed is poverty and having no hope is riches; a man when he has nothing to hope for is independent.' Again Mohamed is believed to have said: "Two defects cannot be found together in a Believer. Avarice and evil-disposition." Giving of alms is strongly recommended in Quran, jointly with prayers. The Quran says: "Woe unto those who pray, who are unmindful of their prayers, who make a show and refuse help to the needy." "The upper hand is better than the lower hand; the upper hand bestows, the lower begs."

Circumcision, though strictly not necessary, yet is held by the Muslims to be an ancient divine direction confirmed by Islam. This rite was practised by the Arabs ages before Mohamed.

The third necessity of religious practice is fasting. It has been called the gate of religion. Mohamed used to say, "The odour of the mouth of him who fasts is more acceptable to God than the odour of musk." There are three degrees of fasting, (a) Restraining the belly and other parts of body from satisfying their craving and lusts, (b) Restraining the eyes, ears, tongue, hands, feet and other members of the body from sin, and highest of all, (c) Fasting of heart from worldly cares and restraining the thoughts from every thing besides God.

There is an express command in the Quran to fast in the month of Ramadan, from the point when the new moon first appears till the appearance of the next moon; during this time they must abstain from eating, drinking, and lying with women from day-break till sunset. After sunset they are permitted to refresh themselves and to eat and drink and to enjoy the company of their wives till day-break. The reason why the month of Ramadan has been chosen is that in that month the Quran was sent down from Heaven.

The pilgrimage to Mecca is another fundamental religious practice. The Muslim before setting out on his pilgrimage, must (1) Repent of his sins, restore what has been unjustly taken, pay his debts, pay the allowances up to his return, return pledges, provide the means of journey, give alms, (2) Choose as suitable companion a pious and charitable man, (3) Before starting say a prayer of two Rak'as and read the suitable verses of the Quran, (4) On arrival at the door of his house say "In the name of God, in Him I trust", (5) On mounting theanimal say "In the name of God0....", (6) Perform thegreater part of his journey at night and not to dismount till the day has become hot, (7) Not linger behind the Caravan, (8) On ascending to say "God is great", on descending "Praise be to God." The "Miqat" are the starting places, where the pilgrims collect. Mohamed appointed five such places of meeting. When the pilgrim has reached his respective Oliquat he has to observe five customs. He bathes and cleans his whole body. He divests himself of his clothes and assumes the pilgrim's sacred robe. He must not shave any part of the body. He faces Mecca and makes the Niyya, that is proposes to himself to perform the pilgrimage. He recites, "Here I am for thy service, O God, I am ready." He repeats this every time he ascends a hill or descends into a valley. He has to observe certain customs from the entrance into Mecca to the going round the Ka'ba.

All sorts of strong and inebriating drinks, including wine, are forbidden by express precept at more than one place in the Quran. The reason for this prohibition is that drink gives rise to quarrels and disturbance, neglect and indecencies. Gaming is also prohibited on the same grounds. The Quran prohibits the drinking of blood, eating swine's flesh, the flesh of a being that has died of itself, or is slain in honour of an idol or is strangled or killed by a blow or a fall.

Usury is prohibited in no uncertain terms and the inhuman and superstitious customs (e.g. of sacrificing their children to the idols) followed by the pagan Arabs were abrogated by Mohamed.

Divorce is well known in Mohamedan Law. Adultery in women is severely punishable. Mohamed has laid down rules prohibiting marriage within certain degrees and has also laid down rules concerning inheritances. Theft and injuries to others are governed by the rule of retaliation.

Amongst the ancient Arabs there was a custom to hold four months in a year as sacred during which they held it unlawful to wage war and to incur hostility. The months which were held to be sacred were Al Moharram, Rajab Dhv'lkaada and Dhul'hajja, the first, the seventh, the eleventh, and the twelth. Dhul'hajja is a month in which they perform pilgrimage to Mecca. The observances of these months seemed so reasonable to Mohamed that it met with his approbation and the same is accordingly confirmed and enforced by several passages in the Quran which forbids war to be waged during these months. The sixth day of the week has been fixed for the worship of God.

In brief, Islam establishes a brotherhood of man. A Muslim must treat every other as a brother with friendliness and generosity. It is a religion which gives high prominence to service. The good of humanity and service of man is the service of God. It is a religion of peace, tranquillity and resignation to the Will of God. A Muslim is enjoined to do selfless service of suffering humanity. There is no asceticism in Islam. What is demanded of a man is a contrite heart, sincere repentance and sincere effort to avoid evil and practise truth. It is said : "He needs no other rosary whose thread of life is strong with beads of love, service, charity and renunciation."

CONFUCIANISM

THERE are three religions practised in China viz Confucianism, Taoism and Buddhism. Confucianism is, not a religion in the customary sense. It is not a monastic or priestly order. Confucius did not give a new religion, a new ethical code to the world, but he gave to the world a forceful restatement of the fundamental principles of human morality and ethics. In Confucius we have one of the world's greatest figures—a fountain of ethics and moral philosophy, an inspirer of the highest type, yet very human. Voltaire, in his dictionary of Philosophy, said of him: "By what fatality, shameful may be for the Western peoples, is it necessary to go to the far orient to find a wise man, who is simple, unostentatious, free from imposture, who taught men to live happily six hundred years ago before our vulgar era, at a time when the whole of the North was ignorant of the usage of the letters and when the Greeks were barely beginning to distinguish themselves by wisdom? This wise man is Confucius who, being a legislator, never wanted to deceive men. What more beautiful conduct has ever been given man ever since the world began? Let us admit that there has been no legislator more useful to the human race." To the Chinese, Confucius is the "Uncrowned King of China."

K'ung-fu-tze-Kung (i.e., statesman philosopher Kung) was born at Ch'ufu in the then kingdom of Lu and the present province of Shantung in the vear 551 B.C. The first European scholars who visited China found it hard to pronounce the name; so they turned it into Latin and called him Confucius. His father's name was Shu-Liang-Ho, who held an honourable position. Confucius was three years old when his father died at the age of seventy. Confucius grew up under the loving guidance and care his mother. He studied history, poetrv. philosophy and music. He had a great love for music. At the age of seventeen he completed his education. His first employment was in granary accounts, which he performed wisely and industriously. He employed his spare time in studying and giving instruction to the boys who played around the pasturage. Thus a circle of disciples was formed, who afterwards followed him devotedly throughout his lifetime. He married at the age of nineteen, and divorced his wife three years after marriage. He had one son and two daughters. At the age of twenty-two he began his career as a teacher, using his home as a place for imparting education. He taught history, poetry and the rules of decorum. He sharpened the wits of his students by exposing their fallacies and urged them to cultivate alertness of mind. When a man does not say, "What shall I think of this? What shall I think of this? I can indeed do nothing with him." He required of his students eagerness and earnestness. He had, at first, few pupils but soon the news spread about his kindly heart and a keen intellect and students flocked to him in great numbers. His disciples inform us that "there were four things from which the Master was entirely free. He had no foregone conclusions, no arbitrary pre-determination, no obstinacy and no egoism." He called himself "a transmitter and not a maker." He held such high offices as Minister of Works, Minister of Justice, in his native State. In 501 B.C., that is in his fiftieth year, he was appointed Governor. In the book, Analects, a collection of his sayings, he speaks of himself at different stages of his life. "At fifteen my mind was bent on learning, at thirty I stood firm, at forty I was free from doubt or delusion. At fifty I understood the will of God, I knew the decrees of Heaven; at sixty my ears were receptive of the truth; at seventy I could follow the promptings of my heart without transgressing the boundaries of right." His active life can be summarized as follows :—

After a stay in his youth in Lu, which was interrupted by a journey to the Imperial capital and by a stay in Ch'l, there followed a short but a brilliant period of official activity in his native State. He attained important success in foreign affairs, and he was also successful in enforcing the authority of the Central power upon the rebellious aristocracy. Likewise he succeeded in restoring order and morality throughout public life, so that the State of Lu, which had fallen into complete anarchy, took an upward curve. These practical successes of Confucius do not merely establish that he was a very learned man, but in them one feels that he possessed in the highest degree the technique for regulating the conduct of humanity. In Chuang Tze there occurs an indication of a great change which took place in him in his sixtieth year. There are various indications that he finally decided to relinquish his long and vain attempts to create order by the use of rites and rules of antiquity; and when he returned to a quiet private life in his native state of Lu, we see in him a calm philosopher of great superiority who devoted himself to the study of the teachings of the Book of Changes and who created for the world in his Spring and Autumn Annals, his programme for government—what might be called the foundation plan of Chinese culture. He died at the age of seventy-two. One early morning he was heard singing a mournful song.

"The great mountain must crumble
The strong beam must break
And the wise man wither away like a plant."

His own view of his life and achievement was that of a disappointed man. On one occasion he cried out "Alas, there is no one who knows me." He was much revered and honoured by his people and by the grandees. The activity of Confucius was that of handling down tradition. He has himself said that he was the transmitter and not the Creator. This does not show that he had no creative power or originality. He was indeed a great genius. He believed that regulations of conduct handed down from generation to generation were no empty words but were life-moulds by which people should regulate their conduct. Confucius had an aim of creating such life -moulds for his people. He had no literary ambitions, he sought deeds, effects and re-creations and for this purpose he subjected himself to an intensive study.

He left behind him five classics. The first book which Confucius edited was the Book of Records. We have no knowledge of the sources which Confucius had. These records are not in the form of Chronicles but are rather documents dealing with all sorts of events and negotia tions within the government then in control. The Book of Records contains wise regulations of saintly rulers and lofty admonitions of faithful ministers. The spirit of the entire work is chiefly ethical. The principles propagated by Confucius glimmer throughout the book. The most important part of the Book of Records is the Great Plan in which is given a system for the regulation of human society.

The second is the Book of Odes. It is the best preserved work of Chinese literature. It contains 305 Compositions. The Book of Odes is divided into four parts: (a) Folk Songs, (b) The minor songs of Ya, (c) The major songs of Ya, (d) The Sung and Songs of Praise. It illustrates the nature of known life and exposes the principles of sound morality. The gist of all may be summed up in the phrase "Have no impure thoughts." He once said to his disciples "My children, why do you not study the Odes? They stimulate the mind. They teach observation. They warn against hatred. From them you learn, at home, to serve your father; abroad, to serve your prince; from them you can also learn the names of many birds, beasts and plants." The third is the Book of Changes. In the last years of his life Confucius occupied himself chiefly with the Book of Changes. It contains as great mass of Chinese wisdom. It deals with metaphysics. The fourth is the Soring and Autumn Annals. According to tradition Confucius wrote them in his extreme old age. It is said to be a royal work. The style is historical. He makes the annals of Lu the basis of his labour throughout. It has remained an incorruptible code of political morality through the centuries. The fifth is the Book of History which deals with the events and legends of the early religions of China. To these five books may be added the Discourses and Dialogues. These are not written by Confucius but they are the opinions and pronouncements of Confucius. After his death the torch of his teachings was handed on chiefly by his grandson and disciple, K'ung Chi whose famous essay is known as the "Doctrine of the Mean," this traces the ruling motives of human conduct to a psychological source, "While fully recognising the sincerity and the value of the efforts of the earlier disciples to keep alight what was to them the sacred flame of Confucianism, it must be admitted that the firm hold which these doctrines took upon the imagination of the Chinese people, and which has been maintained with extraordinary persistence throughout some twenty-three centuries past, would never have been brought about but for the genius and labours of Mencius, who now enjoys the title of second Inspired One, bestowed upon him in A.D. 1330." He was born a century after the death of Confucius and he devoted his life to the glorification of Confucianism.

To give an entire picture of the personality of Confucius is an impossibility; however, we may mention some of his distinguishing qualities. He was a scholar, a teacher, a perfect gentleman and a saint. He was economical in living, moderate in desire, exact in manner, refined in form, precise in speech, slow but sure in action, restful and free in mind, pure in heart, altruistic in aim, and ever sympathetic towards man. He was truthful even in detail. He always meant what he said and behaved as he meant. He was typical of the superior man whom he often described. He was methodical in habits, and he had the practice of doing things at the proper time and place. Legend has assigned to his personality forty-nine remarkable peculiarities. He loved authority and discipline, and had a great admiration for antiquity. He bore his greatness with modesty. He was kind, generous and humble. His humility appears from his own Words: "The things which weigh heavily upon my mind are these: Failure to improve in virtue, failure in discussion of what is learned, inability to work according to knowledge received as to what is right and just, inability also to reform what has been amiss." He used to call himself a transmitter and not a maker. He was ambitious of fame and honour, but would not stoop to make dishonourable sacrifices for their attainment. Once he said: "with a meal of coarse rice and with water to drink, and my bent arm for my pillow even thus I find happiness. Riches and honours without righteousness are to me as fleeting clouds." On several occasions he refused high appointments when he found that the appointer was unjust. He possessed a deep knowledge of his, country's history and literature and his ideal was to create a race of righteous rulers, who could protect the state and make people righteous. He was free from prepossessions, arbitrary determinations, obstinacy and egoism. He did not talk about spiritual beings, or extraordinary things, or feats of strength and disorders. He insisted on the cultivation of ethics, loyalty and truthfulness. In his teachings there were four things which he kept in view: scholarliness, conduct of life, honesty and faithfulness. He devoted himself to the study of things human and stressed the actual reality of life. One of his disciples asked, "O Venerable Master! how can I serve the Gods?" He replied, "You do not know how to serve man, yet how can you ask about serving Gods." He has said. "There are three kinds of friendships which are profitable and three which are detrimental. To make friends with the upright, with the trustworthy, with the experienced, is to gain benefit; to make friends with the subtly perverse, with the artfully pliant, with the subtle in speech is detrimental." Again we find him saying, "There are three kinds of pleasure which are profitable and three which are detrimental. To take pleasures in going regularly through the various branches of ceremonial, and Music, in speaking of other's goodness, in having many worthy wise friends, is profitable. To take pleasure in wild bold pleasure, in idling carelessly about, in the too jovial accompaniments of feasting is detrimental." Again we find him saying, "Three errors there be, into which they who wait upon their superiors may fall: (1) To speak before the opportunity comes to them to speak, which I call heedless haste, (2) Refraining from speaking when the opportunity has come, which I call concealment and (3) Speaking regardless of the mood he is in which I call blindness." Again he said: "Three things a superior should guard against, (1) Against the lust of the flesh in his earlier years while the vital powers are not fully developed and fixed, (2) Against the spirit of combativeness when he has come to the age of robust manhood and when the vital powers are matured and strong, (3) Against ambitiousness when old age has come on and the vital powers have become weak and decayed." From these sayings it is evident how much Confucius laid stress upon the actuality of life. He exhorts man to be clear in vision, quick in hearing, genial in expression, respectful in demeanour, true in word, serious in duty, inquiring in doubt, firmly self-controlled in anger, just and fair when the way to success opens out before him. Confucius was a great thinker. It has been said "If he put his head in the clouds, in thought, he never, in fact, took his feet off the ground, and his philosophy helped the average man to find a better adjustment to everyday life." If he was asked a question he never answered in doubtful phrases or in concealed expressions. He answered the queries and gave his decisions in a clear precise and commonsense way.

Confucius is usually regarded as a teacher of morals and it would be an error to class his doctrines as a religion. It is true that he laid great stress upon man's duty to his neighbour, thinking, perhaps, that, without doing so, a blameless life in the sight of God cannot be attained. But it is certain that he had a firm belief in a higher Power. Not only did he believe in the existence of this Deity but he was conscious that in his teachings he was expressing the will of God. In a case of danger Confucius said God implanted the Virtue that is in me, what can this man do to me?" Again in reply to a disciple who asked him what he meant by declaring that nobody knew him, Confucius said: "I do not murmur against God nor do I grumble against man....If my doctrines are to prevail it is so ordered of God; if they are to fail it is so ordered of God." It is fully evident that Confucius recognised the existence of a Supreme Being. Although he did not talk about spiritual beings he did not hesitate to use the name of the Deity in any suitable connection.

We have some interesting remarks of Confucius himself as regards the spiritual world. "How abundantly do spiritual beings make their presence manifest among us! We look for them, but do not see them, we listen to them but do not hear them; yet they enter into all things and there is nowhere where they are not. They cause all people in the world to fast and to put on their best clothes in order to take part in the sacrifices. Then they seem to pass in waves, now over the heads, now at the very sides of the worshippers. They seem to be above us, they seem to be with us. It is said in the Book of the Odes that the coming of the spirits is beyond human calculations, and much more beyond a feeling of aversion. The reason why the invisible are so manifest is that sincerity can never be concealed." From these passages, the Confucian doctrine is quite apparent. There might be something on the other side of life, but we do not know its exact nature and significance, which are too deep for human understanding to unravel, and therefore we mortals have only to understand the knowable phenomena and leave alone the unknowable. In the Confucian view, it is futile to go beyond the observable and intelligible laws of nature and morality. The transcendental has no practical bearing on our earthly life. He has said "How could we know death when life is not yet understood?" Sweeping aside the petty consideration of rites he presented to man a loftier idea of prayer in a pithy sentence "He who has offended against God has none to whom he can pray." The question of mourning rites received some consideration from him. He said, "Authority without mercy, ceremonial without reverence and mourning without sorrow....what have I to do with these?"

Confucius has asserted in several places that all men are divinely good and intuitively wise. In one of his Odes he sings "All men are good at birth. But not many remain so to the end." Confucius was entirely in sympathy with human weakness and did not put man's faith to too severe a test.

Confucius was devotedly attached to the improvement, well-being and welfare of society. The social ideal of

Confucius is harmony. "If everybody feels attached to his kith and kin and respects his superior there will be peace under Heaven." Society, he held, was made up of five relationships namely, husband and wife, of parent and child, elders and youngsters, of Ruler and subject, friend and friend. A country is well governed when relations between these five are duly recognised and promoted; and human conflicts can no longer arise if these perform their parts well. He exerted himself in giving moral training to his people, and he laid great emphasis on virtuous conduct. A virtuous man, according to Confucius, had three awes (1) Awe of Heaven's Decree (2) Awe of great men (3) Awe of saint's words. "Virtue is inquiring with earnestness and inwardly making application." It was the dream of Confucius that all mankind should be composed of Supermen. The ethical system of Confucius attracts us. His ethical sayings are simple, homely and practical. There is much clearness and commonsense in them. Confucius has said that the life of a moral man is an exemplification of the universal order, because he is a moral person who unceasingly cultivates his true self or moral being. The life of the vulgar person is a contradiction of the universal order, because he is a vulgar person who in his heart has no regard for, or fear of, the moral law. He, therefore, holds that the highest human attainment is to find the central clue to our moral being which unites us to the universal order. It is seldom that people are capable of it for long. He then proceeds to give the reason, why there is no real moral life. It is because the wise mistake the moral law for something higher than what it really is and the foolish do not know enough of what this moral law really is. People believe themselves to be wise, but in finding the central clue of the moral law and following the line of conduct in accordance with it they are not able to keep it for long. Confucius has remarked that "A man may be able to renounce the Possession of Kingdom and empire, be able to spurn the honours and emoluments of office, be able to trample upon bare weapons; with all these he shall not be able to find the central clue in his moral being." According to Confucius a'truly moral man is he who unconsciously lives a life in harmony with the universay moral order, and who lives unknown to the world and unnoticed by men. These are men of holy and divine natures. The moral law, says he, is to be found everywhere and yet it is a secret. A man with infinite morality in him is never satisfied, because the mind of the moral man can always conceive of something higher and higher. In discharge of the ordinary duties of life, and in exercise of care in ordinary conversation whenever there is a shortcoming, a moral man never fails to strive for self-improvement. There is thorough genuineness and there is absence of pretence in him. A moral man conforms himself to the circumstances of life. He does not find himself in any situation in which he is not the master of himself. In a high position he does not domineer over his subordinates, and in a subordinate position he does not court the favours of his superiors. He does not complain against God nor rail against men. He says that moral sense is the characteristic attribute of man. Man must feel natural affection for those related to him. The sense of justice is the recognition of what is right and proper. To honour those who are worthier than oneself is the highest expression of the sense of justice.

"However excellent a system of moral truths appealing to supernatural authority may be, it is not verifiable by experience; what is not verifiable by experience cannot command credence, and what cannot command credence, the people will never obey." Therefore every system of moral laws must be based upon man's own consciousness. It must be verified by common experience of men. In whomsoever such moral law is found, every act of his life becomes an example for generations, everything he does becomes a statute for generations, and every word he utters becomes a law for generations. It is only the man with the most perfect divine nature who is able to combine in himself, quickness of apprehension, intelligence, insight and understanding; qualities necessary for the exercise of command: magnanimity, generosity, benignity and gentleness; qualities necessary for the exercise of patience: originality, energy, strength of character and determination; qualities necessary for the exercise of endurance: dignity, noble seriousness, order and regularity; qualities necessary for the exercise of self-respect: grace, method, delicacy and lucidity. Thus all embracing and vast is the nature of such a man. The life of a moral man is plain, and yet not unattractive; it is simple and yet full of grace; it is easy and yet methodical.

"Truth" he says "is the law of God. Acquired truth is the law of man." He who intuitively apprehends truth is one who, without effort, hits what is right, and, without thinking, understands what he wants to know; whose life is easily and naturally in harmony with the moral law. Such a one is a man of divine nature. He who acquires truth is one who finds out what is good and holds fast to it. In order to acquire truth it is necessary to inquire into it, carefully to ponder over it, clearly to sift it and earnestly to carry it out. It is only he. in the world, who possesses absolute truth, who can get to the bottom of the law of his being. He who is able to get to the bottom of the law of his being will be able to get to the bottom of the law of being of other men. He who is able to get to the bottom of the law of being of men will be able to get to the bottom of the laws of physical nature and in turn will be able to influence the forces of creation of the universe and will thus be able to be one with the Powers of the Universe. Truth means the realisation of one's being and moral law means the law of our being. Truth is the beginning and end of existence. It is for this reason that the moral man values truth. Absolute Truth is indestructible, eternal, self-existent and infinite It manifests itself without being evident, it produces effects without action, it accomplishes its end without being conscious.

Confucius possessed a great reverence and love for the old. The golden age of China with its perfectly virtuous semidivine rulers threw a lasting spell on the imagination °f Confucius. He practised the manners of antiquity and he put himself in possession of the forces of the past. He was convinced that those forces are eternal which rule the future. Confucius stands at a turning point in

Chinese history, where the guidance of society passed from the theocratic ruler to the human philosopher.

Confucius taught the art of reasoning not through rules but by means of his sharp intellect, clarity and honesty of thought were the first lessons which he imparted to his disciples. He said the purpose of speech is to be understood. Thought clouded by insincerity and inaccuracy of speech seemed to him a national calamity. A prince who was not princely should cease to call himself a prince; a father who was not fatherly should cease to call himself a father; and a son who did not perform his filial obligations should cease to call himself a son. He said that what was necessary was to rectify the names. For Confucius, names are not mere abstractions but they signify something ideally co-ordinated with actuality. A name is evaluated according to the position which it occupies in his system as a designation. If one compares the ideal and then compares names with reality one can at once recognise whether the name fits or not. For Confucius it is a question of recognising the true names, not only to measure reality by them, but also to be able to reform reality. And how can reality be reformed? One should recognise the cause and then one would succeed in influencing events by giving an imperceptible direction which will lead to the wished-for goal of this development. This, for example, is the reason why Confucius opposes the method of regulating the State by means of laws and punishment. "If one guides by means of decrees, and regulates by means of punishments, the people evade the laws and have no conscience. If one guides through the force of personality and through morals, the people have conscience and attain good." Confucius avoided metaphysics and tried to divert the minds of his disciples from celestial and abstruse subjects. Questions concerning theology did not interest him. When he was asked what constituted wisdom he replied "To give one's self earnestly to the duties due to men, and, while respecting spiritual beings, to keep aloof from them, may be called wisdom. Wisdom, he said, frees one from doubts, morality frees from sufferings, and determination frees one from fear. He had a great passion for morality. When asked about the essence of morality, he said "It is by conquering oneself and by devoting oneself to the laws of beauty that one accomplishes morality. The whole world would turn to morality if it would; for one day, conquer itself and devote itself to the laws of beauty." The keynote and the soul of his philosophy is expressed in the famous paragraphs of the great learning. "The ancients who wished to illustrate the highest virtue throughout the Empire first ordered well their own states, wishing to order well their states, they first regulated their families; wishing to regulate their families, they first cultivated their own selves; wishing to cultivate their own selves, they first rectified their hearts; wishing to rectify their hearts they first sought to be sincere in their thoughts. Wishing to be sincere in their thoughts, they first extended to the utmost, their knowledge. Such extension of knowledge lay in the investigation of things.

"Things beings investigated, knowledge became complete. Their knowledge being complete, their thoughts were sincere. Their thoughts being sincere, their hearts were then rectified. Their hearts being rectified, their own selves were cultivated. Their own selves being cultivated, their families were regulated. Their families being regulated, their states were rightly governed. Their states being rightly governed, the whole empire was made tranquil and happy."

Confucius has given here a gradual process for self development, and the ways by which it flows into the common life to serve the state; these are the (a) Investigation of Phenomena, (b) Learning, (c) Sincerity, (d) Rectitude of Purpose, (e) Self-development, (f) Family Discipline, (g) Local Self Government, and (h) Universal Self-Government. This gives a complete guide to life. In this world of turmoil, the Constituent states are improperly governed, because no amount of legislation can be substituted for the natural social order provided by the family; the family is in disorder because men do not regulate themselves, for they fail to rectify their hearts, because their thinking is insincere. Confucius therefore exhorts men to seek impartial knowledge and their thinking will become sincere and their hearts will be cleansed of unbecoming desires, and when this is effected the world would be peaceful and happy. It is a counsel of perfection and one of the golden texts of philosophy. Confucius said that wisdom grows from the family, and that the foundation of society is a disciplined individual in an orderly family. Self Development is the substance of social development. When asked "What constitutes the superior man?" he replied, "The cultivation of himself with reverential care." In another place he has said, "'A Superior man lives in measure and moderation; the inferior man lives contrary to measure and moderation. Measure and moderation, that is the highest stage; but for a long time it has been rare to find people who are able to make them a reality of life. The Superior man of Confucius is composed of three virtues—intelligence, courage and goodwill. "The Superior man is anxious lest he should not get Truth, he is not anxious lest poverty should come upon him. He is catholic not partisan... He requires that in what he says there should be nothing inaccurate." He is not merely intelligent or scholarly but his character is in high eminence. The foundation of character is sincerity. "Sincerity is the way to Heaven. The attainment of sincerity is the way of men. He who possesses sincerity is he who, without an effort, hits what is right, and apprehends, without exercise of thought, he is the sage who naturally and easily embodies the right way. He who attains sincerity is he who chooses what is good and firmly holds it fast." He acts before he speaks and afterwards speaks according to his actions. "In archery we have something like the way of the Superior man; when the archer misses the centre of the target he turns round and seeks for the cause of his failure in himself. What the Superior man seeks is in himself and what the lower man seeks is in others. He is modest in his speech, but exceeds in his actions; he seldom speaks; when he does he is sure to hit the point. He is moderate in word and deed and in everything. The Superior man conforms with the path of the mean." The Superior man moves so as to make his movements in all generations a universal path; he behaves so as to make his conduct in all generation a universal law; he speaks so as to make his words in all generations a universal norm. When asked by a disciple for a rule of life, Confucius replied, "Do not unto others what you would not they should do unto you." Critics have made various attempts to minimize the value of this maxim for it is in negative form, but we find that this maxim is expressed at many places in a positive form. In the Analects it is stated "To be able to judge others by what is in ourselves may be called the art of virtue. In the highest path are four things which II have not attained—to serve my father as I would have my son serve me; my prince as I would require my minister to serve me; and my elder brother as I would wish my younger brother to serve me; and to act towards a friend as I would have him act towards me." On another occasion he said: "Overflow in love to all and cultivate the friendship of the good." "The good man loves all men; loves to speak of the good in others, is loyal in friendship; wishing enlargement for himself, seeks it for others. A Superior man helps the distressed but does not add to the wealth of the rich. All within the four seas are his brothers." Another disciple, having asked for an explanation of the Chinese term "Charity of heart" Confucius replied in positive words "Love one another." The Superior man's character is an overflowing sympathy towards all men. He is not angered by the excellences of other men; when he sees a man of low worth he turns inwards and examines himself. He pays no attention to slander or violent speech. He is courteous and affable to all but he does not gush forth indiscriminate praise. He treats his inferiors without contempt and superiors without seeking to court their favour. He is grave in deportment; sincere men will not take seriously one who is not serious with them; he is slow in words and earnest in conduct, he is not quick with his tongue or given to clever repartee, he is earnest because he has work to do and this is the secret of his unaffected dignity. He is courteous even to his familiars but maintains his reserve towards all, even his son. The Superior man always acts in a manner which corresponds to his position. He never finds himself in a situation in which he could not maintain his individuality. 'In high positions he makes no demands on those beneath him. In low position he has no expectation from those above him. He lives Simply and correctly and yields himself to the will of God. "The people of low standards" he said "travel upon dangerous path in an endeavour to obtain happiness." When he was asked "Who is a man," he replied, "He who dwells in the wide house of the world, and who stands in correct place in the world, who walks on the straight path in the world and if he succeeds makes common cause with the people and if he does not succeed goes his way home; whom neither riches nor honour can lure, whom neither poverty nor shame can affright, whom neither might nor threat can bend." Confucius sums up the qualities of the Superior man in those words.

"The superior man has his nine things which are subjects with him of thoughful consideration. In regard to the use of his eye he is anxious to see clearly.... In regard to his countenance he is anxious that it should be benign. In regard to his demeanour he is anxious that it would be respectful. In regard to his speech he is anxious that it should be sincere. In regard to his doing of business he is anxious that he should be reverently careful. In regard to what he doubts about, he is anxious to question others. When he is angry he thinks of the-difficulties his anger may involve him in. When he thinks gain to be got he thinks of righteousness." Such men, says Confucius, must be at the helm of the family and the state. Children should obey their parents, the wife her husband, and any deflection of this obedience would lead to chaos. Higher than obedience is the moral law. "When the Command is wrong a son should resist his father and a minister should resist the Prince."

When asked about government he said that the requisites of government are three: "That there should be sufficiency of food, sufficiency of military equipment and confidence of the people in their ruler." In the view of Confucius the first principle, of family or government is sincerity and character. When asked "What do you say to killing the unprincipled for the good of the principled?" Confucius replied "In carrying on your government why should you use killing at all? Let your desires be for what is good and the people will be good. The relation between superiors and inferiors is like that between the wind and the grass. The grass must bend when the wind blows across it....."He who exercises government by means of his virtue may be compared to the north polar star which keeps its place and all the stars turn towards it...." When he was asked "how to cause people to reverence their ruler, to be faithful to him and to urge themselves to virtue?" he replied "Let him rule over them with gravity, then they will reverence him. Let him be filial and kind to all, then they will be faithful to him. Let him advance the good and teach the incompetent, then they will eagerly seek to be virtuous." The first thing necessary for good government is a good example which must be followed by good appointment. "Employ the upright and put aside the crooked. In this way the crooked can be made upright." Confucius thereafter gives exhortations as to how to cleanse the state and direct the people to a higher level of civilisation. It is by avoiding foreign relations and making the state independent of supplies by reducing luxuries of courts and seeking a wide distribution of wealth, by decreasing punishment and increasing public instruction without distinction of classes, by instructing the people in music, which would regulate their hearts and mind and cultivate good manners, that a good Government can be established.

According to the conception of Confucius our economic, social, religious and political lives are one and inseparable. The social, economic, political and religious ideals are centred in ethics. The blood of life is love, and virtue is its backbone. Without virtue life cannot stand, and without love life is death. The development of life depends upon the development of virtue and the outflow of love, rising when virtue rises and expanding when love expands. From the ethics of Confucius we derive five constant ideas. Jen (humaneness) Yi (righteousness) Li (propriety) Chi (wisdom) and Zun (trustworthiness) and the five cardinal principles. The ruler must be respectful, and the ruled loyal; the father merciful and son filial; the husband chivalrous and the wife obedient; the elder brotherly, and the younger reverent, and friends must be trustworthy in mutuality.

We find the central concept of the doctrines of Confucius is found in the expression "Jen". There is no English equivalent to Jen in all its shades of meaning. We may call it humanitarianism or we may associate the word with the idea of mankind, kindness or morality, sincerity, etc. Humanitarianism is innate in human nature. It is a gift of nature which a man has received in order to live. It is the sacred possession of an individual and it is not difficult for him to seek. Humanitarianism expresses itself in love for all mankind. Its root is filial piety.It expresses itself in forms and ceremonials which are the expression of an inner attitude. All forms without the inner attitude are empty. Thus for Confucius, beautiful manners are the correct expression for beautiful inner impulses. "What does not correspond to the law of beauty, that you must not regard; what does not correspond to the law of beauty that you must not heed; What does not correspond to the ideal of beauty that you must not discuss, what does not correspond to the ideal of beauty, that you must not do." For him good manners and music are closely allied. "Manners consist in behaving to everyone as if receiving a guest, in causing no murmuring and in not treating others as you would not wish to be treated by them." Decorum rules conduct, music rules emotions. What he demanded was an unconditioned sincerity towards one's self. If one does not lie to one's self can one hope to be master of one's own mistakes and weaknesses which can be perceived in the mirror of others: "Fighting against one's sin and not fighting against the sins of others; are not secret faults corrected thereby? He insisted that a man must be conscientious and true in speech, reliable and careful in his action, and so capable of advancing. According to him what is necessary is not a theoretical knowledge for its own sake but a practical exercise in and from communion with other men. "Virtue is not cultivated; that knowledge is not made clear if people hear of duty and do not practise it, if people have evil in themselves and do nothing to improve: Those are things which make me sad." The presupposition of learning is constant practice and one thus arrives at correct inner feelings. The man who acquires such inner feelings will desist from doing that to others which he •does not wish for himself. This contact with the universally human element at the bottom of one's soul and the corresponding action, is the one connecting thread in his teachings. Confucius desired to educate dominant personalities, who develop within themselves the force of their individuality, through which they can influence others. For only that which is entirely true in one's life has the power to change others. Mere words and external means accomplish only external submission, but do not attain any real success. For him human society is not a mechanism but a living organism in which an active effectiveness of forces is possible. The nucleus is the family, within which natural feelings of affection need only to be regulated and properly directed. Beyond this is the state, in which what is love in family becomes duty. The next step is mankind. It is the humanity within each individual which, is as much a reality as mankind. "Whoever mistreats himself cannot be advised. Whoever throws himself away cannot be helped. To disregard order and justice in one's word is what is meant by mistreating oneself; to say "I cannot persist in goodness and follow duty" is what is meant by throwing oneself away. Kindness is tranquil habitation of mankind. Duty is the true path of mankind. Whosoever allows this tranquil habitation to stand empty instead of dwelling in it, whoever leaves this true path instead of walking upon it his case is evil."

TAOISM

FROM the early period of Chinese history there prevailed a condition of civilisation which had reached a high stage, and which was different from other civilisations. The progress of civilisation and of religion is simultaneous and we find that the early religion of the Chinese had long passed out of the phases of super" stition. It is generally admitted that the early beliefs of the Chinese were spiritual in their nature. Throughout their classical writings traces are to be found of the recognition of an ever ruling first cause known under different names such as "Heaven" or the "Almighty Ruler" or the Way. We are told in Tao-Teh-King that Tao, as Teh ruled and the World was in a heavenly state. It does not inform us how long the period lasted, but Lao-Tze says that it lasted till Tao ceased to be observed. It has been called the age of Perfect Virtue or the age of Teh and is described as follows:— "In that age, they attached no value to knowledge and did not employ men of action. Superiors were no more than the higher branches of a tree and the people lived freely in the open. They were upright and correct, without knowing that to be so was to be righteousness; they,loved one another, without knowing that to be real goodness; they were honest, without knowing that to be loyalty; they fulfilled their engagements, without knowing that to do so was to act in good faith; in their daily life they employed the services of one another, without thinking that they were conferring or receiving gifts. Because they lived in that way we cannot find any trace of their actions and no record of their affairs, and that is all in their favour and to their glory." Such was the age which is made the basis of the teachings in Taoism by its first exponent Lao-Tze.

Lao-Tze, the greatest of the pre-Confucian philosophers, was born in 604 B.C. in the village Chu-Jhren. Lao-Tze means the Old Master. His real name was Li, that is to say plum. This name was given to him as he was born under a plum-tree. It is believed that the hair on his head was white when he was born. He was endowed with more than ordinary intelligence. Chinese historians inform us how Lao-Tze, disgusted with the intrigues of the politicians and with corruption of the time, and tired of his work as a keeper of the secret archives in the Royal Court of Chore, determined to leave China to find a peaceful and secluded abode in a distant countryside. On reaching the frontier the warden said to him: "So you are going into retirement. I beg you to write a book for me." Thereupon Lao-Tze wrote a book in two parts on Tao and Teh running into over five thousand words. He then went away and no one knew where he died. Such was the origin of Tao-Teh-King which contained the teachings of Lao-Tze. The book is a guide to the conduct of life. It is not dry philosophy or metaphysics. It is not remote from our daily dealings. Tao-Teh-King is one of the marvels of ancient wisdom. It is like a mountain giving birth to three rivers two of which are Tao and Teh (which are the living forces), and the third the King (which is the Book that contains them). The chief characteristic of. the book is that it can be read like any other book on morals which contains all that is high, noble and worth aspiring.

It has been asserted by some scholars that the teachings of Lao-Tze have been inspired by the writings of the past to which he had access. Dr. Legge says: "Prolonged study and research have brought me to the conclusion that there was Taoism earlier than his and that before he wrote Tao-tze-King, the principles taught in it, had been promulgated, and the ordering of the human conduct and government flowing from them, inculcated." There may have been Taoism before Lao-Tze but it does not warrant us to allege that he stole the ideas of the past. Such ideas as of Tao and Teh always exist, they are a part of the constitution of the universe. They have been discovered time and again and each time revealed in a different way to suit the civilization of the times. Lao-Tze discovered them for his people and handed over to them in a new and fresh form. His thoughts were chiefly concentrated on the nature and attributes of the First Cause, known and worshipped in primitive times under the name Tao. This single word forms the key-note, not only of a portion but to the whole of Lao-Tze's thoughts. Lao-Tze's philosophy centres on the two words Tao and Teh (Way and Virtue).

Of the personality of Lao-Tze we have very little information. He is frequently represented as a bald-headed, long-bearded old man riding on an ox, whilst Confucius is often depicted seated in a waggon to which an ox is harnessed. Only scanty knowledge of his temperament can be obtained through the scanty data afforded by his behaviour to Confucius in their only interview, which would lead to a supposition that he was irascible and impatient. Lao-Tze was 53 years older than Confucius. It is said that when Confucius returned to his pupils from his visit to this dying sage, he informed them "I know how birds fly, fishes swim and animals run. But the runner may be snared, the swimmer hooked and the flyer shot by an arrow. But there is the dragon. I cannot tell how he mounts on the winds through the clouds and rises to heaven. Today Hi have met Lao-Tze and can compare him only to a dragon." Like Confucius he was actuated by the highest and purest motives. Although they both accepted in varying degree the great overruling First Cause and were in perfect agreement as to the original perfection of man, they differed widely in their modes of action. Confucius sought to regenerate society by the action of Great Rulers, whose conduct was to be modelled on that of the great examples of the past who, he considered to have illustrated, in their persons, all the virtues it was possible for a man to possess, and he gave a secondary consideration to the Tao, the Great Way, which in the eyes of Lao-Tze was the soul of all things. Lao-Tze was not satisfied with the limited purview of the past, nor could he find the perfection he was seeking for, till he reached the primitive people who were endowed with the knowledge of the Great First Cause. "The Great Universal Mother." Society was then, pure and simple, and free from those defects which became greater with the growth of time until they culminated in a general condition of depravity such as he saw in his own time. According to him society was originally pure because the people knew the Tao. Nature made men and life simple and peaceful and the - world was happy, but when men attained knowledge the complications of life began and life was flooded with misery. He said: "All things in nature work silently, they come into being, and possess nothing. They fulfil their function and make no claim. All things alike do their work and then we see them subside. When they have reached their bloom each returns to its origin. Returning to origin means rest or fulfilment of destiny." This reversion to the eternal law of following nature, or as the Chinese would express it "get hold of Tao" is the sum and substance, of the teachings of Taoism. From the plain facts of Nature Lao-tze concluded that behind the manifold working of nature there exists an Ultimate reality which is incomprehensible, but which manifests itself in laws of unfailing regularity. To this Essential Principle, this power underlying all phenomena of Nature he gave the name "Tao".

According to Tao-Teh-King the nature of Tao and Teh baffles investigation but it says that if we use Tao and Teh we shall know them. The question, "What is Tao?" has been answered by an eminent Taoist, Huai-Nan-Tzu:

"(1) It is that which supports heavens, and covers the earth, it has no boundaries, no limits, its heights cannot be measured, nor its depths fathomed; it enfolds the entire universe in its embrace, and conifers visibility upon that which of itself is formless.

(2) It is so tenuous and subtle that it pervades everything just as water pervades mine. It is by Tao that mountains are high, and abysses deep; that beasts walk and birds fly, that the sun and moon are bright, and the stars revolve in their courses.

(3) When the spring winds blow, the sweet rains fall and all things live and grow, the feathered ones brood and hatch, the furry ones breed and bear; plants and trees put forth all their glorious exuberance of foliage, birds lay eggs and animals produce their young.

(4) No action is visible outwardly, and yet the work is completed, shadowy and indistinct, it has no form. Indistinct and shadowy, its resources have no end. Hidden and obscure, it reinforces all things out of formlessness. Penetrating and permeating everything, it never acts in vain."

Tao then is nature. If we analyze the above description we see that the ideas of substance, immanent power, active energy and incomprehensibility are associated with it. Tao existed as a perfect but incomprehensible Being, before heaven and earth were; is immaterial and immeasurable, invisible and inaudible; is mysterious, yet manifest without shape or form; is supersensuous and hidden from our eyes; is incapable of being named or defined and the book says: "One needs not peep through his window to see Tao, Tao is not there. The further one goes away from himself the less he knows." Tao is in ourselves first. This is unmanifested Tao. But Tao is also manifested. "Tao is the external foundation of all things, is universal progenitor of all beings and only capable of being named by means of the works but he who would gain a knowledge of Tao's nature and attributes must set himself free from all earthly desires. Unless he can do that, he shall not be able to penetrate the material veil which interposes between him and Tao. Tao is only revealed to those who are free from desires. He who regulates his actions by Tao, will become one with Tao. Tao is the source from which all things come into existence and to which all things return, and Tao is the means through whom this takes place. Tao being eternal and absolutely free has no wants or desires, is eternally at rest but never idle, does not grow old, is omnipresent, immutable and self-determined, .loves all things and does not act as a ruler. Because Tao creates, preserves, nourishes and protects all things, Tao is glorified for this beneficence and held in high honour." Tao is the foundation of highest morality, it makes perfect, gives peace and is universal refuge. Lao-Tze's famous disciple Kwang-zse supplements the above definition—"Come I will tell you about the perfect Tao. Its essence is surrounded with deepest obscurity, its highest reach is its darkness and silence. There is nothing to be seen, nothing to be heard. When it holds the spirit in its arms in stillness, then the bodily form will of itself become correct. You must be still, you must be pure; not subjecting your body to toil, not agitating your vital forces, then you may live long. When your eyes see nothing, your ears hear nothing, and your mind knows nothing, your spirit will keep your body and the body will live long; watch over that which is within you, shut up the avenues that connect you with that which is external; much knowledge is pernicious.... Watch over and keep your body, and all things will of themselves give it vigour. I maintain the unity." Here Tao gives immortality and an endless life. The individual has to enter in "darkness and silence" that is to go beyond the limitations of time and space. The state of the individual must pass beyond the sense perceptions. The individual must be pure, that is to say, must be simple, sincere and still. Stillness cannot be attained without purity. Following this the individual would be awakened to the spiritual life and will proceed along the Path to the summit of the great light. Lao-Tze has said that an individual who is good at taking care of his life may travel over the country without meeting rhinoceros or a tiger, and would enter an armed force without fearing its steel. "The rhinoceros would find in him no place to insert his horn, the tiger would find no place to fix his claw, the weapon would find no place to receive its blade." It is, because he goes beyond the reach of death. When one has thus become immortal, evil will have no power over him.

We now come to Teh. Teh is the realisation of Tao. Teh can be summarized in the terms of life, love, light and will. Lao-Tze defines Teh as self-realisation or that which we can do and must do in this present moment in order to be manifestation of Tao. The meaning of Teh can be found in Goethe.'s phrase, "To live determinedly in the whole, in the good and in the beautiful." According to Tao-Teh-King the relationship of Tao and Teh is that if Tao perishes then Teh will also perish. Teh is the manifestation of Tao, and Tao cannot be attained except through the instrumentality of Teh. Teh is multiform but Tao is one. Tao has been said to be Lord of Teh. These two ideas of manifestation and multiformity explain the great diversity of names and descriptions of Teh. Teh has been given two aspects in express language. The one is "eternally feminine" and the other is of "Mother." Teh is the mother power considered morally out of which springs our whole mental, moral, and spiritual life. It has been described as follows:—"The Valley-God never dies; I call it the Mother of the Abyss and She is the root of Heaven-Earth (or all things). She endures for ever and for ever she produces." It must be considered that these signs and forms of Tao-Teh-King bear a transcendental and sublime significance. The Valley-God means nothing else than Teh or Virtue. Teh is presented to us as a power that makes for righteousness a power that has its being in all our modes of existence. A power and a purpose, a will and a way, name it as we may, it exists as a fact and cannot be denied. Teh enters into all human actions. Such a principle as Teh is peculiar to humanity. Action modified by intelligent use of experience, and those actions which are accumulated results of mankind's past experiences is in Chinese called Teh. All feel the motions of Teh. The Tao-Teh-King declares "To produce and not to possess, to act and not to expect, to enlarge and not to control that is Teh." By whatever name it may be called, e.g. God, Reason, Nature, Highest life or it be called Right Justice. Love, Reciprocity of life. Teh manifests itself in human consciousness. Teh is a force, a vital energy with an individual's constitution. This is the universal aspect of Teh.

We shall now deal Teh as a sum total of practical virtue or Wu-Wei as it is called in the Tao-Teh-King. Wu-Wei represents the wisdom of all ages on how to begin to travel on the Path, and how to continue on the Path, and how to be identified with the Path. In Wu-Wei we have the conception of non-action and non-assertion. Wu-Wei defined as a principle for conduct of life means non-exertion, non-interference, non-acting masterly inactivity. That is we must discard all thoughts of helping nature in her work. It is laid down in LXII "Act non-action. Be occupied with non-occupation. Taste the tasteless. Find your great in what is little and your many in few." The Taoist demand is that the people be left to develop their own resources by acting in conformity with nature. Wu-Wei is not a negative force but a most positive one; one of which it is said that though empty it never collapses and the more it is exercised the more it brings forth. Emptiness is called "the abyss Mother" which is the "root of Heaven and Earth" because the sage employs emptiness as a working principle and as he "abandons himself, he is preserved. It is taught "Thirty spokes unite in one nave and by that part which is non-existent (that is the hole in the centre of the nave) it is useful for a carriage wheel. Clay is moulded into vessels and by their hollowness, they are useful as vessels. Roofs and floors, doors and windows are arranged in such a way, that they make a house by the hollowness they produce." We must be such spaces or such emptiness or ought to empty ourselves.

Wu-Wei or non-action is something positive as will appear from the following quotations: "The non-existent enters into all things without any crevice and by non-action there is nothing that may not be done" and "there is no sin which is greater than giving rein to desire and therefore it is advised "shut the lips and close the pertals of eyes and ears and as long as you live you will have no trouble; but open your lips and meddle with things and as long as you live, you will not get out of trouble." Non-action is suitable for a practical world and makes men wise, who can be in the world and rule it and yet not be of it nor lost in it. The Taoist by Wu-Wei becomes a "sage among the unwise, the physician among the sick and a teacher to those who are wise." The place of man's value is not in what he does but is in what he is. The principle of Wu-Wei is that we shall never come to a true reorganisation of society unless we re-adopt as nature enforces it and as Tao-Teh-King teaches that nature everywhere calls for submission. Wu-

Wei does not ask us to ruin ourselves, by becoming oblivious to our purpose and aim in life. It teaches us to still the senses and the fuming desires which act as impediments to the attainment of truth, lt also teaches us to abandon the intellectual notions. Our senses and our intellectual powers are for use and not abuse. "Silence, solitude and lowliness are the soil, the sun, the air in which spiritual life grows. This is Wu-Wei. This is the manifestation of the power and wisdom that is within.

Taoism teaches to "avoid activity and dispense with the use of means." This is called nameless simplicity. Non-action is not to be understood in the sense of doing nothing. The sage takes to non-action because all efforts with a personal purpose are bound to fail. It is therefore said that things are spirit-like and cannot be obtained by active doing. "He who tries to hold them in his grasp, loses them." Things have their own way without reference to our actions. In Tao-Teh-King is given the way as to how we should live. "This is the way of Tao and Teh (or the true Path) to act without thinking of acting, to conduct affairs without feeling the trouble of them; to taste without discerning any flavour; to consider the small as great and the few as many and to recompense injury with love and kindness." If we act in this fashion we are in Teh and follow Wu-Wei. This is the Wu-Wei of individual life. In the aggregate life we are called upon to live according to nature or terms of equality with all creatures and to live a simple life, flit has been said that the simple life has been lost when people began to aim at knowledge rather than life itself. Lao-Tze repeatedly exhorted people to cease pursuing knowledge and to abandon desires. He points to Heaven and Earth as patterns for the sage. They have no personal ends. They do not aim at knowledge nor do they cultivate desires. About the government by the sage Tao-Teh-King says that it consists in employing the hearts of the people, that is of desires. By such non-action nothing is left ungoverned, because Tao and Teh come into play and begin governing. Wu-Wei or non-action on the practical plane appears in a form of humility. It is said: "When a great kingdom takes a lowly position, it becomes a place of concourse for the world, it is the wife of the world. The wife by quietness conquers the man. And since quietness is also lowliness, therefore a great kingdom by lowliness towards a small kingdom, may take that small kingdom, and a small kingdom by lowliness towards a great kingdom may take that great kingdom, so that either one stoops to conquer, or the other is low and conquers. If the great kingdom only desires to attach to itself and nourish others, then the small kingdom will only wish to enter its service. But, in order that both may have their wish the great should be lowly."

Lao-Tze associates with humility what he calls his three precious jewels which are gentleness, economy and shrinking from taking precedence of others. "With gentleness" he says: "I can be bold; with economy I can be liberal; shrinking from taking precedence of others, I become a vessel of the highest honour." These three together with humility are the four forms of Teh which make Wu-Wei possible for us in our daily life. The state of people who act according to nature is like that of a child. A child lives in Wu-Wei as he does not live in self-assertion. The principle of naturalness is the principle of the child's life and this principle may be attained by Wu-Wei.

Simplicity as defined in the Tao-Teh-King is the foundation of culture and inner life. Simplicity is the method of nature that lies at the root of all her doings. If nature is given a personality, then simplicity is one of its attributes. Simple life and smplicity are two different notions. The simple life is only a, compromise and can never produce simplicity and simplicity does not necessarily mean a simple life. Lao-Tze explains how differences grow after the beginning had been made by ignoring Nature's sublime simplicity. "Strive to keep the world in its original simplicity—why so much fuss? The wind blows as it listeth, so let virtue establish itself. The swan is white without a daily bath and the raven is black without dyeing itself. When the pond is dry and the fishes gasp for breath it is no use to moisten them with a little water, compared to their original and simple condition in the pond and the rivers it is as nothing." Lao-tze meant to say that the only way to reform was to restore primitive simplicity. Ignoring simplicity we have been in the mire of curse and confusion. What Will simplicity do for us? Chapter XXII proclaims: "He that humbles himself shall be preserved entire. He that bends himself shall be straightened. He that empties himself shall be filled. He that has worn himself out, shall be renewed. He that puts himself low, shall be exalted." Lao-Tze teaches that by restoring simplicity, the world may be saved from desires and false notions and from sin, restoring simplicity means correcting our perceptions of virtues; by undivided attention to the soul, by restraining passions and letting gentleness sway it, it is possible to become an infant, continue like a child. By purifying the mind of phantasms it is possible to remain without a spot. He says: "Havings emptied yourself of everything guard your tranquility and remain where you are." "Simplicity is restored when self is emptied of everything. Nameless simplicity would produce absence of desire and rest would return and thus the world would regenerate itself. Simplicity is works of miracles and we never can fail essentially in life if we identify ourselves with it.

Lao-Tze has with insight said: "The weakest thing in the world will override the strongest." Tao is quiescent yet leaves nothing undone. The soft and the weak overcome the hard and the strong. Tao is as nothing yet in its activity it is inexhaustible. By non-acting there is nothing which cannot be effected. To remain gentle is to be unconquerable. "Whoever develops Tao in the world will make virtue triumph." "A woman conquers a man by continual quietness. Gentleness is always victorious." 'The celestial Tao does not strive yet overcomes everything." All these quotations fully bear out that according to Lao-tze's teachings the weak has power to overcome the strong. It represens nature's method. Nothing, he says "on earth is so weak and yielding as water yet for breaking down the strong it has no equal, It can get into the most inaccessible places and that without striving. It is therefore like Tao." Though water is soft and pleasant it hides in itself an enormous strength.

Knowledge is not virtue nor is it wisdom. It is said in Tao-Teh-King: "Those who are skilled do not dispute; the disputants are not skilled... When we renounce learning we have no troubles. The sage constantly keeps men without knowledge and without desire, and where there are those who have knowledge, keeps them from presuming to act The ancients who showed their skill in practising Tao did so not to enlighten the people, but to make them simple and ignorant..... The difficulty in governing the people arises from their having too much knowledge. He who tries to govern a state by his wisdom is a scourge to it, while he who does not do so is a blessing." The simple man is less of a peril than a man of learning. A man of learning is a danger to the state, because he regulates society on laws. Laws destroy society. It takes away freedom and free will. Unhampered by laws, the natural instinct of people would move life in a simple and a wholesome way. In ancient days, says Lao-Tze, nature made men and life simple and peaceful and all the world was happy. But when men attained knowledge they complicated life with inventions and intrigues and lost their innocence. The key-note of wisdom is quiet content, and obedience to nature. "All things in nature work silently. They come into being and possess nothing. They fulfil their function and make no claim. All things alike do their work and then we see them subside. When they have reached their bloom each returns to its origin. Returning to origin means rest of fulfilment of destiny. This reversion is an eternal law. To know that law is wisdom."

Knowledge brings conflict and unrest, obedience to our inner self brings stillness. Stillness, says Lao-Tze, returns us to the root or the origin of existence, which can be obtained by silence and solitude. Stillness lies at the back of all motion. Everywhere we perceive action and nothing but action, which causes our personality to break up into two and which breaks off harmony with our higher self. If we permit our higher self to act we shall be in stillness and Tao will take our spirit in arms.

All these doctrines culminate in the conception of a sage who is described thus: "The sage is occupied only with that which is without self-assertion and he conveys his instructions by silence. He does not refuse the world's ten thousand things, but does not possess them. He works but claims not the fruits of his action. He has merit but does not dwell on it and therefore no one robs him of it." The sage and simplicity are two sides of the same truth. Sage is simplicity realised. The sage knows "no distinction, he has 'no loves' but looks upon all men and things as made for holy uses." Separateness does not exist for him. The sage is indifferent to himself and thus becomes the greatest among the men. Because he does not seek his own, he accomplishes his own. As little as he seeks his own so little does he proclaim himself to be the greatest man. By acting in this manner he surmounts the hatred and the irritation of the world. Tao-Teh-King says that the reason for the sage's success and his superiority is that he adapts himself to Tao and therefore he is preserved till the end and becomes a model, an example to others. He bends himself, therefore he becomes straight; he is filled because he empties himself. He toils incessantly for the common good and the toil wears him away but is constantly renewed. This is because to him work is not toil, it is growth, recreation, and laudation of Tao. It is his precious key. The sage never loses his gravity and lives in dignity. He never forgets himself. In his intensity the sage balances the world's immensity. Being one he outnumbers many. Because he rests in the endless, he commands the finite. He is always in the world but the world does not know him. He abandons pleasure, extravagance and indulgence. He is the devotee of beauty, and being rooted in simplicity he can appreciate beauty as nobody else. Again it is said that he does not travel yet he has knowledge; that he does not see things, yet he defines them. His world is the sum total of all the factors of the universe. His world has been described in all that which Lao-Tze says about Tao. He knows that Tao is one and follows the Teh which is neither more nor less than following Tao, for Teh is Tao realised. The sage does not strive nor care for name and distinctions. It has been said by a Taoist: "The man of (virtue) Teh, remains indifferent to his environment. His integrity is thereby undisturbed and his knowledge transcends the senses. As a result of that his heart expands to enfold those who take refuge in it. Such is the man of complete virtue." It has been said of one who does not strive. "He will bury gold in the hills and cast his pearls in the seas and not strive for wealth or fame. He will not rejoice in old age nor grieve over early death, nor will he pride himself on success or feel sorrow in failure. He will not feel rich because he ascends the throne nor glory because he rules the world. His real glory is to know the one, Tao, and that all things are but phases of the one."

"His heart is not set upon anything, he has no fixed opinions or opinions which he calls his own. He lives in the universal so how can he opine on particulars. He accommodates himself to the minds of others. He universalises his heart and thus becomes a saviour. He becomes a saviour by simplicity."

Lao-tze says that by setting value on rare things of sense we disturb our peace of mind, lt is said that the human heart is not radically wrong. The book says that Tao is the guardian of all things and does not even forsake those who are not good. It also says that Teh nourishes all things, increases them, protects them and Watches over all things.

The real Taoist is "both-and" not "this or that"; he is the reconciliation of opposites. Tao-Teh-King says:

"Who his manhood shows
And his womanhood knows
Becomes the Empire's river
All come to him, yea, all beneath the sky"

and he is

"The simple child again, free from all stains
"Who his brightness knows

And his blackness shows
Becomes empire's model
He in unchanging virtue arrayed
Man's first estate, the absolute
Who knows his fame
And guards disgrace
Becomes a spacious valley
And men come to him from all beneath the sky"
and in him
Hail the simple infant.

The principle of naturalness is the principle of the child's life and this principle .may be attained by Wu-Wei. Nature is like Teh. Teh is life and Tao is structure. They cannot exist apart. Nature is incarnate and is manifested in suffering and sacrifice. She does not live for her lone self. She is part of another. She is consuming herself every moment. Lao-Tze wishes to accept nature as his guide. "Nature is natural activity, the silent flow of traditional events, the majestic order of seasons and the sky; it is the Tao exemplified and embodied in every brook, rock and star; it is that impartial impersonal and yet rational law of things to which the law of conduct must conform if men desire to live in wisdom and peace."

The reason, says Lao-Tze, why heaven and earth are long enduring and continue long, is bectuse they do not live of or for themselves. Therefore the sage puts his own person last and yet it is found in the foremost place. "It is better to leave a vessel unfilled than attempt to carry it when it is full. If you keep feeling a point that has been sharpened the point cannot long preserve its sharpness. When gold and jade fill the hall, their possessor cannot keep them safe. When wealth and honours lead to arrogance, this brings its evil on itself. When the work is done, and one's name is becoming distinguished, to withdraw into obscurity is the way of Heaven." An individual must free himself from self-consciousness in what he does and of all satisfaction in the result of his doing. Under the guidance of Tao the individual works for himself and others. Tao seeks to withdraw an individual from the attractions of what is external, and pleasant to the senses and imagination, and to maintain the primitive simplicity of men's ways and manners. Lao-Tze gives an example of muddy water and says that it can be made gradually clear by allowing it to be still; and it is stillness which can secure the condition of rest. Lao-Tze says of himself: "I alone am listless and still, my desires having as yet given no indication of their presence." Further he goes on to state that when we renounce learning we shall have no trouble. After renouncing learning an individual finds an end to the trouble and anxieties of his mind. By acquiring Tao the heart empties itself and the partial becomes complete, the crooked straight, the empty full, the worn out new. He whose desires are few gets them, he whose desires are many goes astray. Therefore the wise man holds in his embrace the one thing which is humility and manifests it to all the world. He becomes free from self-display and therefore he shines; from self-assertion and therefore he is distinguished; from self-boasting and therefore his achievementisacknowledged;fromself-complacencyand therefore he acquires superiority. It is because he is thus free from striving that no one in the world is able to strive with him. The empty shall become full, if taken literally, is the hollowness of a cavity in the ground which is sure to be filled by overflowing water. He who empties himself acts in conformity with the Tao, and he is directed by it. Such an individual will be omnipotent in his influence over all others. The Tao in him will restrain loquacity. As to an individual who does not pursue the Tao, he is described as one who stands on his tiptoes and is unable to stand firm or one who stretches his legs but is unable to walk.

The Tao-Teh-King says "Gravity is the root of Tightness, stillness the ruler of movement." The individual who cultivates these qualities must not give way to lightness of mind or hasty action.

Lao-tze teaches how things can be dexterously used.

"The skilful traveller leaves no traces of his wheels or foot steps; the skilful speaker says nothing that can be found fault with or blamed; the skilful reckoner uses no tallies; the skilful closer needs no bars or bolts, while to open what he has shut will be impossible... In the same way the wise man is always skilful at saving men, and so he does not cast away any man; he is always skillful in saving things and so he does not cast away anything.

The characteristic of a man of Tao, such as he was in the primeval time, is denoted by humility and simplicity, and an artless freedom from all purpose. He is the man who knows his manhood's strength and he still maintains his female feebleness. He knows the attraction of the white yet he keeps himself in shadow and thus he becomes a pattern of humility. He knows how glory shines but he loves disgrace. We hail in him a simple infant man.

The kingdom or throne is a "spirit like Vessel." This has become a common saying among the Chinese. Lao-Tze says "The Kingdom is a spirit like thing and cannot be got by active doing. He who would so win would destroy it." This idea is based on the immunity of spirit from all material law and it shows the uncertain results of attempts to deal with it according to ordinary methods.

It is said in Tao-Teh-King: "He who knows other men is discerning, he who knows himself is intelligent. He who overcomes others is strong, he who overcomes himself is mighty. He who is satisfied with his lot is rich; he who goes on acting with energy has a firm will. He who does not fail in the requirements of his position continues long; he who dies and yet does not perish has longevity." In this it is taught that possession of Tao confers various distinguished attributes. To the selfish, unprincipled, and ambitious men Lao-Tze says; "When one is going to weaken another he will first strengthen him; when one is going to overthrow another, he will first have raised him up; when he is going to despoil another, he will first have made gifts to him."

Lao-Tze says that Kings and princes call themselves "Orphans" and "man of small Virtue" it is because dignity finds its firm root in its previous meanness and what is lofty finds its stability in the lowness from which it rises. It is only by Tao that the world can be won. It is said that he who devotes himself to learning seeks from day to day to increase his knowledge but he who devotes himself to Tao seeks from day to day to diminish his doings. He who thus diminishes and carries on the process of diminishing, arrives at doing nothing on purpose and having arrived at this point of non-doing then there is nothing which he does not do. So in the process of diminishing, he clears himself of all coarseness about him, and he puts it away till he becomes oblivious of all that was bad in it. He then puts away all that is fine about him till he has forgotten all that was good in it. Having diminished the wrong and also diminished the right, the process is carried on till they are both forgotten. In such a state passion and desire are both let off and his virtue and Tao are in union, and though he does nothing, he allows all things to do their own doing and all things are done.

To trust in one's force is contrary to the Tao. The strength of an individual is more in weakness and humility. He says: "Man at birth is supple and weak; at death firm and strong. So it is with all things. Trees and plants in their early growth are soft and brittle, at their death dry and withered. Thus it is that firmness and strength are the concomitants of death; softness and weakness the concomitants of life." Hence he who relies on his strength of his forces does not conquer and therefore the place of what is firm and strong is below and that of what is soft and weak is above.

Lao-Tze compares the way (or Tao) of Heaven to the method of bending a bow. The higher part of the bow is brought low and the lower is raised up. In the same way Heaven diminishes when there is superabundance and supplements where there is deficiencv. But the way of man is different from this; for he takes away from those who have not enough, to add to his own superabundance. Lao-tze's advice is to "Abandon your saintliness (This is a hint to the priest and preachers) put away your cleverness (This is a hint to the so called learned people and statesmen), and the people will be benefited a hundred-fold. Abandon your charity and put away righteousness; and people will be more brotherly and more kind; put away your riches and scheming and there will be no robbers or frauds (that is a hint to those who establish charities like universities, hospitals, museums after they have amassed enormous wealth by robbery of all kinds"). Culture is insufficient for the highest purpose.

> "Hold fast to that which will endure,
> Show thyself simple, preserve thee pure
> Thine own keep small thy desires poor."

SUFISM

VARIOUS scholars have given a variety or meanings to the word Sufi. Some associate it with the word "Sufa" i.e. purity; others think it alludes to 'Ashabus' or the people of the bench, and some associate it with the word wool, owing to the fact that in the ancient days of Islam, woollen garments were worn by the ascetics as a distinctive dress symbolising poverty, renunciation of the world and all its joy. The term Sufi first came into use in (815 A.D.).

It is believed that Sufism is Islamic in origin and Mohamed was its originator. He (Mohamed) is said to have been the recipient of a two-fold revelation—the one embodied in the contents of the Quran, the other within his heart. The former was meant for all and is binding on all; the latter was transmitted to the chosen few through a line of succession. Hence it is that Mohamed's knowledge is described as being 'ilm-i-Safina", book knowledge, and "ilm-i-Sina", heart knowledge. The former is incorporated in the doctrinal teaching of the Ulama. The latter is strictly esoteric, the mystical teachings of the "Sufis." Sufism is, according to Mohamedans, indigenous to Islam and they see the germ of it in certain passages in the Quran. There are other scholars who have traced an Indian origin of the movement. The later development of Sufism is influenced by Indian mysticism and oriental Christian mysticism.

The chief characteristic of early Sufism is the renunciation of worldly pleasures and the fear of God and His Judgment. "The way of the Sufis was regarded by the ancient Muslims and their illustrious men—the companions of the Prophet, the successors and the generation that came after them—as a way of Truth and Salvation. To be assiduous in piety, to give up all else for God's sake, to turn away from worldly goods and vanities, to renounce pleasure, wealth and power, which are the general objects of human ambition; to abandon society and to lead in seclusion a life devoted to the service of God—these are the fundamental principles of Sufism which prevailed among the companions and Muslims of old time." It is apparent that the foremost phase of Sufism was extreme asceticism which was the result of the Islamic Conception of God, which was, as has been said by Bevan Jones, such as to "produce fear and servility, also littleness and formality in life and practice." Allah is one to be feared rather than loved. Islam would, as it were, propound as the greatest Commandment of all "Thou shalt fear the Lord thy God."

The early Sufis were orthodox in their beliefs and practices. They attached great importance to the traditions and teachings of the Quran. The chief characteristics of their creed were self-abandonment, self-mortification, piety, quietism in its super-excessive form. Among these early Sufis there also existed a class of people who, besides leading an ascetic sort of life, practised meditation and contemplation, leading to ecstasy and vision. Rabia the Sufi woman saint speaks, thinks and feels in terms of devotional theism. 'God, if I worship thee in fear of hell, burn me in hell. And if I worship Thee in the hope of paradise, exclude me from paradise. But if I worship Thee for Thine own sake, withold not thy everlasting Beauty." Devotions, inspired by self-interest are work done for wages, but devotions inspired by sincerity are work done to serve God. "Perfect love proceeds from the lover who hopes naught for himself. What is there to desire in that which has a price? Certainly the Giver is better for you than the gift." The sayings of Abu Said include several definitions of Sufism, which are:—

(1) To lay aside what thou hast in thy head, to give what thou hast in thy hand, and not to recoil from whatsoever befalls thee.

(2) Sufism is two things: to look in one direction and to live in one way.

(3) Sufism is a name attached to its object, when it reaches its ultimate perfection it is God.

(4) It is glory in wretchedness, and riches in poverty and lordship in servitude, and satiety in hunger, and Sclothedness in nakedness, and freedom in slavery, and life in death, and sweetness in bitterness.

(5) The Sufi is he who is pleased with all that God does, in order that God may be pleased with all that he does.

(6) Sufism is patience under God's Commanding and forbidding, and acquiescence and resignation in the events determined by Divine providence.

(7) Sufism is the Will of the Creator concerning His creatures when no creature exists.

(8) To be a Sufi is to cease from taking trouble; and there is no greater trouble for thee than thine own self, for when thou art occupied with thyself thou r emainest away from God.

These definitions show that Sufism lays a great stress on quietism and pantheistic self-abandonment.

It has been said that there are innumerable ways to reach God. Yet the way is but a single step. "Take one step out of thyself, that thou mayest arrive at God." He who knows himself as not-being knows God as Real Being. This knowledge according to Sufism cannot be obtained through the intellect, nor can it be learned hut it is given by Divine illumination. Man is not freed by his own exertions but by the grace and help of God. The attainment of selflessness is independent of human initiative. A power not his own pulls him towards the Goal, but this requires on his part an inward striving. Towards the end of the eighth century (A.D.) a new phase was added to its development which was the discussion of theosophical and gnostic speculations. At this period of time certain non-Islamic and extraneous elements such as pantheism, theosophy, gnosticism and ecstasy were associated with the original conception of Sufism. Mansoor the wool-carder by trade was the greatest of all among the early pantheists. With such admixture of concepts, the Sufis were considered heretics till the advent of (Imam-al-Ghazali who assured to Sufism a firm place in Islam. He is the greatest theologian

Islam has produced. He conceived the unity of God not in a negative manner as absorption in God and identification with Him. He followed the Christian conception of Unity, in an ethical Code. He said Tawhid i.e. Unity, and Tawakhul i.e. Trust, , are inevitably bound together. We find in him a forerunner of establishing ethical and spiritual concepts.

The classic period of Sufism begins with 13th Century A.D. which was marked by the advent of three great mystical poets. These were Faridu'd-Din Attar, Jalalud-Din-Rumi and Shaykh-Sa'di. Their writings have influenced much the religious concepts of the Muslims in the East. Faridu'd-Din Attar has, in Mantiqu't-Tayr, in an allegorical mode pictured the ascending rungs of the Mystics' progress to establish Unity with God. The soul is likened to birds setting out in flight, and after passing through seven valleys which are Search, Love, Mystic Apprehension, Detachment, Unity, Bewilderment and Annihilation, come to the abode of Simurgh. Jalalu'd-Din-Rumi is another great poet mystic of the classical period, commonly known as Mawlana, that is "our master." He is the author of the most widely known poetical works on mysticism, the Mathnawi-i-Manawi i.e. spiritual couplets. It has been given the name of Quran in Persian language. He has contributed the highest mystical literature, and is widely studied in the East. In his work entitled Diwan he has given a description of the man of God, the God-intoxicated without any outside agency, who is lost in bewilderment at the unreality of the world. His origin is supernatural but his worth is clouded by the body. He is beyond all formal concepts of religion, whose true knowledge can be gained through mystic intuition.

The third great poet of this period is commonly known as Sa'di. His 'Gulistan' that is Rose Garden and 'Bustan' that is Orchard are well known. Bustan treats in verse of ethical concepts. His ethics are based on expediency.

With Gulshan-e-Raz of Shabtari and the poets Rafiz and Gami the last phase of the development of Sufism closes. In Jami "the mystical and pantheistic thought of Persia may be said to find its most complete and vivid expression. One of the towering conceptions in his doctrine is that of the Absolute as the Eternal Beauty. Voicing the famous concept "I was a hidden treasure and I desired to become known. Therefore I brought the creation into being in order that I might be known." He said that God is the Eternal Beauty and the purpose of His creation is to manifest that Beauty. Beauty leads to love and love to Bliss. All duality melts. The lover and the beloved become one. Through perfect beauty, perfect love is attained and through perfect love perfect Bliss is attained. God is conceived as eternal beauty and it lies in the nature of beauty to manifest itself. Thus the purpose of creation is to manifest the beauty of God. The passion for beauty is a means to link the Soul to God."

Indian Sufism has its roots in the mystic speculations of Persia where it had reached its height in the 15th century A.D. As regards the development of Sufism Evelyn Underhill writes: "Mohamedan mysticism appearing in the eighth century in the beautiful figure of Rabia (717-831) and continued by martyr Al Hallaj (Mansoor) in 922 attains literary expression in the 11th century, in the confession of Al Ghazali (1055-1111), and has its classic period in the 13th century in the works of the mystic poet Attar (1140-1234). Sadi and the saintly Jalaludin (1207-1273). Its tradition is continued in the 14th century by the rather erotic mysticism of Hafiz (1300-1388) and his successors in the 15th century by the poet Jami (1414-1492). In its course of development it has imbibed elements which were foreign to the true spirit of Islam. It departs to a great extent from the early Islamic Creed preached by Mohamed in its doctrine of God, in its outlook in life, and in its conception of the relation of man to God. But it must be admitted that in spite of it having imbibed the various foreign elements it has maintained an abiding place in Islam."

Bevan Jones has succinctly expressed the Sufi practices and experiences to find Union with God. "Sufism speaks of advancement in the spiritual life as a 'journey' and the seeker after God as a 'Salik' or Traveller. Its teaching is intended to guide the traveller to the attainment of perfect knowledge of God, the only reality, diffused through all things. Subsequently the wandering Soul is led onwards by slow stages and through the experience of certain states along a path to the desired goal of Union with God, called absorption in Reality." The great mystic Ghazali has said: "Allah hath seventy-thousand veils of light and darkness. Were He to withdraw their curtain then would the splendours of His Aspect surely consume everyone who apprehended Him with his Sight." In seeking to have Union with God the soul has to pass through seven stages and after the Soul overcomes the sensual and the earthly things it finds Union with the Eternal Being. These seven stages are as follows.

(1) The first stage is of Service of God. At this stage the Soul purifies itself by repentance which is described as "the awakening of the Soul from the slumber of indifference to awareness of his evil ways and a sense of contribution for past sins."

(2) The second stage is that of love. Man's love towards God in the form of Veneration seeks to satisfy his Beloved and becomes impatient in his desire to have a vision of Him and cannot rest with any one except Him, and remembers Him. He is cut off from all association and habits, and renounces all sensual passions and turns towards love, submitting himself to the law of Love, and he knows God by His attributes of perfection. His heart becomes devoid of all earthly desires and takes to pover ty; as has been said by a Sufi writer: "the poor are the richest of God's creation... they dispense with the gift for the sake of the Giver."

(3) The third stage is of renunciation "Zuhd". When the Soul has been purified from all sensual desires the mystic proceeds towards his journey towards God and aims at renunciation of all buy God. At this stage he feels "the Beloved is all in all, the lover merely veils him. The Beloved is all that lives, the lover a dead thing."

(4) The fourth stage is of knowledge or gnosis, in which the aspirant contemplates the nature, the attributes and the works of God. "Gnosis is the life of the heart through

God and turning away of one's inmost thoughts from all that is not God."

(5) The fifth stage is ecstasy in which the thrill is produced through contemplation and repetition of His name. Prof. Nicholson says "The whole of Sufism rests on the belief that when the individual self is lost, the Universal Self is found or, in religious language, that ecstasy affords the only means by which the Soul can directly communicate and become united with God." There is no hell but selfhood, no Paradise but selflessness. Hell is where thou art and Paradise here thou art not.

(6) The sixth stage is reality in which the heart is aglow with the true nature of God and becomes pure from the self as flame from the smoke.

(7) The last stage is the union in which the aspirant sees God face to face. This stage precedes the final annihilation and subsistence. A famous Sufi writer has said that "that man is a sufi who is satisfied with whatever God does or God will be satisfied with whatsoever he does."

In manifesting itself the Absolute has to pass through several stages of devolution. The aspirant in order to find Union with the Absolute has to traverse in obverse order. prof. Nicholson speaking of the ascent of the aspirant says: "Man is the microcosm in which all attributes are united and in him alone does the Absolute become conscious of itself in all its diverse aspects. To put it in another way, the Absolute having completely realised itself in human nature returns into itself through the medium of human nature; or, more intimately God and man become one in the perfect Man—the enraptured prophet or saint, whose religious function as a mediator between man and God corresponds with his metaphysical function as the unifying principle by means of which the opposed terms of reality and appearance are harmonised. Hence the upward movement of the Absolute from the sphere of manifestation back to the unmanifested Essence takes place in and through unitive experience of the Soul.'

"Ruh,"the spirit, and "Nafs" the self are contra-distinguished by the Sufis. "Nafs" forms the evil in man which comprises. lust, desires and passion which the aspirant has to subdue and conquer. The aspirant must "die to the self" by a process of mortification. The lower self is to be purged of all the evil elements. The Sufi in order to attain his goal has to place himself under a guidance of a "Murshid" (leader) commonly known as "Pir" and he has to submit himself to his Pir. He thus becomes a "Murid", a disciple. (It is believed that the Pir is able to infuse spiritual power in the "Murid" and it is he alone who can lead his "Murid" from the first to the last stage of his journey of annihilation. The Murid must mystically always bear his "Murshid" in mind and become mentally absorbed in him. This is carried to such a degree that he sees the master in all men and in all things. The Pir should be worthy of imitation, he should have perfect knowledge, both theoretical and practical, of the three stages of the mystic life, the Law, the Path and the Truth; he should be entirely free from bodily desires so that nothing of his lower self remains in him. The sufi aspirant in the course of his journey has to perform certain acts of devotion which are (1) Namaz, the ritual prayer. (2) "Tilawat", the recitation of Quran, (3) Award, repeating a set form of prayers. Besides these, he has also to perform the special acts which are the acts of self-mortification, remembering God and contemplation. It has been said that outward and inward purification must go together.

Sufism teaches its followers to believe in saints. The saints are the chosen friends of God whose teachings arc to be venerated and followed, their legends to be recapitulated, their names to be invoked in times of stress and strain, and pilgrimage to be performed to their shrines and tombs. The pilgrimage to tombs is held in high esteem, as, according to Sufis, saints do not die but they merely depart from one habitation to another. It is said that 'he who hurts a saint has allowed himself to make a war on him." An undiscernible hierarchy prevails among the saints, of which the highest is Qutbe on whom it is believed that the kingdom of the world rests.

Sufism centres round the personality of its several Pirs. It is they who have given innumerable forms, all of which are the expression of the inner experience of the founders. A Sufi in spite of his distinctive belief and his mode of living is above all a lover of God and as such he stands in different relation to God from others except from those who are its followers.

Sufism has appealed to the masses chiefly because of the element of love and of the inspired works of the founders which speaks in a language that is easily understood. "Is there a lover in the world? Then I am he. Here then the gist. The soul of the soul I am he. Cup-boy and lees, minstrel and cup, lute string and song, sweet heart and lamp, wine and carouse all these I be." Love is the essence of God's essence and it is the highest form in which God is worshipped. It appeals to the deepest emotions of men and rouses in them a longing for God. Sufism has provided to men of diverse aptitude a variety of ways by which he can give vent to his spiritual feelings. There is nothing rigid or stern.

The essence of God is Pure Being. He is the highest manifestation of the Essence, embracing all that is manifested. Creator appears in the form of the Creature and conversely the Creature in the form of the Creator. Since it is the sum of attributes, it is invisible, though visible everywhere in its effects. Mercy and lordship are the primary aspects of Divinity. His first mercy is bringing the universe into existence out of Himself. His manifestations pervade everything and His perfection is displayed in every atom, He remains one in the many. God does not lend his attributes to the things. The things are a part and parcel of His attribues. The Universe is like ice and God is the water. Sufism in speaking of the oneness of God attributes to Him unity of Essence, unity of Attributes and unity of Acts. There is only one God without any second and all the manifestations whether in acts, or attributes though appearing to be diverse countless and different are centred in that oneness. All actions and attributes of men are of God. Such manifestation is effected through Divine Effulgence called 'Tejalli", and only a mystic can comprehend it because his illumination is Divine. It is said: "Tejalli then on the Divine side represents the outgoing Effulgence of the

Divine towards the creature and on the creaturely side the-illumination which draws the creature back to the Divine." The Divine descent is the corresponding mystic Ascent. In his upward path towards union with God, the aspirant receives light of illumination in varying measure through the self-manifestation of the Deity in the following upward path. The first is the mystic illumination of the Divine Acts; in which the Absolute makes himself evident by negating the acts of his creature arid establishes His own. This deprives the creature of his strength, power and will. It becomes plain to him that human agency is nothing, that he has no power or will of his own and that all things are done by the power of God. The second is the mystic illumination of Divine names; in which when the Absolute manifests himself in one of His names then that one is completely drowned in the radiance of that Name and if one invokes God by that Name the man will answer him because the Name is applicable to him "Like a single person wiith two names thou cannot miss by whichever name thou callest him." The third is the mystic illumination of Divine attributes in which the essence of the mystic is gradually invested with the attributes of the Absolute till the mystic possesses the whole range of attributes in perfection. God puts in the main body, without incarnation, a spiritual substance which is of God's essence and is neither separate from God nor joined to the man in exchange for what He deprived him of. They receive this illumination in proportion to their capacities, strength and resolution. The fourth is the mystic illumination of Divine Essence in which all relations, modes, adjuncts and aspects are cast off. At this stage, the aspirant becomes a perfect unit or the universal helpmate to whom all resort for aid. The essences of all things that exist are drawn to obey him. He subdues the sensible world by his might and does what he will by his power.

"Fana" or Annihilation is the state which precedes that of "subsistence." Annihilation is the annihilation of the consciousness of manhood and subsistence is the subsistence in the contemplation of God-head. This is explained by a Sufi writer as: "It is an imperfection to be conscious in one's actions that one is a man, and one attains to real manhood when one is not conscious of them, but is annihilated, so as not to see them and become subsistent through beholding actions of God. Hence all actions of one are referred to as of God, not to one's self and whereas man's actions that are connected with himself are imperfect, those which are attached to him by God are perfect. Therefore when anyone becomes annihilated from things that depend on himself he becomes subsistent through the beauty of God-head." In simple words, the essence, the attributes and actions of the aspirant become the essence, attributes and actions of God. The enraptured Sufi who has passed beyond the illusion of subject and object and broken through to the oneness can either deny that he is anything or affirm that he is in all things.

Sufism teaches that there is no other actor than God and all things which exist for which a name can be found, as well as the originator, the initiator, the cause and the effect is God who has second. When a man understands this, then he will not look elsewhere, but will be in fear and awe of Him and put utter trust and confidence in Him alone.

In Sufism the Absolute Being in its primary State is conceived as unalloyed Essence, devoid of all attributes and relations which forms the first place of the Triad in the emanational system. It conceives that this Essence from the state of bare existence gradually becomes qualified by acquiring modes, adjuncts, relations and aspects which are in the Absolute Being and not separate from it. The Sufis base their view on the tradition of Mohamed which says "I (i.e. Allah) was hidden in treasure. I desired to become known and I brought creation into Being that I might be known.

"The second plane of the Triad is the Reality of Mohamed. The world is a manifestation of that reality. Thus Mohamed is conceived by the Sufis as the final and complete revelation of the Absolute who existed prior to the existence of creation.

The third plane of the Triad is Unity in diversity.

Thus the single Essence, as to Its being absolutely void of the individualisations and limitations, is creative Truth and in respect of the multiplicity and plurality by which it displays its veilings in individualisations, is the created Universe.

According to Sufism the entire creation belongs to the world of Command, that is to say, has been brought into existence by the Command of God and therefore non-material, or to the world of creation that is to say brought into existence from pre-existing matter and therefore material. These two worlds together form the microcosm. Man in contrast is called microcosm, possessing five elements of Alam-i-Amr which are heart, spirit, consciousness, mysterious and deeply mysterious and five elements of Alam-i-Khalq which are ego and the other four elements earth, water, fire and air. Each of these elements is called Latifa, subtle substance. The Latai'f (plural of Latifa) connected with Alam-i-Khalq constitute the physical side of human life and the other five which are connected with Alam-i-Amr are the organs of spiritual communication with God. Their relative position is described in the following way. The place of heart is said to be on the throne of God. Mohamed is said to have received revelation. "My earth and my heaven contain me not but the heart of my faithful servant containeth Me"—and above it in ascending order are Ruh, Sin, Khasi, Akhfa. Somehow they are connected with the inner life of man. The aim of every Sufi is to awaken these five Latai'f into active remembrance of God and through them to receive 'Tajalli', the Divine (Illumination.

A Sufi through mystic subtleties gropes his way to find that which will assuage the deep hunger of his heart. "Our whole work in this life is to heal the eye of the heart by which we see God."

Complete negation of individuality requires complete affirmation of the Universal self which is expressed by the Sufis "Abiding after passing away." He abides in God and yet he goes out towards created things in a spirit of love towards all things in the virtues and works of righteousness. He by his words and actions exhibits and diffuses around him a divine life. The Sufi describes a Perfect man as a man who has fully realised his unity with God in whose likeness he is made. This realisation is experienced by prophets and saints. The Perfect men are not only the Prophets but "Superlatively elect" amongst the Sufis, that is, the Walis. An ecstatic state of oneness with God constitutes the Wali. He performs two important functions as a mediator uniting one and the many and as a cosmic power, and as such he brings relief to the afflicted. These beliefs follow as a result of the conception of God and man. According to Rumi the essence of God's essence is love. Before the creation, God loved himself and through love revealed Himself to Himself. Then desiring to see that love-in-aloneness that love without duality He brought forth from non-existence an image of Himself endowed with all His attributes and name. Rumi says:

"I am He whom I love and He whom I love is I.
"We are two spirits dwelling in one body.
"If thou seest me thou seest Him.
And if thou seest Him thou seest us both."

In simple words it says that Being is one, that all apparent differences are manifestations of reality. The phenomenal is the bridge to the Real. The phenomenal world is no illusion. It exists as a self-revelation of the Absolute. "We ourselves are the at tributes by which we describe Him, our existence is merely an objectification of His existence, God is necessary to us in order that we may exist, while we are necessary to Him in order that he may be manifested to Himself." The Universe is like ice and God is the water of which it is made.

The Sufis do not believe evil to be permanent. Jill cites the tradition : "My mercy precedeth my wrath" and infers that while the latter attribute is a mode of Divine Justice, Mercy is essential and prevails in the end.

The Sufis believe that it is by losing the egocentric life that we attain the latent and undiscovered life which in the spiritual part of our being we share with the Divine. "When the heart weeps for what it has lost, the spirit laughs for what it has found" and, to find the latent, the present moment, say the Sufis, is the only aperture through which the soul can pass, out of time into eternity.

"Past and future veil God from our sight.
"Burn up both of them with fire, How long
Will those be partitioned by these segments like a reed!"

So long as a reed is partitioned it is not privy to the secrets nor is it vocal in response to lip and breathing.

SHINTOISM

EVER since the dawn of history the Japanese have inhabited the group of islands skirting Eastern Asia. The first inhabitants occupied the whole group of islands but were driven to the north and to the east by immigrants. One strong group of the aboriginals settled down first in the island of Tsukushi (Present Kyusu) and along the northern coast. This group became the chief stock of the race and was destined to become the rulers of the whole country. In addition to these there came other invaders probably Malayans and established themselves on the Southern Coasts. During this period emigrants from China and Korea carried out the activity of civilising the chief stock, It must be said that in spite of the constant influx of new people, the people of Japan achieved national unity comparatively early in history. This is due to the fact that they had hardly any sense of race division or antagonism. The primary cause of the establishment of national unity consisted in the character and ability of the chief stock. Their belief, that they descended from the heavenly gods,—among whom the supreme deity, the Sun-Goddess,—was the protectress of the royal family and of the nation,—kept up the ties of Union. Their inherent character enabled them to assimilate new-comers; it also enabled them to adopt the various forces of civilisation and religion which were introduced; it enabled them also to convert the extraneous element to their own advantage, in their effort to make progress. The island thus became a repository for various literatures, cultures, arts of the Asian continent, But it must be admitted that the old Shinto owes little to any outside source. It is an independent development of Japanese thought. The Japanese had no writing until the introduction of Chinese learning early in the 5th century A.D. Kojiki, which is believed to date from 712 reciting the old myths and traditions of the Japanese is the first source book. Another work which followed close on is known as Nihongi. In the 18th and 19th centuries some learned commentaries were written on these two works. The above-mentioned works give a tolerably complete account of the old state religion of Japan. The Shinto principle is the background of Japanese culture, code of ethics, family and national structure. It has vitalised and reinforced their social, national and religious lives. The history of Japanese religion and morals shows an interaction of various influences which have supplemented their growth in combination rather than in antagonism. Thus we see that Confucianism came to Japan and gave impetus to a development of her national life. Confucianism furnished materials for social institutions, political organisations and systematization of moral precepts. Confucian influence in Japan was conspicuous in the sphere of legal, educational and civil institutions. Thus Chinese metaphysics and religious practices contributed to the development of the old Shinto religion. Buddhism, when it first appeared, supplied their yearning for the beyond, but at a later stage gave vitality to the religious life of the people by instilling in them universal ideas, and refining their religious sentiments. A saying compares the three religious and moral systems found in Japan to the root, the stem, and branches and flowers and 'fruits of a tree. Shinto is compared to the root, embedded in the soil of people's character and national traditions. Confucianism is seen in the stem and branches of legal institutions, and ethical codes and Buddhism made the flowers of religious sentiments bloom and give the fruits of religious life.

It is believed by the Japanese that 'The God who originally founded the country is the God who descended from Heaven and established their state in the period when Heaven and earth became separated and when the trees and herbs had powers of speech: "On the basis of this primitive conception a system has been established and attempts have been made to found the national ideas on the worship of the Deity who originally established the state." This belief and worship is known by the name of Shinto or Kami-no-michi which means the "way of Gods" or the "God like way." It may be called the national religion of the Japanese. Shinto is fundamentally not so much a religious system having high philosophy and complicated rituals as a complex of ancient beliefs and observances which have remained comparatively unchanged.

The deity or spirit is called Kami. Primarily it means superior, sacred or miraculous and is applied to many other things, besides deities such as nobles, the authorities, etc. The Kami are high, swift, good, rich-living but not infinite, omnipotent or omniscient. Motoori, the Great Shinto theologian says: "The term Kami is applied in the first place to the various deities of heaven and earth as well as to spirits which reside in shrines. Moreover birds, beasts, plants, trees, seas, and mountains and all other things which deserve to be dreaded and revered for the extraordinary and pre-eminent powers which they possess are called Kami. They need not be eminent for nobleness and goodness but malignant and uncanny beings are also called Kami if only they are objects inspiring awe. Among Kami who are human beings I need hardly mention first of all the successive Mikados ... .Then there have been numerous examples of divine human beings both in ancient and modern times who, although not accepted by the nation generally are treated as gods.... Amongst Kami who are not human beings I need hardly mention Thunder. There are also the dragon, the echo, and the fox who are Kami by reason of their uncanny and fearful natures...."

Shinto religion is inspired by love and gratitude rather than by fear. The three greatest Gods, namely, the Sun-goddess, the food goddess and the god of earth are all beneficent deities, though they are wont to send a curse when offended by the neglect of their worship. Their worshippers come to them with joyful feelings. There are some, like the Fire god, Thunder god and the god of the Rain-Storm, who are malignant deities, who have to be propitiated by offerings. The Kami possesses two essential attributes, namely, sentiency and superhuman power. Sentiency attributes sense and will to the great elemental objects and phenomena. Super-human power carries with it the idea of transcendent power derived from the contemplation of the mighty forces upon whom we are dependent. We have therefore two classes of deities, Nature Gods and Man Gods, the first being the result of personification, and second of deification. It is generally believed that Shinto gods are the result of deification or ancestor worship. This conception is erroneous, for all the great deities of the older Shinto are not Men but nature gods like the Sun, Moon, Earth, Sea, Mountain, Rain, Fire, Thunder or they are satellites of Nature gods e.g. the Mikados. In imitation of the Mikados who selected the Sun-goddess as their ancestral deity, the clans in ancient times selected others as their patron gods to whom they paid special worship. These deities were called Ujigami that is to say "Surname-deities." In later times the Ujigami ceased to be patron gods and simply became local deities. There is very little trace of any religious worship of individual men in Shinto. Living Mikados were styled Kami but their godship was more titular than real. The Nature gods of Shinto are primarily the actual material objects or phenomena regarded as living beings. The ancient Japanese characterised these gods very feebly and indeed most of them were supposed to have no characters at all. Shinto is highly polytheistic and numbers its deities by hundreds. The gods of the ancient Shinto are on the whole unspiritual beings. Their dealings are modelled on those of living men and women. Some of the gods are represented as having "Mitama" or souls which reside invisibly in temples and are the means of communication between Heaven and earth. The "Mitama" is represented in the shrine by a concrete object called the God-body. It may be a mirror, a sword or a jewel. In the course of development of Shinto they have acquired a figurative meaning. They symbolise wisdom, courage and benevolence or intelligence, will and love in Shinto theology. These three are the holy ensigns of royalty of the sovereign emperor. They are supposed to symbolise the dynamic working of the Great way and so they are found in the forefront of every Shinto shrine popularly known as Mishi-tomoe or the three big commas. With few exceptions such as these, Shinto has no idols.

Shinto books do not directly lay down the doctrine of the immortality of the soul. There is a land of Yomi to which we are told that some of the gods retired at death. It is represented as inhabited by various personifications of death and disease but not by human beings or their spirits. The two great classes of deities, Nature gods and Man gods have a tendency mutually to encroach on each other's sphere so that ultimately they become assimilated under the one general term of Kami. Thus the Sun-Goddess does not merely give light and heat, but is the protectress of agriculture and the ancestress of the ruling family. Susa No Wo, the Rain-storm-god provides mankind with useful trees. He and his wife are regarded as gods of wedlock. Inari, the grain god, is an answerer of prayer. Suitengu is the protector against perils of the sea, burglary, etc.

In Shinto mythology three deities are said to have sprung out of primeval chaos, which was like an ocean of mud veiled in darkness. The head of the triad was the Heavenly Central Lord, and the two subordinates were the High-Producing and the Divine-Producing. This latter couple symbolised the male and female principle of generation and are sometimes identified with the divine male (Kami-Rogi) and the divine-female (Kami-Romi) who are invoked in rituals. The first triad vanished without leaving any posterity and was followed by a series of similar ones who were generated spontaneously from one another. All these came out of chaos and vanished. The last couple of the series was the male-who-invites (Izana-Gi) and the Female-who-invites (Izana-Mi). They descended on the earth to produce the terrestial world. They united and gave birth to many things,—water, winds, mountains, fields, mists, fire, flood. Finally this divine couple begot the ruler of the world, the Heaven-illuminating Goddess; the Moon Ruler and the valiant swift Impetuous Hero. The realm of light was assigned to the Sun-goddess, the realm of night to the Moon-Goddess; while the ocean together with the myriads of hidden treasure were entrusted to the Swift-(Impetuous. After the disappearance of the primeval couple the world was transferred to the dual rule of Sun-goddess and the Swift-Impetuous, who possessed traits of the storm-god. The Sun-goddess was bright and beautiful in features, unrivalled in dignity, benign, honest and meek in temper. She ruled wisely, giving light and life to all. She was the protectress of the rice fields. She was the presiding deity of peace and plenty. On the other hand her brother Swift Impetuous was wild, arrogant and disobedient and disregarded all his duties. Swift Impetuous ravaged the domain of his sister, destroyed rice fields. Being distressed at his doings she hid herself in a cave with the result that darkness and disorder prevailed in the worlds. She was induced to come out by myriads of deities, and light and order, peace and plenty were restored. The triumph of the Sun-goddess over her brother secured her the rule of the world. The above narrative has two aspects, in its bearing upon the belief and the life of the people. As a myth of solar phenomena it represents the beliefs of an agricultural people and their reverence for the Sun. Politically the same beliefs resulted in the predominance of a certain family who worshipped the Goddess as their progenitrix. Thus the Sun-goddess embodied life-giving power and wise rulership at the same time. In the former aspect she is associated with a male counterpart, the High Producing Deity. There is, however, a female counterpart who is even to-day worshipped besides her at Is'e the most holy of the Shinto sanctuaries. On the other hand the outrageous Swift Impetuous was banished. The place of exile is on the northern coast of Japan. It was there in fact that a tribe claiming their descent from him established themselves and resisted the solar race. One of his sons was the great evil-doer who was the source of all evil; while another son, the Great Law-Master worked for the welfare of the people in association with his partner the small Prince of Renown who is regarded as the chief of medicinemen.

It might be of interest to know why the sun is considered as a female. Women held a far more important and independent position in ancient Japan than they did in later times. Several of the ancient Mikados were women. Old Chinese books call Japan the country of queens. Women chieftains are frequently mentioned. Some of the important monuments of the old literature were the work of women.

In ancient Japan, the sacred and the secular were imperfectly differentiated from one another. "Miya" meant equally shrine and palace. The Mikado was at once the high priest and sovereign of the nation. In the oldest legends he appears frequently in a sacredotal capacity and even at the present day, he takes a personal part in some of the Shinto rites.

The Shinto Shrines are marked for their simplicity and there are no complicated rites. Offerings were in the older Shinto, regarded as token of respect. The general object of making offerings is to propitiate gods or to expiate offences against them. The offerings were of rice, cakes, fruits, vegetables, edible sea-wed, flesh of deer, pigs, hare and birds.

Purity holds a prominent position in Shinto. Actual personal dirt was obnoxious to the gods, as is evidenced by the frequent mention of bathing and putting on clean garments before the discharge of religious duties. Sexual acts of various kinds, incest, interference with virgin priestesses, menstruation and child birth, were accompanied with disabilities for the service of the gods. Disease, especially leprosy, wounds, and sores involved various degrees of pollution. The death of a relative, attendance at a funeral, touching a dead body, all incapacitated a man temporarily from the discharge of religious duties. On the approach of a festival the intending participant was specially careful to avoid all possible sources of pollution. The great ceremony of Shinto religion is known as 'Ohonihe', which means "great-food offerings." (Its cardinal feature was the Mikado's offering in person to the gods the first-rice of the new harvest. Praying for harvest was another important ceremony of the State religion. One of the most important State ceremonies which is still kept up is the Nai Shido Koro so called from the Chamber in the palace where it is performed. It is here that the regalia are kept, consisting of mirrors, which represent the Sun-goddess, a sword and jewel or jewels. The ceremony which is performed by the Mikado in person, was formerly in honour of these sacred objects but is now apparently addressed to the tablets of the Emperors.

It is commonly said by writers on Shinto that it has no ethics. Enthusiasts of the pure Shinto made a virtue of such a lacuna by declaring that moral precepts and ethical systems have become necessary for the depraved. They said that the ancient Japanese were innately good and therefore they needed no exhortations of goodness. It is certain that Shinto had no ethical doctrines as compared with Buddhism and Confucianism; nevertheless the ancient Japanese had a type of morality which suited their culture. It was to this morality that religion gave its effective sanction in the great purification festival. This festival gives an insight into the religious and moral concepts of ancient Shinto. To their thinking,, on a lower plane, defilement, disease and guilt were contagious evils, which could be physically transmitted either to an animal or to some inanimate object; and on the higher plane it was believed that gods could be invoked to take away these evils by propitiating them with offerings. It was believed that the offerings of food and other things were propitiatory and that gods hearing the potent words of the liturgy would remove both physical and moral uncleanliness. Purification offerings, however, were sent off in a boat and cast into the deep sea. Offences were distinguished, between heavenly misdeeds—so called because they are like those perpetrated by Susa No Wo in the myth, and earthly misdeeds. It will be found, however, that no distinction is made between crimes against person or property, skin disease, or calamities.

"Now of the various faults and transgressions to be committed by the celestial race, destined more and more to people this land of this peaceful rule, some are of heaven, to wit, the breaking down of divisions between rice fields, filling up of irrigation channels, removing water pipes, sowing seed over again, flaying alive, flaying backwards. These are distinguished as heavenly offences. Earthly offences, which will be committed, are the cutting of living bodies, the cutting of dead bodies, leprosy,

Kokumi (a disease); incest of a man with his mother, or daughter, with his mother-in-law or step-daughter, bestiality; calamities from creeping things, from the high gods and from high birds, killing animals, bewitchments." These are the primitive notions of offences. Shinto in later times gave ten precepts which are:—

(i) Do not transgress the will of the gods.
(ii) Do not forget your obligations to your ancestors.
(iii) Do not offend by violating the decrees of the State.
(iv) Do not forget the profound goodness of the gods through which calamities and misfortunes are averted and sickness healed.
(v) Do not forget that the world is one great family.
(vi) Do not forget the limitations of your own person.
(vii) Do not become angry even though others become angry.
(viii) Do not be sluggish in your work,
(ix) Do not bring blame on the teachings.
(x) Do not be carried away by foreign teachings.

Later, Shintoism lays a great stress on sincerity and purity. The first and surest means to enter communion with the Divine is through sincerity. Wherever there is sincerity there is virtue. Sincerity is a witness to truth. It is the mother of knowledge and it is one single virtue which unites Divinity and man in one. As regards purity it has been said: "Leave the things of this world and come to me daily with pure bodies and pure hearts." "To do good is to be pure and to commend evil is to be impure." Purity that is required is both external and internal. The heart of the person before you is a mirror, look into it for your reflection. Again it has been said that the beginning of righteousness is the admission of your own fault.

The domestic rites of Shinto are simple. In a corner of one of the rooms of the house is a shelf on which stand tablets or strips of paper inscribed with the names of the gods particularly revered, especially the Sun-goddess and other deities of Ise, and the tutelary god of the owner's calling. Images, in imitation of Buddhist statues, are sometimes found on this shelf. On the shelf are placed two jars, a pair of vases to hold flowers or leaves and a miniature lamp.

Religious duty also inspires followers of Shinto to visit nearby temples, to participate in festivals, and to make pilgrimages to distant shrines.

It must be noted that, for about a thousand years, Shinto existed in combination with Buddhism. Under the rule of the Takugawa Shoguns came a revival of the national consciousness. One aspect of his was to promote the study of Japanese, history, literature and learning. Of the scholars who thus devoted themselves to the task were Mabuchi (1697-1769 A.D.) Motoori (1730-1801) and Hirata (1776-1843). It was they who inspired the people to revive pure Shintoism.

We have mentioned that in Japan there are among the people few who are exclusive Buddhists or exclusive Shintoists. I shall therefore summarise the development of Buddhism in Japan.

Between the years (552 A.D. to 577 A.D.) unsuccessful attempts were made to introduce Buddhism in Japan. It was in the reign of Shotoku Taishi (593-628 A.D.) that Buddhism became the religion of the court and the nobility made haste to follow the fashion. Shotoku was a man of high character and remarkable learning. In the second article of his instructions for officials he strongly recommended Buddhism. "Zealously venerate the three jewels. The three jewels are the Buddha, the Law, and the Order." His example and influence did much to further the spread of Buddhism. Buddhism seemed to be an integral part of the new epoch. The reforming emperor Kotoku (645-654) honoured the religion of Buddha and despised Shinto. Till the eighth century Buddhism flourished chiefly at Court and in official circles. Gyogi taught that in ancient times the Buddha had appeared in Japan as Kami to bless the people of the land. This formula caused a fusion of Buddhism and Shintoism, and Buddhist images were set up in Shinto shrines, and the native Kami was worshipped in the Buddhist temples. Buddhism thus made rapid progress among the common people. Many things contributed to its success. The first reason was that the gods of Buddhism were more human than the vague gods of Shinto. The Gods of Buddhism were more compassionate. The voluminous scriptures, the high repute and learning of the priests, impressed the common mind. One great field which Buddhism had to itself,—and which Shinto lacked,—was the conception of future life after death; this vividly impressed the imagination of the people. The eleventh and twelfth centuries witnessed the rise of Buddhist sects. During this time can be noticed the decline of Buddhism from its pristine virtue, but its recuperative power was by no means exhausted, and a contemplative (Zen) sect was founded by a monk. The Zen sect preached that neither learning nor retirement from the world was necessary but the great means to attain salvation was to discover the essential Buddha in man's own heart. The ideas of the Zen sect presuppose rather a philosophic nihilism. Through the various recognised spiritual disciplines, with emphasis on open-hearted searching and on the use of competent instruction, the aspirant would awaken into an experience and insight that would transcend the possibility of explanation in speech. In the thirteenth century another sect called the Jodo Sect came into being, and exercised an influence among the people. The central theme of the Pure Land school is faith and devotion. They held that salvation could not be achieved by man's own strivings but that it is bestowed by the grace of Amida Buddha. This became popular and was patronised by the Emperors; Amida Buddha has promised that whosoever calls upon His name shall be born again in Pure Land and there, in Amitbha's paradise will be made perfect. The said Pure Land school made forty eight vows, which are recited by many Japanese Buddhists. This form of Faith implies a philosophic idealism. At the heart of ultimate reality is the compassionate wisdom revealed in the Infinite Love and unquenchable light of Amitabha. Shiran developed this doctrine further and there was division and Shiran's followers called themselves "Jodo Shin-Shu" (commonly called Shinshu) "The true Pure Land Sect." The Shin Shu Sect grew rapidly in numbers and power and is today the most numerous and vigorous of the Japanese Sects. The essential feature of this sect was monotheism, and it emphasised man's inability to achieve salvation by his own powers; his dependence on the power of another; the infinite compassion of Amida, who, before innumerable ages, provided this way, by which even the weakest and the most ignorant could attain salvation. This doctrine aroused opposition from the various sects and a reactionary movement was started by Nichinen. The last of the great divisions of Japanese Buddhism, the Lotus sect was that of Nichiren, which preached salvation through learning Lotus Law. But to the masses the abstruse doctrines and scholastic controversies signified little or nothing. To them the Pure Land sects give a better inspiration than the Holy way pointed out by Nichiren. Thus the Japanese had many varieties of Buddhism, and a man could choose any. He might seek self-realisation and bliss through the quiet practices of Zen (Meditation), or he might follow the fiery Nichiren into the Lotus Sect and find salvation through Lotus Law, or he might follow the Spirit Sect and fast and pray until the Buddha appeared to him in flesh, or he might be conforted by the Pure Land Sect and be saved by faith and devotion. Japanese Buddhism found room within its ancient theology and its pantheon for the doctrines and deities of Shinto. The Buddha was amalgamated with Amaterasu and a modest place was set apart in Buddhist temples for the Shinto Shrines. It has been said: "For it was not the Buddha's Buddhism that came but it was the Mahayana Buddhism of gentle Gods like Amida and Kwannon; of cheerful ceremonial, saving Bodhisattwas and personal immortality. Better still it inculcated with irresistible grace, all those virtues of piety, peacefulness and obedience which make a people amenable to Government; it gave to the oppressed such hopes and consolations as might reconcile them with their simple lot; it redeemed the prosaic routine of a laborious life with the poetry of myth and prayer, and the drama of colourful festival; and it offered to the people that unity of feeling and belief which statesmen have always welcomed as a source of social order and pillar of national strength."

The Mahayana literature of Buddhism is devotional rather than philosophical, and it was Mahayana Buddhism that spread in Japan. Mahayana Buddhism has exercised a wide appeal in Japan and China, which is expressed in the viewpoint of the Pure Land school and that of the meditative Zen school.

The Buddhist priests of the earlier centuries were men of devotion, learning and kindness. Success, however ruined the later priests and many of them became lazy and greedy. Under the Tokugawa regime (1603-1868) the priesthood had degenerated to the lowest rank. Thus during the eighteenth century, Buddhism seems to have lost its hold upon the nation. Mabuchi and Motoori led the movement for the restoration of Shinto. In the restoration of 1868 Shinto was at first proclaimed the religion of the state and was placed under special ministry. Buddhism was no longer recognised. This lasted for some time but thereafter both Shinto and Buddhist priests were put under the supervision of a special ministry. The constitution of 1889 acknowledges no state religion and guarantees complete religious liberty. Shinto continues to be the religion of the imperial house and of the court. Thus Shinto enjoys prestige though not the legal status of a national religion.

JAICO PUBLISHING HOUSE

Elevate Your Life. Transform Your World.

ESTABLISHED IN 1946, Jaico Publishing House is home to world-transforming authors such as Sri Sri Paramahansa Yogananda, Osho, The Dalai Lama, Sri Sri Ravi Shankar, Robin Sharma, Deepak Chopra, Jack Canfield, Eknath Easwaran, Devdutt Pattanaik, Khushwant Singh, John Maxwell, Brian Tracy and Stephen Hawking.

Our late founder Mr. Jaman Shah first established Jaico as a book distribution company. Sensing that independence was around the corner, he aptly named his company Jaico ('Jai' means victory in Hindi). In order to service the significant demand for affordable books in a developing nation, Mr. Shah initiated Jaico's own publications. Jaico was India's first publisher of paperback books in the English language.

While self-help, religion and philosophy, mind/body/spirit, and business titles form the cornerstone of our non-fiction list, we publish an exciting range of travel, current affairs, biography, and popular science books as well. Our renewed focus on popular fiction is evident in our new titles by a host of fresh young talent from India and abroad. Jaico's recently established Translations Division translates selected English content into nine regional languages.

Jaico's Higher Education Division (HED) is recognized for its student-friendly textbooks in Business Management and Engineering which are in use countrywide.

In addition to being a publisher and distributor of its own titles, Jaico is a major national distributor of books of leading international and Indian publishers. With its headquarters in Mumbai, Jaico has branches and sales offices in Ahmedabad, Bangalore, Bhopal, Bhubaneswar, Chennai, Delhi, Hyderabad, Kolkata and Lucknow.

SINCE 1946